Testimonials for Female Homosexuality in the Middle East

Elegantly written, *Female Homosexuality in the Middle East* will be a significant text to scholars in the fields of lesbian studies, queer histories and Middle Eastern studies. Not only does it bring to light important historical material from the medieval period, but it intervenes in long standing theoretical debates and lights a way forward for further consideration of female homosexualities outside the western framework.

Dr Rebecca Beirne, *Televising Queer Women*, Editor

One is immediately struck by the lucidity and openness of Samar Habib's analysis: it is felt both in the force of her exposition, and her keen sense of significant detail.

Professor Ivor Indyk, *Heat Magazine*, Editor-in-chief

....convincingly challenges purely constructionist theories of sexuality that insistently represent sexuality as an entirely socio-cultural phenomenon. ... innovative, critical and landmark work.

Associate Professor Joseph Pugliese, Macquarie University

The novelty of this book lies in its author's willingness to take nothing for granted. Habib's work shows not only that just about everything you assumed about Arab culture and its understanding of queer sexualities was wrong, but that a careful reappraisal of the historical record also necessitates a reinvestigation of arguments about historicist and essentialist understandings of sexual identity. This book will make an important contribution to arguments about queer identity at the same time as it corrects many faulty assumptions about Arab culture and history.

Dr Melissa Hardie, The University of Sydney

Samar Habib has a rare insight into literature and writes with a lyrical clarity that is even rarer. Dr Habib's monograph *Female Homosexuality in the Middle East* is outstanding scholarship.

Dr Wayne Pickard, The University of Sydney

Routledge Research in Gender and Society

1. Economics of the Family and Family Policies
Edited by Inga Persson and Christina Jonung

2. Women's Work and Wages
Edited by Inga Persson and Christina Jonung

3. Rethinking Households
An Atomistic Perspective on European Living Arrangements
Michel Verdon

4. Gender, Welfare State and the Market
Thomas P. Boje and Arnlaug Leira

5. Gender, Economy and Culture in the European Union
Simon Duncan and Birgit Pfau Effinger

6. Body, Femininity and Nationalism
Girls in the German Youth Movement 1900–1934
Marion E. P. de Ras

7. Women and the Labour-Market
Self-Employment as a Route to Economic Independence
Vani Borooah and Mark Hart

8. Victoria's Daughters
The Schooling of Girls in Britain and Ireland 1850–1914
Jane McDermid and Paula Coonerty

9. Homosexuality, Law and Resistance
Derek McGhee

10. Sex Differences in Labor Markets
David Neumark

11. Women, Activism and Social Change
Edited by Maja Mikula

12. The Gender of Democracy
Citizenship and Gendered Subjectivity
Maro Pantelidou Maloutas

13. Female Homosexuality in the Middle East
Histories and Representations
Samar Habib

Female Homosexuality in the Middle East

Histories and Representations

Samar Habib

Routledge
Taylor & Francis Group
NEW YORK AND LONDON

Routledge
Taylor & Francis Group
270 Madison Ave,
New York NY 10016

Routledge
Taylor & Francis Group
2 Park Square,
Milton Park, Abingdon,
Oxon, OX14 4RN

Transferred to Digital Printing 2009

International Standard Book Number-10: 0-415-95673-0 (Hardcover)
International Standard Book Number-13: 978-0-415-95673-4 (Hardcover)

Library of Congress Cataloging-in-Publication Data

Habib, Samar.
Female homosexuality in the Middle East : histories and representations / Samar Habib.
p. cm. -- (Routledge research in gender and society ; 13)
Includes bibliographical references and index.
ISBN 978-0-415-95673-4 (hardback : alk. paper)
1. Lesbianism--Middle East. 2. Lesbianism--Islamic countries. 3. Homosexuality--Middle East. 4. Lesbianism in literature. 5. Lesbianism in motion pictures. 6. Arabic literature--History and criticism. I. Title.

HQ75.6.M628H33 2007
306.76'630956--dc22 2006039037

ISBN10: 0-415-95673-0 (hbk)
ISBN10: 0-415-80603-8 (pbk)

ISBN13: 978-0-415-95673-4 (hbk)
ISBN13: 978-0-415-80603-9 (pbk)

Visit the Taylor & Francis Web site at
http://www.taylorandfrancis.com

and the Routledge Web site at
http://www.routledge.com

For Rebecca and the women about whom this is written

Contents

Acknowledgments

This study would have been impossible without the support and encouragement of peers, family and friends. I take a few moments here to acknowledge at least some of my debts to others. My first thank you should go to Rebecca Beirne for putting up with me, challenging my ideas, and for translating copious orientalist studies written in German. I should also thank the wonderful and dedicated Interlibrary Loan staff at Fisher Library, the University of Sydney — without them I would not have been able to acquire most of the material reviewed in this book. I would also like to thank my intellectual predecessors who have forged solid grounds of research upon which I am able to build; in particular I thank E.K. Rowson and C.E. Bosworth for their exceptional and inspiring scholarship on Arab (cultural) history. I would like to thank my doctoral supervisor, Melissa Hardie for having the insight to encourage me into entering what seemed to be a risky research project at the onset. Dr Kate Lilley, from the University of Sydney, has provided a number of useful comments and suggestions that have helped along the years. Dr William Christie provided the technical and administrative support needed with flawless endurance; his approachable style is inspiring. I would also like to thank Dr Luke Ferretter for his insightful comments on the early drafts of chapter IV. I also thank Professor Margaret Harris and Dr Margaret Rogerson for their excellent advice and encouragement. The blind reviewers at Routledge made invaluable observations which led to constructive revisions of the manuscript. I would also like to thank Mr Benjamin Holtzman and Ms Erica Wetter, my editors at Routledge, and the online academic journal *Entertext* for featuring my work on more than one occasion. Finally, I could not have achieved this without the moral support of my family and friends who have taken care of my R&R time: Rebecca, Dianne, Amal, Rima, Samer, my parents, Michael, Amal (the second), Riyad, Sammy, Rami, my aunties Zouka' and Samira and my drinking mates Wayne and Ken. I would also like to thank Keara, Lara, Theo and Bridie for putting up with me throughout this long haul upwards.

Transliteration legend

ء = '

a = أ

b = ب

t = ت

ṭh = ث

J = ج

ĥ = ح

kh = خ

d = د

th = ذ

r = ر

z = ز

s = ص = س

sh = ش

d̲ = ض

t̲ = ط

t̲h̲ = ظ

å = ع

gh = غ

f = ف

q = ق

k = ك

l = ل

m = م

n = ن

h = ه

oo = و

y = ي

Where the 't' is silent åt = عة.

Note: Wherever possible, Arabic names that appear frequently in English (e.g. Youssef Chahine) are retained in their generally known English spelling. Names which appear in a predominantly Arabic context have been transliterated according to the legend above. Names which appear in English works with their own system of transliteration have been simplified in quotation.

Abbreviations

al-Aghani: Kitab al-Aghani by Al-Asfahani, Abu Faraj.

al-Asĥab: Kitab Nuzhat al-Asĥab fi Muåsharat al-Aĥbab by al-Samaw'uli.

Muĥadarat: Muĥadarat al-Udaba Wa Muĥawarat al-Shuåra wa al-Bulagha by al-Asfahani, al-Raghib.

MT: al-Maktaba al-Turaṭheeya: a hypertext database of classical Arab literature accessible at http://www.alwaraq.com.

al-Muntakhab: al-Muntakhab Min Kinayat al-Udaba wa Isharat al-Bulagha by al-Jurjani.

Nuzhat: Nuzhat al-Albab Fima La Yujad Fi Kitab by Tifashi, Aĥmad.

Rashd: Rashd al-Labeeb Ila Muåsharat al-Ĥabib by al-Yemeni, Aĥmad.

Salwat: Salwat al-Aĥzan Lil-Ijtinab ån Mujalasat al-Aĥdaṭh Wa al-Niswan by al-Mashtooly.

PART I

Introducing studies on female homosexuality and contemporary critical theory

1 Introduction

Contemporary views of female homosexuality in the Middle East

This study of homosexuality in the Middle East is by no means an isolated event, though perhaps unique in its predominant focus on female homosexuality. Nor is it isolated from a host of interdisciplinary connections and implications. It is at once the product of literary analysis, historical research, comparative and cultural study, theological research and research of contemporary medical literature. However, at the same time that this study is expansive, it is also necessarily limited. I have limited myself to the study of female homosexuality in the Middle East, precluding other relevant and important groups to this kind of inquiry. In doing so I wanted to narrow the search, to focus exclusively on one of the many letters in LGBTIQ. My choice falling on the "lesbian" category is, of course, not an incidental one. Together with the fact that neglected primary information on the subject existed, I also felt that my enquiries would benefit from a host of emotional truths and experiences that informed a considerable cultural knowledge in my possession. The study of male homosexuality, at any rate, is a much easier one to achieve, with significant precedents springing to mind, written in English, Arabic and French.[1] To the contrary, studies on female homosexuality in this region are relatively unknown, which resonates with the neglected history of female sexuality in general. In the course of my research, I have discovered material from the Middle Ages to the present that has not been discussed in a modern context.

When one encounters material on the study of homosexuality in the Middle East, female homosexuality is treated, if at all, as some kind of secondary and unusual phenomenon. I have viewed a wide range of modern literature, which deals only slightly with female homosexuality in connection with: Arab cultures, Islamic civilizations, Semitic communities, "Middle Eastern" geographies, and such. What is curious is that the study of female homosexuality precedes the widespread enforcements of homophobic ideologies. This is, of course, only in reference to the particular regions in space and time that are covered by the literary[2] artifacts I deal with.

My research adventure began early in my last undergraduate year when I was writing a paper on Eve Sedgwick's *Epistemology of the Closet.*[3] I had recently acquired a Lebanese novel entitled *I Am You.*[4] A friend had told me that it was the first full length work of fiction devoted to a *lesbian* protagonist living in what is (possibly the late 1980s of) war-torn Beirut. Naturally I was intrigued — a novel that basically *outed* even the concept of "lesbian" to a culture so adamantly decided against sexual freedoms of any sort! In addition the very concept of a native Arab lesbian seemed incongruent with the popular theoretical trend of constructionism, which dominated the fields of queer theory and gay and lesbian studies at the time this project was beginning. *I Am You* signaled the entry of a very peculiar literary production into the world of published Arabic material. The centre of this text is a woman who is exclusively attracted to other women and who is unable to negotiate a form of bisexuality that was expected of her by her society (i.e. regular marriage and sex with women on the side). In the Lebanon of the novel, and indeed the Lebanon we know today, it is marriage which dominates the cultural bond between reputation and imputation — there are no other acceptable forms of socializing — at least not visibly. And so it seemed befitting to apply Sedgwick's *Epistemology of the Closet* to something which would, at first, seem incongruent. After all, many a theorist had warned us in the discourse against confusing physical acts of homosexuality with anything which remotely resembles Western notions of "lesbian" identity. The course teacher to whom I had delivered my paper in a class presentation suggested that I should consider this subject as a postgraduate research topic in addition to my planned translation of *I Am You*.

Since then I have translated *I Am You* and I often reflect on the innocence with which I first beheld it. There it was, an artifact, the first of its kind, I thought, the beginning, the crack in the ceiling which has oppressed innumerable sexual beings who could not fit the basic social contract of marriage and children. After *I Am You* I began to search for other texts containing possible references to female homosexual acts — naively assuming á la Foucault that female "homosexuality" in the Middle East was non-existent. I encountered a series of writings, curiously published within a three-year span between 1999–2002, which dealt rather mercilessly with homosexuality and various sexual "aberrations" of the similar kind. In these heavily solipsistic, God-fearing texts, the devil was the prominent originator of homosexual sins and activities. I deal with this material briefly later on. I also encountered Aĥmad Ibn Yusuf Tifashi's thirteenth century text *Nuzhat al-Albab*. I consider this text to be key to the argument I put forward and for this reason I dedicate chapter 4 entirely to a close reading of it. This text reveals that there can be no doubt as to the existence of female homosexuality, *at least* as a category, in the premodern Arabian imagination. In addition, the means and the rhetoric with which this material is written, strongly suggest a view of human sexuality which contrasts sharply with modern (Arab) orthodox notions of sexual pleasure and functional concepts of sex.

In translating from Tifashi's chapter, I relied on Jamal Jomåt's modern edition, published in 1992. Jomåt's text is reliable and is compiled by the editor from manuscript versions, one of which he perused at the Royal Library in Copenhagen, while the other two are to be found at the National Library (BNF) in Paris. Jomåt's introduction to the text relies heavily and without acknowledgment on Salaĥ Adeen al-Munajjid's *al-Ĥayat al-Jinsiya åind al Årab/Sexual Life among the Arabs*,[5] so much so that Jomåt may be Munajjid writing under a pseudonym or vice versa. Munajjid's study was published in 1958 and reprinted in 1975, on both occasions by Dar al-Kitab al-Jadid in Beirut. It is perhaps one of the best and most comprehensive scholarly works on a history of sexuality among Arabs, in which Munajjid traces the evolution of sexual customs among pre-Islam Arabs through to the radical changes that Islam brought with it in terms of sexual prohibitions and social (re)organization. Curiously, in an academic style which resonates with but precedes Foucaultian habits, Munajjid is not thorough in his footnotes. However, he does write with a well deserved and thoroughly researched authority on the subject. I have often followed the trail of many a statement made by Munajjid to find that, even though he did not footnote his sources, his claims were still true. Munajjid could not have fathomed the momentous importance of his work — that it was to become a rare scholastic feat to be ignored and abandoned for the better part of three decades, as the Lebanese (civil) wars droned on and brought with them a host of political and social problems which seemed to be more pressing than frivolous study into human sexuality.

Since Munajjid's work, Jamal Jomåt has been a leading figure in restoring medieval Arab erotology to modern availability. As well as preparing a modern edition of Tifashi's *Nuzhat al-Albab*[6] in 1992, he also re-introduced the ever-popular (particularly in the West) *al-Rawd al-Åttir fi Nuzhat al-Khatir*[7] (*The Perfumed Garden* first translated into English by Richard Burton in 1886) two years earlier. In 1994, Jomåt also brought to modern availability the compilation of Abu Nuwass's poetry *Jocularity and Amusement* — a collection of his lewd poems collected and first published in 1898 — more congenially re-titled for a twentieth century readership as *The Forbidden Texts*.[8] Jomåt also belongs to that rare breed of Arabic-writing intellectuals who seek to liberate Arabic discourse on sex from the moral restrictions placed by orthodox (and solipsistic) scholars who are his contemporaries. Jomåt's introductions to his compilations tend to contextualise the erotological material within a sociohistorical framework which sees these works as symptoms of a progressive Arabian intellectualism and sociability.

On the other hand, the predominant literature on homosexuality in Arabia is written from a moral and religious high ground, which sees the existence and acceptance of homosexual practices as indications, not of intellectualism, but of moral and intellectual degeneration. In these writings there can be no argument about the moral baseness of the subject and the biological, or purely mental, degeneracy it implies. These texts tend to rely rather dubiously on the kinds of evidence they bring to discussion. An exemplary text is Muntasir Mut͟hhir's *al-Mutåt al-Muĥarama/The Prohibited Pleasure*[9] first published in 2001. In his concluding statement, Mut͟hhir calls for a moral war, in an anxious tone that conveys the sense that the very constitution of decency and humanity are verging on extinction as a result of homosexuality. For example, he writes:

> ...those will come who will complete or add to, or better present what we have here presented...Our greater aim has been in putting a limit to "sexual deviation" in all of its manifestations. And this book is a loud cry, should it find those to hear it, which calls for functional cooperation and participation in saving humanity's ark, which is in danger of sinking. (Mut͟hhir, 197)

Mut͟hhir includes a chapter on crimes committed by homosexuals to legitimize his claim that these individuals are unwholesome and threatening to the natural order of the human cosmos. In addition, throughout the text, Mut͟hhir's writing is coloured with adjectives and adverbs (such as "depravity" [*rathala*], "baseness" [*nathala*], "vileness" [*khi'sa*], "ugly and depraved habit" [*åda qabiĥa wa marthula*]) to contextualise his unmistakably moralistic view of his homosexual subjects. He makes a number of rather odd leaps of logic as well, such as in the instance where he ascertains that the execution of Plato (for his homosexuality) was a moment of "awakening" for the Greeks, who suddenly realized that "what vanquished their strength and swords and degenerated their sciences, was no other than their immersion in sodomy and sexual deviation [whilst] in contrast, the Romans [being conquerors of the Greeks at this point] ... [executed] every sodomite they found" (Mut͟hhir, 18). Mut͟hhir's knowledge of homosexuality is also dubious since he fails to establish a logical basis for his protestation against homosexuality and often conflates and confuses transgendered identities and pedophilia with homosexual ones. What he takes for granted as the most blatantly obvious: that homosexuality is a disease of the will and the body, is perhaps the point of his argument's aporetic disintegration.

Mut͟hhir's ultimate failure in being convincing is not necessarily because he comes from an irrational religious prejudice, but rather because he fails to produce any genuine knowledge of the subjects he treats. He fails to demonstrate that he has any understanding of the deviants' humanity beyond their sexual preference. Even the nature of their "deviance" is poorly represented to a readership which, due to the intellectual vacuum and censorship surrounding the subject, is unlikely to contest him on any of the points he makes. In his chapter entitled "Sodomy and Tribadism: Between the Law, Science and Medicine" he writes:

> Scientist have asserted that for every man there is a feminine side, similarly for every woman there is a masculine side ... so if the woman possessed a great deal of "male" traits then there appears the tribade in her, and if the man possessed a great deal of feminine traits thus appears the homosexual (read as sodomite) male. However it is possible for sexual deviance NOT to occur in such individuals despite this, if the environmental conditions and religious inclinations in which they are reared are good. It can be noted that in the tribade there is a weakness of maternal instinct and an absence in inclination towards men or being impressed by them, she is continually attempting to imitate them and competes with them ... There also appears in her a tendency towards controlling her husband .... masculine (read as male) features appear in her face, she also has thick skin prone to developing pimples. Her hair is closer to baldness at the forehead .... hair also spreads throughout her body in which muscles grow .... As for the medical point of view .... deviant sex is the primary source for catching the dangerous immune deficiency disease, known as AIDS, which is an illness known to eliminate human beings within months because it is a virus which targets blood cells. (Muthhir, 186)

Highly reminiscent of obsolete medicine, some form of phrenology, it seems almost pointless and excruciating to have to sift through these claims and show their logical and evidential fallacies at every turn. And yet this is precisely the nature of the literature on homosexuality available to a curious readership. Even Muthhir's basic explanation of AIDS fails to take into account the difference between AIDS and HIV or the relationship of lesbian sex to the contraction of HIV, or the heterosexual or non-sexual transmission of the virus.

Muthhir's textbook and its Orthodox "No" which permeates the subject of homosexuality for Arab cultures (whether religiously devout or not), is preceded by Khatib Ådnani's *al-Zina Wal Shuthooth Fi Tarikh al-Årab* (1999).[10] In fact, Muthhir reiterates a considerable number of concepts presented by Ådnani, who in turn, reiterates them on behalf of a number of premodern Muslim scholars, oftentimes without acknowledgement. What both authors fail to do is take into consideration those texts written *by* other Arab scholars, ancient or contemporary, whose temperate views on homosexuality and scientific methodology of enquiry, tend to originate from less exclusive and stringent theological and social beliefs.[11] Ibrahim Maĥmood's *al-Mutåt al-Maĥthoora* (2000)[12] is a more ambiguously written and rigorously researched work on the history of homosexuality among the Arabs. It offers the usual Orthodox "No" to homosexuality a little more vaguely and hesitantly, yet it assumes the abjection of homosexuality without seeking to prove this or to delineate its rhetorical axioms as such. Maĥmood's presentation of evidence, however, is also heavily biased and resonates, at least in the theological discussion, with the texts abovementioned.

The main argument against homosexuality espoused in these kinds of texts, whether explicitly or implicitly, is as follows:

1. God has decreed against unlawful acts of sex. Homosexuality has been forbidden in the Torah, Quran and the Ĥadiţh. Therefore, the matter is indisputable, or so it seems, from the onset for believers. Both Sodomy and Tribadism were originally introduced to Lot's people by the devil disguising himself as an old man who showed men sodomy, and then as a woman, showed women tribadism.[13] Therefore, homosexuality is the work of the devil not God (Muthhir, 37; Maĥmood, 107).
2. Homosexuality was forbidden by God and is undesirable because it is unnatural, and because it negates the purpose of sex — which is childbearing — it indicates an individual's desire for self-annihilation (Maĥmood, 273).
3. Homosexuality is a contagion which, if allowed to exist liberally, will spread and cause the annihilation of humanity due to lack of interest in breeding or inability to breed.[14]
4. Homosexuality spreads and causes diseases—namely AIDS (Muthhir, 189; Ådnani, 110).
5. Homosexuality itself, if not simply a sign of sheer moral degeneration, is then a disease or biological defect.

This argument is fundamentally flawed at each turn.

Points 1 & 2. The claims that homosexuality is strictly forbidden in the Quran is disputable. I deal with this issue in chapter 3 where I trace this idea to its medieval origin and attempt to contextualize its rise and wide dissemination in relation to the centuries which precede it. The Quran is much more ambivalent toward homosexuality than the Torah or the New Testament. Even the aĥadiţh which discuss homosexuality have been suspected, at least by *one* medieval intellectual, of being forgeries. A dispute as regards the view of homosexuality in Islamic theology exists, but it has not been properly attended to. Other theologians were either accepting or clearly tolerant of homosexuality, sometimes reflecting a culture of tolerance hidden from the traditional view of the canon — among such thinkers were Yaĥya Bin Akţham (explicitly), Tifashi and (implicitly) Ibn Ĥazm.

Point 3. Scientific studies carried out in the latter portion of the twentieth century suggest that homosexual behaviour is apparent in a number of species across the ecosystem.[15] Some scientific theories for homosexuality have attempted to find functional purposes for it, indicating a trend in nature towards diversification to ensure continuity and survival.[16] However, the "functional" basis of homosexuality seems to be more elusive than the functional basis scientists have unquestionably assumed for heterosexuality (i.e. procreation), which suggests that a review of our certainty of the latter is in order if we are to come to a more comprehensive understanding of the various functionalities of sexuality or sexualities. I delve into these concepts of functionality in the next chapter.

Point 4. No scientific study to date has pursued the question of whether homosexuality is indeed contagious or not but I suspect that this is because the answer is self-evident. Some research is required in order to ascertain whether permissive cultures have increased the ratio of homosexual-acting to heterosexual-acting individuals. Although it seems that in sexually repressive cultures instances of homosexuality are greater, albeit that this form of homosexuality is sometimes "opportunistic." Further research might help us better substantiate the notion that a society composed predominantly of sexual deviants[17] (which is the fear lurking behind Orthodox denunciations) would be either equally or less harmful to the process of creation and human existence than a society constituted predominantly of "law" abiding individuals.

The most significant scientific research into homosexuality has been conducted in order to determine whether homosexuality contains essentialist (biological) determinants or not. The scientific community continues to be divided on the subject. A number of studies have concluded that homosexuality possesses heritable (i.e. genetic) factors particularly in women.[18] Some studies have attributed the difference in behaviour between hetero and homo *men* to differences in brain structures in respective groups. This theory was engendered by Simon Le Vay in his *The Sexual Brain* (1993)[19] and was further developed as a sociological question in *Queer Science* (1996).[20] Even here, in the realm of scientific research, there are but few enquiries into female homosexuality — I discuss this relevant literature briefly in the next chapter.

Point 5. At the onset of the AIDS epidemic in the Reaganesque 1980s, AIDS was for some time a Sodomite's disease, and the easiest form of transmission of HIV continues to be anal intercourse (which is often associated with homosexual acts between men). Attitudes towards AIDS and its connection to male homosexuality in particular have eased, considering that the disease now unfortunately affects infants, heterosexuals and those in third world countries much more than the "American Sodomites." Sexual promiscuity meant increased likelihood in contraction of STDs and their dissemination, this was and is seen as a sign from God: as one preacher on the Christian Right famously put it: "Homosexuality is the disease, AIDS is the cure."[21] The idea that homosexual sex in itself created HIV is an idea of something impossible; the idea that homosexual behaviour singularly spreads HIV/AIDS to heterosexuals and infants and third world countries is also insubstantial.[22] Finally, exclusively lesbian sexual activity is counted as the category which faces the lowest risk of HIV infection.

Point 6. Homosexuality, given current social statistics, is certainly abnormal, that is, it is a deviation from the norm. Medical concepts of homosexuality are no longer fashioned to fit the current (internationally held) medical definition of disease, although it has been previously considered in Western countries as such.[23]

There is much to be disputed in the arguments set forth by Mu<u>thh</u>ir, Ådnani, Maĥmood and their predecessors, on various levels the least of which is the personal. One text which is situated in a rather peculiar position within this particular discourse on homosexuality is Ålia Shuåyb's book *Kalam al-Jasad* (2001).[24] Shuåyb, a Kuwaiti scholar, is one of a handful of Arab intellectuals, within the three-year period of 1999–2002, who approaches the subject with what appears to be true scholastic intent. Her research methodology is admirable and it reveals a great deal about female homosexual behaviour indigenous to Arab Gulf countries, for example the survey she conducts with one hundred female university students yields some rather astonishing results:

> ...fifty-three percent of [these] women admitted that they would love a woman if it were not for the objections of religion and society ... and sixty per cent of women admitted to having an inclination towards the love of women ... and seventy-nine percent of women admitted to having inclinations towards other women but that they attempted to repress or ban this. (Shuåyb, 25)

Unfortunately, however, Shuåyb's ideological precepts leave a lot to be desired, as the author is not able to shun the pressure placed on her by society and the academy to take a condemning moral stance. At no point is she able to consider the possibility that homosexual feelings may not be as damaging to the social fabric and the moral cosmos as is stringently believed. Nor is Shuåyb able to stray too far from modern Orthodoxy, for she writes in one instance:

> The Islamic doctrine prohibits anything which contradicts natural sexual relations and those which are outside the framework of marriage, because of what they contain of phantasmal and imagined pleasure. It is irrational to assume that there is pleasure in the prohibited sexual act, for it provides no benefit and it contradicts good instead of achieving it, since it causes much pain and has a negative impact on the individual, his family and society at large and because it contradicts the

> Heavenly order of marriage whose goal is reproduction — homosexual relations are not able to produce this. (Shuåyb, 35)

Shuåyb does not explain why non-reproductive but perhaps fulfilling erotic sexual encounters provide "no benefit" or why they might contradict "good" rather than achieve it, except by simply relying on the commonplace recourse: homosexual acts do not lead to progeny and this must mean that they are evil. Furthermore, the book is a study, not only of female homosexual practices in the Arabian Gulf but also of prostitution. The implication being that the two behaviours are a result of some deficiency in social relations (between men and women) and that these two can be fittingly categorized together and in juxtaposition. On the motives behind homosexual relations between women, Shuåyb writes:

> The woman can be comfortable with another woman and she experiences neither fear nor embarrassment to mar or murk her pleasure particularly in the absence of the male scent and the male member and the thick and coarse hair and penetration and erection. There is no pain in female homosex and no problem of the hymen or the responsibility of remaining chaste; there is only comfort, pleasure and complimentarity. (Shuåyb, 23)

It is interesting that Shuåyb contradicts her own statements that she made only a few pages earlier where it was "irrational to assume that there is any pleasure in the prohibited" sex act, by telling us of the many advantages of female homosex, all of which, amusingly, perhaps tautologically, revolve around the notion that there are no men involved. While in a way Shuåyb's work is reliable for the sociological methodology it deploys, and while it reveals to us intricate social and cultural constructions of Gulf homosexualities, it remains unconvincing in its inability to fathom homosexuality outside the framework of religious prohibitions and inadequate heterosexual relations. The focus is once more on the "homosexuality" which is a recourse, which is not innate, homosexuality which is *unnatural*.

A traditional constructionist may wish to argue that this is so because this is the nature of Gulf homosexualities, that is, there are no homosexualities such as those we call "innate" here. A considerable deal of evidence and relationships forged over some years of research cause me to disagree forcibly on this point. As I discuss in the next chapter, the problem with social constructions of sexuality is that these constructions are in themselves heavily ideological and tend to focus on "ideologies" as though these are the only possible means of understanding the visible world. For instance it might be argued that no such thing as "homosexuality" takes place in Kuwait or in Lebanon — that it is only homosexual behaviour, not orientation/identification, which takes place.

Interestingly, Ålia Shuåyb's study reveals a little about these homosexual acts native to the lives of Kuwaiti mariners from previous generations:

> The men used to set sail in search for pearls or travel with the intention to trade in India etc. And the women used to stay alone at home, taking care of their duties as mothers and as domestic managers in the kitchen .... But at the end of the day and after doubly difficult labour [as she assumes the chores of both man and woman in her husband's absence] the woman is left feeling deprived of emotional and moral support as she finds herself in need of tenderness. And because the husband's absence was long there emerged a need for finding a person to fill the moral and emotional emptiness left by this absence and it was then that a need for a female lover and intimate emerged. (Shuåyb, 31)

Shuåyb quotes her now elderly subjects and further explains that these relations took place to the knowledge of both husbands and wives and that the homosexual relations came to an end upon the husband's return from his long travels. She further illuminates us, through discussion with one of her interviewees, that similar conduct took place aboard the ships on which the men voyaged (Shuåyb, 32). Constructionists will be quick to see this as an example of culturally variant homosexual beahviour, to demonstrate that the "modern homosexual subject" (who is exclusive for one thing) does not possess a universal component, or that a certain sexual component (such as homosexual behaviour) does not constitute identity. Luckily we *do* now know that there are many examples of "homosexuals" in the Middle East, with one pair being prosecuted for having a homosexual marriage ceremony. And even though what Shuåyb reveals may very well be true, this in itself does not and cannot negate the possibility that "homosexuals" existed before the term was coined.

It has always been assumed that "Gay Weddings" are a recent Western phenomenon brought on by the Civil Rights movement in the 1970s. This is one reason why Boswell's *Same Sex Unions in Premodern Europe* (1994)[25] was greeted with much protestation. Similarly, until recently, it could not have been thought that the Arabs living in their native homelands experienced life-long love relationships with members of their own sex. In contradistinction to such a mode of argumentation we have recently begun to learn that homosexual women and men in the Middle East have performed private marriage ceremonies[26] (those who are found out are usually prosecuted, hence the obscurity and invisibility of this phenomenon). Evidence of "Gay Weddings" in the Middle East only appears in the media when the "perpetrators" are caught and incarcerated, with the exception of Noura El-Ĥakeem's recent, short column "Not First, But Welcome" in which she informs us:

> Recently there were two news items about gay marriages in Muslim countries that have received a lot of international coverage. One was from Egypt, with Kuwaiti men getting married. The other from Pakistan, with Afghan [sic] men getting married. Are they firsts? No.
>
> Why are western media always terming our lives "first", according to their knowledge? What do these people know about our struggles in our countries? I consider myself young and I have been blessed to know many lesbians unions [sic]. I have also heard [sic] many male celebrations. If somehow one of them is exposed to the media, will their union be considered the 'first' in the Arab world? Even if we all know it is not?
>
> In 2002, as an Egyptian woman in my Egyptian circles, I married my longtime girlfriend [of eleven years] Zainab.[27]

At the site of these texts, both homophobic and homophilic, published so closely together at the turn of the twentieth century and the beginning of a new millennium, it is difficult to imagine that social attitudes about homosexuality can ever truly begin to shift in the Arab world. The prejudice seems too deeply embedded and the believers are so adamant about their beliefs. The literature available to those who are curious about the subject will do nothing but dissuade them from an ideology which liberates the human mind into accepting a variety of the body's desires. While I have heavily criticized the assumption by these Arab scholars that homosexuality is some sort of parasitic evil, I should also point out that a theory which attempts to prove the opposite of this is almost equally dubious — in the same vein that heterosexuality as common "good" is equally dubious to establish. Prejudice against homosexuality has been so resilient and has survived throughout the ages precisely because homosexuality itself can be appropriately categorized as a deviance. Being outside the norm — i.e. abnormal — opens the phenomenon to various rhetorical vulnerabilities which cannot be defended against indisputably. In this realm of prejudicial thinking, imaging homosexuality as a virus, or an aberration is not entirely fantastical since it indeed threatens the foundations of "normal" moral society by threatening its increased dilution (though by no means the extinction of the species as enthusiasts like Mu<u>th</u>hir and Shabazz suggest). Homosexuality suggests a different form of organized society, different ways of conception and procreation which do not at all resemble the so-called natural world of the animal kingdom, which has no doubt inspired religious doctrines on sexual behaviour, where the male rules supreme and the female acts as a recipient.

The gender binary is central to Orthodox Islamic religious doctrine, where men and women are ascribed specific social roles based on their gender; deviations from the gender binary (through homosexual couplings, masculine women, effeminate men etc.) in which social constructions are geared towards progeny, are seen as not only undesirable but as contradictions of the Creator's intention (Shabazz, 1–2 & 5). This is one possible reason as to why transgenderism is more acceptable in countries like Saudi Arabia and Iran (both of which condemn homosexuality with sentences that can be as harsh as death) than they have been accepted elsewhere both in the Arab and Western worlds. The logic behind this acceptance is not a tendency towards openness and acceptance of gender deviance, but rather what informs the impetus is an obsession in keeping and maintaining the distinction between men and women. If a man believes that he is a woman then he must be reduced to that social status, otherwise, if he dwelled among other men, whilst believing he is a woman, then he would be committing grievous injury to the orthodox tradition of social relations. Similarly, if a woman believes that she is a man, she must not dwell in the ranks of women, although she will never be *fully* received in the ranks of men.[28]

A great irony dwells in the current climate surrounding the surge in transsexual surgeries in the Arabian and Persian gulfs. This is more than simply good news for repressed individuals who are born with transsexual inclinations, who are now able to transform their bodies into who they believe they truly are. The murkier side of this positive aspect will be the assimilation of homosexual men and women within this binary gender paradigm. Effeminate men, masculine women and those who admit an overwhelming desire for sexual experiences with members of their own sex will all be threatened by a solution to their deviation which will conflict with their sense of identity. The "solution" or reparative therapy for homosexual desires might soon become transsexual operations, as it once had been shock therapy or hormone replacement therapy. This homosexual gender reassignment will preserve the heteronormative order of the "human" cosmos and the binary gender paradigm: Men who desire to be penetrated by other men will be turned into women, while men who desire to sodomise other men, may continue to be thought of as manlier for it.

It would be confounding to intellectuals born of this cultural, social and traditional climate to come to terms with the concept of the feminine lesbian or even more confounding a lesbian who is a sexual "bottom." Indeed, none of the studies cited above seem to be able to recognize feminine female homosexual subjects. Since there is no epistemological or discursive means, either for the medical professionals or the academics of the Gulfs, to understand homosexuality in its atomic variations, it will be relegated to a deviance which can be eradicated through surgery: "Approval of gender changes doesn't mean approval of homosexuality. We're against homosexuality .... But we have said that if homosexuals want to change their gender, this way is open to them."[29] What is even more peculiar is Ayatollah al-Khomeini's part in making transsexual surgeries legal in the Islamic Republic of Iran. Khomeini "had pronounced on gender problems in a book written in 1963, when he indicated there was no religious proscription against corrective surgery" *for intersexed individuals*. It was not until Maryam Molkara, a MTF transsexual, pleaded with the Ayatollah in person that she was able to acquire "a letter addressed to the chief prosecutor and the head of medical ethics giving religious authorisation for her — and, by implication, others like her — to surgically change their gender."[30] Molkara's story is exemplary of the flexibility of even the most Orthodox Islamic systems of thought and should serve as a reminder that simplistic understandings of any culture or social organization are fundamentally flawed. Nevertheless, a similar plea for homosexual desires has yet to achieve such a success in the Islamic Republic, and this is complicated by the fact that the Quran has not been silent in regards to sodomy, whereas in contrast it makes no mention (prohibitory, deprecatory or otherwise) of either hermaphroditism or transgenderism.

The main argument *against* homosexuality insinuates that homosexuality is in itself an infliction of violence on the innocent and the God Fearing and the righteous. The story of Lot's people reflects an archetypal impression, deeply seated within Hebraic religious cultures, which couples homosexual behaviour with sexual aggression among a host of other deplorable activities. The story of Lot's people does not vary terribly much from the Torah to the Quran and within it resonates that deep seated hatred, resentment for the reviled, sexually fluid enemies of God. Homosexuals (here perhaps omnisexuals) are equivocated with perpetrators of sexual assault, violence against the innocent and weak (presumably) heterosexual protagonist(s). In the dogmatic rhetoric it is always the homosexuals and the sexual deviants who are perpetrating violence against the nation, society and culture.[31] Ironically, acts of violence perpetrated *against* homosexuals, whether state controlled or individually based, currently constitute the great bulk of violence involving homosexual deviance.[32] As Vasu Reddy notes in his examination of "Homophobia as Hate Speech in Africa", homophobia is "a discourse of power, dominance and control which is not merely a form of patriarchal oppression, but a kind of performative communication that produces discourses about homosexuals in order to misrecognize them."[33] Reddy also adds that homophobia as "a form of persuasive discourse is engineered to arouse emotion around the subject it despises" (Reddy, 167). The discourse Reddy examines intricately in his article is entirely commensurable with the rhetoric of present Arab critics writing on the subject, not to mention that it is also the same rhetoric imposed on the discourse of homosexuality as early as the Arabian middle ages, and it has resounding similarities with any rhetoric motivated by the vilification of homosexual orientation. What occurs in the orthodox discourse is always a conflation between sexual orientation or preference and a host of sexual violations: pedophilia, assault and bestiality, the three of which constitute violation since consent is not possible, is not sought or is coerced.

The representation of homosexuality that I have discussed above is shared by the great bulk of Arabs living in the Middle East. Individuals who touch on the topic (should it be raised) are frequently expected to hold a homogenous and negative view of homosexual behaviour. Due to the prevalence of homosexual behaviour which is not homosexual, but which is opportunistic at best, people in the Middle East have difficulty in distinguishing the desire to be homosexual from the activity of homosexuality. To some individuals, who may have at some point engaged in homosexual activity, this experience is not pleasant, and is rather a substitute for another experience (with the opposite sex) which is more difficult and risky to attain. Such has been the nature of the reception and understanding of homosexuality until recent years and it is no wonder that homosexuality is thought to be an act, rather than an orientation, even as early as the times of the prophet who seemed to have been more interested in the prohibition of the *act* of homosex rather than the desire for members of the same gender.[34]

The famous Cairo52 case, well documented in a newly released (May 2005) documentary *Dangerous Living*,[35] brought the subject of homosexuality qua sexual orientation or preference rather than sexual acts to the forefront. Fifty-two men engaging in revelry on the amusement boat *The Queen Boat* in Cairo, Egypt, were arrested on May 11, 2001. Of the fifty-two men who were arrested, fifty faced charges of "habitual debauchery" and "obscene behaviour" (since, similar to the Lebanese penal code, homosexual behaviour is not specifically outlawed, but it is classified by prosecutors and law enforcers as an aspect of unnatural sex acts or obscene behaviour).

In both Kuwait and Saudi Arabia, the authorities have had to stamp down on "Gay Weddings" — these are not merely "sex parties" which involve tourists and married men;[36] these are indications of intimate, *homosexual* partnerships. The trial of three Saudi men charged with "homosexual acts" and "child-molestation" resulted in their execution on January 1, 2002, whilst various other arrests have taken place in Saudi Arabia where punishments included prison terms and lashings for men involved in homosexual activities *and relationships*. Nevertheless, we must take into account that even in the most repressive societies, on the atomic level, things are never as dire as they appear. Mubarak Dahir, a freelance writer and journalist who has traveled extensively throughout Arab and Muslim countries and frequently reports on the nature of "gay life" in those countries, seems to be of the opinion that execution for homosexual acts alone is near impossible. He writes:

> I was able to do in-depth interviews with five gay men — three in Riyadh, the largest city and the seat of government, and two in Jeddah, the country's most progressive city. I found these men worrying more about how to meet others for sex and companionship, how to date and keep their sexual orientation secret, whether they would be forced by their families to marry, and what to wear to show off their bodies. Getting beheaded was just about the last thing on anyone's mind.[37]

INTRODUCING SOME OF THE INDEX TERMS

I wrote this book with high fidelity to the research conducted. Instead of naming the subjects of this study as "lesbians" or else something much longer (like woman-woman eroticism in the Arabic Middle Ages), I refer to them by a literal translation of the term assigned to them culturally (and, significantly, not the name some of them assigned themselves). I hope in doing this, I demonstrate that although the terms and concepts espoused by ancient languages, describing sexual behaviour and feeling, do refer to something uniquely different from our own words, that in the end, we might be looking at our human condition which precedes or exists independently of our language of it. Below is a brief introduction to the literal translation of some terms.

Luṯi (Literal translation is "of or pertaining to [the prophet] Lot") describes a male engaged in the act of homosexual sodomy and it comes from the biblical prophet Lot. The Judaic story of Lot is recounted in the Quran and a man being referred to as a *luṯi* is seen to be one engaging in homosexual activities (coupled with bestiality, alcohol drinking, gambling, sexual assault and general wickedness) on a regular basis. *Liwaṯ* is a noun which may be understood as "Sodomy" in its classical sense — i.e. it is not only the active partner (the sodomite) who is a *luṯi*, but so are the sodomized, and thus they both perform *liwaṯ*. On one occasion I was able to find the use of the verb *laṯa* (engaged in sodomy) in relation to a woman (i.e. *laṯat*). In a section dedicated to "women devoid of good taste", al-Suyuṯi[38] describes such a woman in the following way: "she grinded (*saĥaqat*) as a girl, sodomised (*laṯat*) and fornicated in her old-age" (9). Here *laṯat* is very peculiar. It is possible that this verb was used under poetic license since the use of this term in relation to women is not evident elsewhere in the literature. However, it is possible that al-Suyuṯi was, in fact, referring to a particular sexual practice which involved women performing sodomy, or an act which is similar, on others.[39]

For female homosexual behaviour, the term most commonly used in both past and present Arab-speaking cultures is *suĥaq* — which has nothing nearly as flashy as a biblical association. *Suĥaq* means grinding, as in pepper or some such herb. Others prefer to derive the meaning of *suĥaq* from the original word *saĥq* which, besides grinding, also means eradication, complete and total destruction. Particularly, the image of the grinding of saffron has been most heavily associated with woman-to-woman sexual action. Anatomically speaking, the word "grinding" is in reference to the rubbing of clitorises against each other, or presumably, against the lover's or beloved's body parts. On one occasion *suĥaq* or *suĥaqiyya* (i.e. the woman who practices *suĥaq*) were used to denote simply clitoral masturbation, most references, however, refer to sexual relations between women — both voluntary and circumstantial, both long term and short term. In referencing female homoeroticism as *Suĥaq* (rubbing or grinding) woman-to-woman penetration does not seem to have been known to the male Muslim scholars who wrote on the subject. When women performed sexual acts on each other these were always thought to have involved surface grinding, for in the patriarchal imagination, penetration could only be attained with the male presence. By the same token, when men and women engaged each other in intercourse this was always going to involve penetration and therefore the term *suĥaq* came to be known as the exclusive property of homosexually acting women. Medieval Arab scholars rarely indicated whether there were "active" and "passive" parties amongst the "grinders" and in most cultural interpretations of the Quran and the aĥadiṭh both parties involved in the homosexual act are equally culpable.

The use of the term *mukhanaṭh* refers to an effeminate male, sometimes it is also used to refer to a hermaphrodite (*khunṭha*) or to an individual who has been castrated. When referring to a *mukhanaṭh* in the context of sodomy, the effeminate homosexual male is the intended conveyance — such a male is always presented as one who enjoys being sodomised, and who seeks sodomy liberally and has a tendency to dwell amongst women even though regularly speaking this would be seen as a grave transgression.[40] A masculine grinder was referred to as a *mutathakeera* (male-like-woman), and she was a woman who took on the "mannerisms of a man", and according to al-Samaw'uli, competed with men for the affections of women.

More contemporary terminology includes a*l-miṭhliya*, which is a translation of the word homosexuality. The root word is *miṭhil* which translates as "alike" or "similar", hence referencing the term "homo" as in "same" or "alike." The concept of *al-Jins al-ṭhaliṭh*, or "The Third Sex" appeared some time in the 1970s and it appears to be a conflation or confusion of hermaphroditism, transgenderism and homosexuality — all three categories of "deviance" being seen as indications that individuals with these "conditions" are neither man nor woman, thus occupying the space of a third sex. The expression *al-shuthooth al-jinsee* (which translates literally as sexual abnormality or sexual deviance) was imported from homophobic 1950s Western sexology,[41] but the expression continues to feature today as the most popular term used for "homosexuality" in Arabic-speaking countries. Its popularity is no doubt due to the moral finality associated with the subject of homosexual desire.

WHAT IS A HOMOSEXUAL?

I am not able to avoid giving an account of the constructionist critique of essentialism particularly when I have assumed a predominantly essentialist mode of inquiry. As David Greenberg rightly chronicles, constructionism grew as a response to unsophisticated essentialist and often homophobic qualifications of homosexuality.

> With the destruction of the homosexual-liberation movement at the hands of the Nazis, historical research on homosexuality virtually ceased. By default, most scholarly discussions of homosexuality were medical or psychiatric. The physicians and psychiatrists who wrote of it were primarily interested in its causes, prevention, and treatment and saw little reason to turn to history of the social sciences. Their training led them to view sexuality as presocial and individual, so that the ways it was expressed and the responses it received could not be illuminated by knowledge of their social context. (Greenberg, 4)

Constructionist histories of sexuality were born to counteract negative and dogmatic literatures (which were, coincidentally, also essentialist) while also initiating the project of gay (cultural) historiography. The effect has been a slow institutionalization of constructionism and rejection of essentialism in social and cultural studies (while medical literature is still predominantly interested in the essential quality of human sexualities). Even though a complex essentialism has not been disproved, it has not been revisited or considered seriously in recent gay historiography.

The best discussion of the essentialist/constructionist conflict is found in Edward Stein's introduction and conclusion to *Forms of Desire*, in which he clearly distinguishes the fundamental difference between essentialism and its successor.

> One cannot be a social constructionist and still think that sexual orientation is innate .... [while an essentialist] is committed to there being transcultural, law-like generalizations that can be made about the nature and origins of sexual orientation.[42]

Since constructionism's victory over essentialism within gay historiography in the late 1990s, there have been some re-considerations that have placed the soundness of constructionism into question. This is no more apparent than it is in the evolution of David Halperin's writing and analysis from his early work *One Hundred Years of Homosexuality* (1989) to *How to do the History of Homosexuality* (2002). By his own admission, "the overriding purpose of *One Hundred Years* ... was to win the once-vehement debate between essentialists and constructionists over the constitution of sexual identity."[43] As this quotation indicates Halperin argued for an uncompromising view of (Greek and therefore all) sexuality as consisting of ideological precepts and social programming, which are incommensurable, almost incomparable to, other paradigms of sexual identification — particularly modern (Western) ones.

In contrast to earlier works, Halperin's introduction to *History of Homosexuality* summarizes admirably some of the theory of constructionism's weaknesses and renders essentialism a greater complexity, but *without* inviting us to consider it more seriously. Whereas Halperin's career was consolidated the moment he took out a radical line against structuralist or formalist accounts of history, it soon became apparent that constructionism had simplified essentialism in such a way as to render only the most fundamental essentialism obsolete. And the reaction against essentialist and predominantly homophobic theories of sexuality had not taken into account the possibility of a more radical essentialism, which could work to corroborate studies of social and cultural constructions.

And yet I wonder if it isn't after all naïve to assume that the only "historicism" (the name Halperin imparts on the new-millennium, revised, constructionism) applicable to a history of homosexuality is that which emphasizes the ultimate "alterity of the past" (Halperin, 2002, 17) — its distinctness. This approach is unsatisfactory in its inability to tell us the significance of the transhistorical and transcultural similarities. At the same time, Halperin-style historicism can recover the archaeological remains of the missing and vital context (the spirit of the text?), and this is crucial to developing or maintaining a non-delusional body of knowledge. However, empirical evidence suggests that there are patterns in history. Or rather, patterns in the constitution of the human species which cause them to perpetuate significantly similar sexual behaviour.

Even though the tension around, and oftentimes contempt for, essentialism has eased,[44] encouragement to revise essentialism remains to be seen. This monograph attempts to consider the potential contributions of essentialism to gay historiography more seriously. I attempt to demonstrate throughout this work why it is not necessarily a historical crisis to refer to "medieval gay people." I feel that the unique evidence brought up by a history of Arabic homosexualities tends to support an essentialist framework, although it can be equally useful for constructionists who seek meaning in alterity. As such, I do not wish in this book to challenge the precepts of my predecessors so much as to contribute to the smaller field of essentialist inquiry. Luckily for me, my work comes at a time when the heated debate has considerably subsided, despite the fact that institutionally, constructionist (or historicist) studies find ample support opportunities[45] while, particularly with the rise and rise of gender studies and queer theory, the essentialist perspective is still being unlearned. And further, it is clear that the essentialism which emerges after the old essentialism gets the boot, will be a different one — a hybrid more resistant to the molecularizing power of the constructionist framework.

To illustrate one of my primary motivations for taking up an essentialist approach, I quote Halperin at length:

> Abelove pointed out that just because feudal peasants work with their hands and factory laborers work with their hands, it doesn't follow that feudal peasantry should be described as the form that proletarianism took before the rise of industrial capitalism. Of course, if you want

> to describe feudal peasantry that way, well, you can, and the claim even makes a kind of sense.[46]

Perhaps we could use the above analogy in a better way to demonstrate what Halperin admits only as "a kind of sense." It is not the quality of working with hands under which it is best to genealogize the temporally continuous relationship between feudal systems and capitalist ones. Rather, I would have said that factory workers and feudal peasants shared an inequality of profit from their labour — i.e. they are bound in hierarchies of power and business within which they are the most productive and the least rewarded. Of course, choosing an arbitrary category such as "working with hands" is not doing justice as an equivalent to the theoretical application of categories of sexual behaviour to various historical periods and situations.

The constructionist view, as Sedgwick pointed out, is negated by the concept of atemporality.[47] There is no inherent quality to time that makes past cultures automatically different to contemporary ones, on the contrary, the continuity of time itself makes an essentialist, panoramic survey of sexualities all the more important. And further, the constructionist viewpoint has a limited, singular view of homosexuality, much as medicalized models of the 1950s did, which is based upon a Eurocentric model of modernity. When these theorists talk about "the modern homosexual" the homosexual to whom they are invariably referring is from industrialized, first world, capitalist societies. As Stein notes, "different cultures produce different forms of sexual desire and different types of people" (Stein, 347). The focus on first world homosexuals has also been rendered problematic by postcolonial theorists who were keen to apply queer theoretical concepts to third world settings.[48] Just as the present is never a singular homological event, neither is the past.

More contemporary theorists take a more moderate perspective, acknowledging discontinuities as well as continuities within sexual erotic systems; they nevertheless continue to exhibit a strong bias in favour of cultural constructions.[49] Ultimately however, the last few years have seen considerable dissipation in the hostility towards essentialism, as constructionists began to ponder "the perennial features of the erotic system" and the postcolonial critique of the narrow categories of "modern" and "homosexual" (that somehow came to mean white, middle class, in a first world nation and predominantly English speaking). But even despite this adjustment, essentially-inclined theoretical frameworks are not encouraged, or at least they are overlooked. Perhaps this is due to no more than the fact that the Humanities produces many more historians and literary analysts than it does produce culture-analyzing, art-critiquing physicists.

Edward Stein has provided considerable insight into the particularities of the essentialist/constructionist battle, and he rightly observes that there are multiple strands and various levels of complexities when it comes to both theories of sexuality and sexual orientation. He does, however, demonstrate the strategic discovery needed to put an end to the conflict:

> Is it possible to develop a theory of sexual orientation which involves transcultural, objective categories ... or are the categories merely culture-dependent ones. This is both an interesting and important empirical answer, such an empirical answer will, if found, begin to settle the controversy between social constructionists and essentialists. (Stein, 353)

My response here is not to jump to hasty conclusions, or to affirm the strength of one position over another (although the recent neglect of essentialist inquiry is unfortunate), but to present to you the evidence of (a medieval) Arabian epistemology of sexuality, desire and identification, whose features feel strangely contemporaneous with recent discourses on sexuality. As a result, we are able to suspend the tenuous "categorical," metonymic and nomological conflict produced by essentialist and constructionist considerations. I expect that the reader will come to conclusions that better suit her or his previous experience and body of knowledge, as I do not think that my own, individual interpretation is as important as knowing that theoretical biases inform these interpretations in any case. However, while the interpretations are indicative of subjectivities, the writings themselves, the literary artifacts that present themselves in the material I review do not seem to be compatible with the constructionist tenet that "sexual orientation is" *not* "innate." And therefore at the very least, the evidence I present in the following chapters moves to reveal the calcification that has built up around the *concept* of sexuality-as-a-concept. Ultimately, the paradox of essentialism and constructionism is that neither alone can give a convincing account of being.

2 Constructing and deconstructing sexuality

New paradigms for "gay" historiography

Why do you blame me?
If you were to see how beautiful his eyes are
You would say that my preoccupation and my
late nights are not too high a price to pay
Why do you blame me?
Lovers' prisoner, O my melted heart,
From the wave of fragrance and the silken hair
Which rustles on the cheeks and then takes flight
...
And the people reproach me and what am I to do my heart?
They want to forbid me from him why my heart?
From the day his love touched my heart
It opened the door to yearning
And he is my lover, and he is my fortune
And he is the light to my eyes and my heart
And he is my youth and my relatives and all my beloveds
And the people reproach me and what am I to do my heart?
They want to forbid me from him why my heart?
—From *Why Do You Blame Me?* sung by Åbd al-Ĥalim Ĥafeth

Imagination is more important than knowledge.
—Albert Einstein

CONSTRUCTING SEXUALITY

Åbd al Ĥalim Ĥafeth[1] was not the first or last Arab singer to sing songs which seem to us (in translation), at first, celebrating his love for another man. In fact, Arabic song lyrics, at least in the twentieth century, are full of examples of this sort of song: where the male singer sings to one whose pronoun is "he," but where the "he-lover" (*ĥabibi*) is nearly always understood to be in actuality "she," wherever the singer happened to be male. The origins of this peculiarity might have something to do with the Andalusian love poem of the late Middle Ages and various other forms of poetry written by men and *for* men[2] (but this is only speculation and I cannot prove it). On the other hand, Folk wisdom tells us Arabs that this happened because it would have seemed too rude for a man to sing so fervently of this kind of passion to the "her" pronoun. This kind of explanation is quite insufficient considering that songs were sung to "shes" as much as "hes," and female singers were never expected to sing to the "she" pronoun in order to appease customary tastes. The most reasonable explanation might be one which appeals to grammatical rules, where the "He" refers to the lover, whose masculine state is also neutral in language. And without much thinking, it makes sense to natives of Arab culture: the song is not homoerotic; Åbd al Ĥalim Ĥafeth is not singing to another man, this is not evidence of the widespread acceptance of homosexual feelings and inclinations throughout twentieth-century Arabia. What this is, is peculiar, adding to the complexity of cultures reared on sexual forbiddance and convolutions. It is precisely this kind of cultural idiosyncrasy, referring to a woman as a man by another man who is in love with her, that scholars rummaging through the history of sexuality need to be aware and afraid of. The interpretation of text is so heavily cumbersome and burdensome, especially for those of us who are looking for things which were forbidden from writing, and who are looking into things whose context is no longer particularly clear or accessible.

For similar reasons, which cast doubt on the interpretation of little remaining evidence, John Boswell's research in the 1980s sparked a great deal of constructionist resistance to ideas of "gay history" and notions of "sexual identity." Resistance occurred precisely due to the ambiguity of context which surrounds the kinds of historical and literary artifacts needed to produce knowledge of transcultural and transhistorical "sexuality". Boswell's works *Christianity, Homosexuality and Social Tolerance* (1980)[3] and *The Marriage of Likeness: Same-Sex Unions in Pre-Modern Europe* (1994)[4] left a three-fold legacy which helped define the constructionist position at the same time that it defied it. Firstly, Boswell introduced into the discourse the idea that tolerance of homosexuals existed in the early Christian church. Secondly, dealing with manuscript evidence before him, he introduced us to an even more radical notion: same-sex marriage ceremonies in Medieval Europe. Thirdly, he took for granted that such a thing as "gay people" always existed. His critics in turn asserted reasonable disputes and doubts regarding the translation of the texts and Boswell's interpretations of them.

Among these criticisms was the notion that the church is in large part responsible for anti-homosexual attitudes, borrowing from the Judaic Levitical tradition which preceded it, and therefore, Boswell should not have dismissed or ignored the role of the church in configuring present attitudes.[5] As far as same-sex unions are concerned, the critics showed that Boswell was not able to prove that the ceremonies were ones involving lovers .... they could have indeed involved friends, or "brothers" in the non-sexual sense.[6] Most importantly, Boswell's idea of Medieval "gay people" (perhaps I should say gay men) was the one most ardently contested and was seen as incredibly anachronistic. This final point of dispute was marked by a constructionist fervour which was rising within the academy at the time, and which continues in its influence to this date, where sexuality began to be seen purely as a social construct — this in itself being based on the notion that sexual categories were evidently in the process of evolution and devolution and that these categories themselves, which reflected society's understanding of sexuality, were unstable and were indelible from cultural ideologies and systems of thought.[7]

To some extent, the notion that identity is constructed should be self-evident. Not only the "gay" identity but any identity incumbent on a phenomenon restricted to a particular sociohistorical context. For example, could there have been any Christians before the birth of Christ? This leads us to the question which is at the heart of the matter: is "gayness", what Boswell defined as a "conscious…erotic inclination toward [one's] own gender" (Boswell, 1980, 44), something which appeared as a *result* of homophobic attitudes (the coining of the term "homosexuality"), or at least which appeared due to a moment in history (such as the Gay and Lesbian civil rights movements of the 1970s?), or due to religious strictures, as Johansson reasons:

> … the Christian Church itself, by mercilessly outlawing all forms of homosexual expression and even feeling, unwillingly and unwittingly created the homosexual identity that emerges in modern times as the subjective reflex of the theological-forensic notion.[8]

What institutional homophobia most likely *did* do was engender the phenomenon of Gay Pride and the creation of a Queer Nation or an international LGBT collective consciousness, however it seems dubious and illogical that, as Johansson suggests above, the prohibition of certain sexual acts then lead to the creation of a people who did not previously exist and who now existed solely for the purpose of performing (exclusively) these prohibited sexual acts. It would seem more logical to fathom that such people *did* exist but *for whom contemporary gay semiotics and epistemology was nonexistent.* But one cannot rob these individuals of the most basic conscious knowledge of themselves as different from the dictates of standard social sexual currency.

Although we cannot delineate which factors of human behaviour are affected by innate responses and biology and which are affected by social learning, we can always take a guess precisely by comparing cultures from different historical and geographical contexts. For example Aĥmad Bin Moĥamad Bin Åli al-Yemeni (d. 845)[9] tells us that there were two kinds of *grinders*: "Some of them love grinding but do not hate the penis," while the "second kind is a woman who is masculine (*mutathakeera*) in appearance and this *becomes apparent in her from an early age*. She competes with men and resembles them and haughtily rejects submitting to them. She rejects being fucked and undermines penises and competes with men over deflowering other women, and she equals the men in jealousy over, and protection of, women."[10] Would it be unfair and anachronistic of me to refer to al-Yemeni's second type of woman as *similar to* a butch, top lesbian? When I learn later from al-Yemeni that some such women also take for their pleasure, young adolescent men by rubbing themselves against the young men's anuses and I learn even later that some women prefer sexual relations only with beardless (feminine) young men, does it then become implausible that homosexuality existed? We might interpret this evidence to suggest that women's sexual orientations were not geared towards genders but rather towards passion for the feminine or the masculine, regardless of gender. In this way it would be difficult to establish that these women were homosexual or that homosexuality existed. In a similar vein in regards to this subject in antiquity, Halperin has argued:

> The most salient *erotic* distinction made by the ancients rested not on a physical typology of anatomical sexes (male vs. female) or even on gender differences (man vs. woman) but on the social articulation of power (superordinate vs. subordinate social identity).[11]

Hence, the logic continues, the "homosexual" was nonexistent, because the concept was not possible given the hierarchy of social relations which, as Halperin argues, encompassed nongendered power relations. But for the Arabs of the Medieval Islamic empire, as persuasive and sophisticated as the above possible analysis sounds, it is difficult to imagine power relations organized in any manner more obvious than those which are gender based, if only because the entire social and cultural structure of Islam was originally based on the distinction between the place and role of both men and women. A ĥadiṭh related by Ibn Åbbas (a companion of the prophet) and which appears in Saĥiĥ al-Bukhari as well as other transmissions, demonstrates once more that men and women with atypical gender behaviour were seen as transgressive: "The Prophet cursed effeminate men and masculine (man-like) women, and he said, take them out of your houses."[12]

Furthermore, al-Yemeni continues in his catalogue of the behaviour of these "masculine" grinders who are not interested in erotic relations with men, while the more feminine ones behave bisexually, and should prefer the penis given the right encounter with the right-sized male:

> This woman [another *type* of grinder] can be rescued from doubt to what is just and extracted from mood to truth by a skilled man who is rich in ways of intercourse and who can offer her various forms of fucking, until she finds one she prefers and which agrees with her appetite, and who then administers it to her. (*Rashd*, 124)

At what point does it become anachronistic to read al-Yemeni's writing within a feminist framework which critiques the deluded phallocentric misogyny of patriarchal ignorance of female (homo)sexuality? And is it not peculiar that, even through al-Yemeni's patriarchal biases, the behaviour of individuals who can be loosely categorized as "lesbian," "gay," "bisexual," "femme," "butch," "top," "bottom" and "queer" can still be glimpsed through his moral filter? Do not these masculine behaving women, who choose so-called "passive" feminine women for their sexual partners *resemble*, at least loosely and basically, those women whose history is better documented in the the United States of the 1950s and 1960s — the generation of adamant lesbians living exclusively through the butch/femme dichotomy, whose communities were closely documented by the likes of Nestle, Kennedy and Davis?[13] I have asked a great number of rhetorical questions in order to delineate that the search for intercultural differences has become so politically charged that a search for trans-histocultural similarities is seen as a faux pas. However, in the state or collation of what we find *repeated* in history and not the *new* or different in history, exists the theoretical axiom upon which Boswell's concept of medieval "gay people" stands.

It would seem that while it is important for historians of sexuality to be aware of their own "alien" involvement in the making of the sexual past (history), it is still possible to refer to "homosexuality" and "gayness" according to the terms of a monolithic language — as a single set of pronouns, nouns and adjectives — which suffice in a comprehensive and generalist approach to the study of human sexuality. As Boswell put it:

> It is true that there were no terms in common use in Greece or Rome to describe categories of sexual preference, but it does not follow that such terms were wholly unknown: Plato, Athenaeus, and other writers who dealt with the subject at length developed terms to describe predominant or exclusive interest in the opposite gender. Many writers, moreover, found it possible to characterize homosexuality as a distinct mode of erotic expression without naming it.[14]

But Boswell and his military of critics were all heavily interested in male homosexualities — Classical and Medieval alike. In the meantime, studies of female homosexuality flourished in the latter part of the twentieth century, but these mostly involved European cultures and literatures beginning in the early modern period. Very few studies consider female homosexuality in Antiquity or the early Middle Ages. Bernadette J. Brooten's *Love Between Women* gives us one of the rarer insights into female homosexuality of a specific period between the second and fourth centuries A.D. Brooten discovered three manuscripts of Greek love spells intended for use by women (in "Upper Egypt") to "attract other women" and she compellingly discloses that:

> these binding spells are formulaic, they do not reveal the internal dynamic of these women's relationships. Nevertheless, the spells do provide evidence that: (1) actual historical women in this period desired erotic attachments to other women and were willing to go to some lengths to consummate these relationships; (2) some nonelite women from Upper Egypt (relative backwoods in comparison with the urban centers in which Seneca the Elder, Juvenal, Martial, Paul or Clement of Alexandria wrote) experienced homoerotic desire; and (3) some social support for woman-woman relationships must have existed for those women who commissioned the spells, at the minimum on the part of the scribes who composed them.[15]

Brooten is further intrigued by the male-centred *representations* of "female homoeroticism in terms of an active/passive duality, with one of the women playing a 'male' role" (Brooten, 75). She suspects these interpretations of being flawed and because of a lack of evidence she concludes that the "spells do not reveal the internal dynamics of these women's relationships" (Brooten, 76). Because the spells followed a formulaic language of violence and conquest, Brooten could not discern whether the language of "violence" and "conquest" in the spells reflected how women organized their homosexual relations socially, or whether they understood themselves and their relations as replicas of heterosexual unions. Indeed, what we cannot determine from the literature available to us is the ideological precepts of the subjects that this literature treats, occasionally, however, we become privy to glimpses. In al-Yemeni's ninth century text, the following poem, which he claims is written by a grinder, appears:

> ...my vagina succeeds and glimmers with a cheek and a freckle
> like a dot of musk swinging above the crescent
> revealing a pure mouth, smiling pearls
> in which there is a savory saliva
> instantly sweet to taste.
> And a fine neck as slender as the gazelle's
> For what I have seen of her beauty —
> And O how much have I seen! —
> I say glory to whomsoever molded beauty from clay
> To create a perfect creature made of beauty
> I came to sip from her and her extreme thirst is at a well
> If that is prohibited (*Ĥaram*) then this is not lawful (*Ĥalal*)
> (*Rashd*, 131–132)

The poetess begins by candidly describing what is the site of an oral sexual scene (cunnilingus), and moves from the eroticism that her imagery invites to a much more serious confrontation with the popular prohibitory ideas (in regards to sin and sexual behaviour) of her time. Throughout this poem it is unclear who is perceived to be active or passive, given that the recipient of direct sexual stimulation is also actively gazing, touching and tasting at the same time. Later on in the poem the poetess makes an appeal to the theologians, firstly by subtly invoking images of the Maker, who is here equated with the benevolent figure of the artist — "glory to whomsoever molded beauty from clay." Glory, the poetess suggests, is to the undefined "whomsoever" (God?) who has created "a perfect creature made of beauty." The poetess places herself as an ally of the very force that is often used to condemn and reprimand her desires, becoming an agent for the admiration of God's creation. And then she criticizes tradition for forbidding (*ĥaram*) her very intense adoration and desire by saying that if something as essential as the quenching of one's thirst can be forbidden, then that forbidding in itself *is* unlawful: "I came to sip from her and her extreme thirst is at a well, If that is prohibited then this is not lawful." al-Yemeni, a male Muslim scholar whose views of homosexual behaviour involve repudiation and refusal, nevertheless gives a woman, through citation, the opportunity to elegantly and rhetorically defend her conception of desire and beauty and sexual love (and the thirst for it) in such a way that is aimed at orthodox religious figures such as himself. This pluralistic conveyance of various points of view is eliminated in the years succeeding the 1250s, which incidentally coincides with Boswell's description of European cultures.[16] al-Yemeni's entertainment of this sort of citation suggests to us, much in the same fashion that Brooten's discovered spells suggest, that same-sex desire between women was prevalent and known for its prevalence (otherwise the author would not have been so compelled to write an exposition on it); that these sexual relations were (sometimes) motivated by desire for the female form (rather than replacement of the absent male) and that such women (or one of these women) possessed an intellectual sensitivity alerting her to her social position as an oppressed outcast, fighting against bigotry which was most probably inseparable from religious belief.[17] This poem also tells us that spiritual or religious belief should not be seen to be in itself the originary site of homophobic prejudice, since the Maker can still be celebrated, precisely for creating the womanly "Beauty" that the verse immortalizes. This is a point about the separation of religious/spiritual belief from homophobia for which Boswell has been widely criticized.[18]

Citations such as these, which imply some sort of psychological insight into what Boswell might have dared to call "gay women's lives", are rare. Most medieval writings on and citations of grinders are usually fashioned to imply a male-centred view of female homoeroticism – in which such feelings and inclinations are predominantly social. Whether as the result of "restriction imposed on [women], where they are unable to be alone safely and privately except with other women,"[19] or whether it is for fear of pregnancy or the contumelious word (*Rashd*, 125) homoeroticism was rarely depicted as a celebration of a particular sexual orientation. However,

I must disagree with critics such as Halperin, that this must then mean that no such sexual orientations existed, or that no individuals had conceptualized this, if only because occasional evidence seems to suggest the contrary. Particularly in relation to Halperin's criticism of Brooten's interpretation of evidence, it now appears to be even more likely that these "love spells" were exactly what they appeared to be, since there is irrefutable evidence that women formed both erotic and romantic relationships. al-Yemeni writes:

> The first woman to set grinding was the daughter of *Ĥ*assan Yamani. She came by Nuåman Bin al-Muthir and so he took her to his wife Hind. She fell madly in love with her. Hind was the best of the folks of her time, she was completely without excesses. The daughter of Ĥassan did not cease to deceive her and to deceptively depict (*tuzayinu*) grinding for her and to say: in the union of two women there is a pleasure that cannot be between the woman and the man. To safeguard herself from scandal and knowing that her appetite can be satisfied without accusation or fear of punishment, they had intercourse (*ijtama'ata*). Hind discovered a pleasure that was even greater than the other had described and their amorous desire for each other increased — and it had never been so between women before this. (*Rashd*, 123)

It is interesting to note how this is a case of one woman being corrupted by the insistence and deceptions of the other, also note how very simply al-Yemeni asserts that this is the first instance of female homosexual love ever recorded in history — a sort of Madam and Eve myth of biblical proportions. To Yemeni, this love affair between the lady-in-waiting and the wife of a Nestorian Christian king,[20] is the genesis of the distasteful practice ("It has never been so between women before this"). One wonders where Ĥassan Yammani's daughter *learnt* that homosex was as wonderful as she depicted (*Zayanat*) to Hind. How did she devise her seductive charms and arts, if indeed this *was* the very first historical instance of such a thing? At any rate, al-Yemeni's story of homosexual genesis is nevertheless much more forgiving than the latter versions, after all he describes the protagonists in a sympathetic light:

When the daughter of Ĥassan died Hind sat at her grave all the time until people began to use her case for their sayings. al-Farazdaq said:

> I was devoted to you in a time that you bestowed kindly
> Like Hind was devoted to Ĥassan Yammani's daughter
> (*Rashd*, 123–124).

Yemeni provides further proof of the existence of women who preferred sexual intimacy with women and who were clearly involved in romantic relationships:

> Then after them [Hind and Yammani's daughter] came Rughum and Najda — they romanced each other and they became famous for their grinding until Rughum's brother was taunted for his sister's behaviour. So he waited until he came upon them one day as they were having intercourse. So he killed Najda and took his sister away with him. Rughum began to incite Najda's people to kill her brother and a war erupted between them. This serves as an indication of the greatness of the pleasure they find in grinding as well as an indication of their preference for grinding over the pleasure with men. (*Rashd*, 124)

It is unclear what the social status between the two women in this narrative is, however, it is clear, if we assume that al-Yemeni was writing historically, that their love, as the love of the two women who preceded them, became well-known both outside and within their immediate community. Yemeni's writing also makes it clear that homosexual relationships of this kind were not widely accepted, for what would motivate Rughum's brother to kill her lover if it was not for a sense of shame and embarrassment? However, it is also clear that Najda, who engaged in this relationship, was nevertheless loved by her family and her people to the point where her *lover*'s appeal to them would incite them to engage in a vengeful war against the people housing her killer. If either Rughum or Najda were total outcasts or assumed to be so by the narrator, the dynamics of the story would have been different: the story might not have even survived or have been thought worth telling, and the outcome for the various characters would have been different. If their relationship did not also bring forth with it negative thoughts and associations then the behaviour of the brother might be difficult to rationalize.

From the very little information Yemeni provides it is impossible to discern who Rughum and Najda are. Were they women of prominence? Were they of Muslim, Christian Arab or Byzantian tribes and which century and geographical space did they inhabit? We can at least assume, since they come *after* Hind and Yammani's daughter, that they existed in post Nuåman al-Muthir's rein, which ends in 554 A.D and before 845 A.D when the author of this text dies. Somewhere in between the seventh and ninth century this story either takes place or becomes part of the oral history which Yemeni thought worth mentioning in the mid-ninth century. With these tales of not simply homoeroticism but lifelong love supposedly taking place in a time period shortly after Brooten suggests that marriage between women was commonly known in Egypt, Halperin's criticisms — that Brooten was applying herself into the narrative of the ancient texts, and seeing "marriages" where there were none — fall by the wayside.

For Halperin female homoeroticism is a "social and discursive production...a culturally constituted category of both erotic arousal and social organization." Halperin continues, asserting that Brooten's analysis in *Love Between Women* is flawed because she treats female homoeroticism as "a *thing* — a single, stable object that can be viewed from different perspectives" (Halperin, 1998, 561). Later in his article he adds that "Brooten's consistent anachronisms are all the more bizarre because almost all the evidence with which she has to deal reflects ... not the experiences of ancient women but the fantasies, jokes, abuse, or moral judgment of hostile male authors" (Halperin, 1998, 572). Instead of negating Brooten's thesis Halperin and other constructionists would be better to make the conflict as clear as possible. Their conflict with those working with a blended framework (of essentialism and constructionism) is one of axioms and maxims; it is in fact a conflict over semantics and the historicizing of concepts. In criticizing Brooten and also in others' similar criticism of Boswell, Halperin fails to dismiss the reality of certain types of evidence which speak plainly of homoerotic *relationships*, which strangely resemble more contemporary settings (but are in no way identical). At no point did Brooten simplify the cultural constructions of sexuality and assimilate them entirely into a model befitting her own culture's configurations and while Halperin does indeed call for a sensible way for us not to neglect or abuse the particular context which produced these writings, we in turn cannot be too shy about delving into our common humanity as a resource for interpreting these texts.

In face of this harsh criticism, brought about by a forum published in *GLQ* in 1998, Brooten defended her work against accusations of being anachronistic and self-projecting, but her defense was rather peculiar. She wrote:

> In *Love Between Women* I voice skepticism about contemporary genetic and neuroscientific research on sexual orientation ... Halperin and I share the view of significant historical discontinuity. Further, many of us lesbians simply do not experience ourselves as having known that we were like that since were five years old, as we hear from many of our gay male friends. And many of us are surprised to fall in love with a man or be married to a man but find ourselves falling in love with a woman. I also think that the innateness argument, as seductive as it may be, is not the best political strategy.[21]

What is implicit in Brooten's argument is that it is primarily the "many... gay male friends" who experience homosexual desire as early as the age of five. At such an early age it is safe to say that those who experience homoerotic desire are informed only very little by cultural and environmental milieux and thus the notion of the "innate" tends to present itself as self-evident for sexually deviant subjects who experience an early onset of homosexual inclinations. Of course, Brooten is mistaken if she suspects that it is only the "gay male" who experiences such an early onset of homosexual desire. For many others the onset of erotic desires occurs later in life, and for some there occurs a drift from one orientation to another or even a life-long oscillation between the two — the possibilities and formations of orientation are endless. What is not known is the various natures of innateness, for at what point does homosexuality in an individual come about? Pre-natally, at the moment of conception, peri-natally, by the age of seven etc.? I satisfy myself with the notion that there are various forms or ways in which infants are either born homosexual, or *born to become* homosexual. Brooten asks for the abandonment of the possibility of the "innateness" of sexual conduct because simply it is a bad "political strategy." What underlies Brooten's comment is the intimidation and recoil of those who sought a transhistorical and transcultural "gay" historiography at the hands of the heavy weights of the academy. Regardless of what fruit the pursuit of essentialist or universalist components may bear, regardless of the truths this methodology might help uncover, if any, Brooten suggests that we abandon it because, simply, it is "not the best political strategy."

Another remark made by Brooten which appeases constructionist theoretical preference and which requires examination is "the view of significant historical discontinuity." Constructionists are quick to castigate anyone for "projecting themselves" into the historical past because this assumes a kind of continuism which, they say, simply isn't true. Even though continuity is self evident, most simply in the passage of time itself, cultures are seen to be existing in separate bubbles of space and time. However, in truth, to suggest that there is something *other* than historical continuity is to suggest that cultures suddenly vanish, cease to exist and that at the site of this vanishing, brand-new cultures appear. For exactly what occupies this necessary pause, this space, which is the discontinuity so often emphasized by constructionists? At some point in the past "homosexuality" did not exist, much in the same way that at some point human beings altogether did not exist, but I cannot believe that the existence of homosexuality per se spans a period a little over a century.

In their introduction to *Hidden from History*, the editors provide a thorough and highly useful genealogical review of the emergence of homosexual historiography. They write that many "social constructionists would argue that ... the constitution of "sexuality" and of identity itself must be the subject of inquiry."[22] They add to this that those "interested in the lesbian past have faced the very practical problem of a relative absence of records concerning same-sex sexual activity by women ....[An] emphasis upon romantic friendship as the normative form of lesbianism," and this, the editors argue, led to a binarized conflict within "lesbian" historiography. On the one hand, intimate friendships, which were devoid of (or not bearing any apparent) sexual intent, were subsumed under the banner of "lesbianism" or homoeroticism (as in the case of Adrienne Rich's Lesbian Continuum and "woman identification" and Lilian Faderman's work on "Boston Marriages" in *Surpassing the Love of Men*),[23] while other critics defended against this notion — either for fear and horror of female homosexuality, or precisely because they saw the sexual element as inseparable from the lesbian subject. The editors further point out that "gay history has necessarily engaged profound philosophical questions concerning the definition and constitution of the self ...yet such exploration has been impeded by the lack of consensus concerning the essential characteristics even of contemporary gay or lesbian identity and culture" (Duberman et al., 7). It is intriguing that the *impediment* to homosexual historiography has been encountered during the process of defining the essential characteristics of the subject itself — what is homosexuality, if it is not a late nineteenth century clinical term?

Within this work, and in the same vein as Joan Nestle, as far as homosexuality is concerned, the essential element we are in search for is the (at least predominant) psychic desire for sexual intimacy with members of one's own sex, even if this desire is not acted on and even if it does not result in relationships.[24] In the case of Arabian women however, evidence suggests that not only sexual intimacies but life-long partnerships took place. In addition, sexual desires and urges are not entirely the result of social constructs and while new categories are continually being synthesized and re-synthesized, these shifts (in synthesis) do not necessarily denote the *invention* of new individuals to fit the criteria of the category, but rather that the category is born of the collection of individuals who converge about a particular and noticeable similarity. What is essential in homosexuality, as it is viewed in this study, is the role of sexual desire, even though many forms of homosexual activity are not expressions of homosexual desire but heterosexual desire or even a largely un-sexual desire to overpower or control or the desire to please or appease (outside the context of the sexual), or to gain social advancement. As Boswell has argued, the fact that "no two social structures are identical should require no proof; and since sexual categories are inevitably conditioned by social structure, no two systems of sexual taxonomy should be expected to be identical .... But to state this is not to demonstrate that there are no constants in human sexual epistemology" (Boswell, 1989, 24).

By contrast to this approach to the theoretical dilemma of sexuality Valerie Traub warns that we should avoid the creations of

> static models ... under which all historical variants would be gathered, organized and codified. To offer the tribade and the friend, for instance, as the Ur-figures of lesbian history would be as mistaken as to insist on the transhistorical nature of *lesbianism*. To do history of sexuality is not to turn a blind eye to perennial features of the erotic system, but neither is it too quickly to assume homology when not every facet repeats.[25]

Traub is one of the more eloquent interrogators of models of discourse on sexuality within which cultural differences are subsumed by similarities and yet even Traub acknowledges that we must *not* "turn a blind eye to perennial features of the erotic system" — it is unfortunate that she does not tells us why we must not turn a blind eye on the *continuity* of sexuality. Precisely because of such an omission, Traub implies a superiority of one mode of theorization over another — the success of one analytical model (interrogation of cultural differences/historical discontinuities) and the failure of the other (interrogation of cultural similarities). This emphasis on heterogeneity produces, *ironically*, homogeneity in the analytical tools available within the discourse, and analysis which does not pay close attention to the *differences* quickly becomes suspect, colonial, imperialist, rather than being potentially humanist, universalist, materialist.

Traub also notes the concept of "historical continuism" and she asserts that within "the subdiscipline of lesbian history, the search for historical foremothers has been, and continues to be, a primary motivation, and the logic of temporal continuity — and the related issue, similitude — has served as a governing paradigm" (Traub, 331). Unfortunately, as Traub notes, these notions of "continuism" and "similitude" are grounded in concepts of patriarchal supersystems and the repeated influence that these systems have over women's lives. The search for continuisms and similitudes which are less related to patriarchal taxonomies and disciplines and that are more closely related to women's interest in women are less noted. What continues to figure in the historical continuism noted by Traub is the presence of the male discourse and in this way homoerotic desires among women continue to be figured as indelible from and driven by (inadequacies in) social relations between men and women under patriarchal ideologies. This is criticized only under-handedly by Traub who writes that "to assume that patriarchal culture utterly frames the experience of women is to grant masculinist discourses too much power" (Traub, 332). I would venture to add that what it suggests is that female homoeroticism is then seen to be born of poor relations between women and men, and not as a desire as independent from heterosexual desire as heterosexual desire is usually seen to be independent from homoeroticism. Traub then ventures to ask "how [one is] to postulate a continuism that is not naïve. What would a sophisticated continuism look like? Unfortunately the answer is not clear" (Traub, 333). Traub has asked the right question here and even though the answer may be unclear for many of us, it is a noteworthy project to pursue the engendering of a "sophisticated continuism" which involves the question of homosexuality per se.

DECONSTRUCTING SEXUALITY: LOOKING FOR A SOPHISTICATED CONTINUISM

In search of this "sophisticated continuism" I propose that we venture beyond our own species and to look outside the human genome to find instances of homosexuality apparent in other species. To make things truly complicated, I would like to suggest that what is essential about sexuality, which precedes cultural configurations and socializations of the individual, not only exists for humans across the cultures and the ages, but is evident in various species of which we know. The most amusing and delightful of my ensuing evidence that I bring to this discussion, is the recent rise in the reporting on incidents of homosexuality in penguins. Earlier last year (Feb 2005) a zoo in Bremen, Germany, "imported four female penguins from Sweden in an effort to tempt its gay penguins to go straight."[26] This took place shortly after the zoo keepers became aware that despite many mating instances a group of six penguins were not reproducing. These penguins were soon discovered to be all male. In an effort to assist the Humboldt Penguin species (which is endangered), the zoo keepers announced that they intended to introduce female penguins to the group of six, some of whom were now, strangely, attending to an egg-shaped stone as though it were a soon to be hatched offspring (at least this is how we explain this behaviour).[27]

The international news agency Reteurs quickly reported that the zoologists' attempts "sparked protests from gay groups" who saw this introduction of the females as an attempt on the zoologists' part to force heterosexuality on the penguins. Several months later, other reports came in that the Penguins rejected their new female guests and remained "true" to each other. And this is by no means an isolated incident. In New York City a "gay" penguin couple has become somewhat of a celebrity pair and the anthropomorphizing of the penguins and subsuming them into the gay and lesbian rights movement can at times be hard to swallow (after all, they're not paying attention to interspecies differences which I believe to be much more pressing than human intercultural differences!),[28] but the similarity is striking as it informs a very highly charged theoretical debate about what is innate and what is learned behaviour. It is, of course, still plausible that homosexual behaviour is learnt.

Similarly to this largely undocumented phenomenon of "gay" penguins (and I am more reluctant to use gay for penguins than I am for humans of previous ages), the work of Joan Roughgarden in *Evolution's Rainbow*,[29] stands as testimony to the existence of homosexuality and transexualism across species. Roughgarden writes that the

> notion of a universal male or female template [i.e. male = masculine/active; female = passive/feminine] is clearly false. Let's focus specifically on the males who would seem most clearly to violate the universal male template: The feminine males. The third male gender in bluegill sunfish consists of males that look like females. Are such cross-dressing animals rare? .... we might have to consider that being a feminine male might be adaptive in itself. (Roughgarden, 93)

Roughgarden's delightful work has been criticized for its imaginative blend of human concepts (such as "cross-dressing" here) with animal concepts and for various other treatises; however, the evidence that she brings to discussion (like Brooten and Boswell) cannot be disputed as being false. Roughgarden notes how scientific reports on

> feminine males are marked by deceit rhetoric [as opposed to other less malignant possibilities] and sensationalism. Reports of masculine females are scanty, suggesting underreporting.... [Nonetheless] courtship [between female lizards] in an *asexual* species is almost exactly the same [as male/female copulation/courtship]. One of the females copies the male role down to the last detail. One mounting female was even seen everting her cloacal region to contact the cloacal areas of the mounted female. Courtship between female whiptail lizards is not a sloppy parody of male-female courtship left over from its sexual ancestry, but an intricate and finely honed sexual ritual. (Roughgarden, 126, emphasis mine)[30]

Of course, as someone heavily invested in theories of sexuality and sexual behaviour, I am not at all impressed with Roughgarden's notion of "copying", that the female "copies" male copulation behaviour, as this term tends to suggest that the male is the possessor of an original behaviour which was then studied and replicated by an imposter, but Roughgarden atones for this error when she notes that this "is not a sloppy parody of male-female courtship... but an intricate and finely honed sexual ritual." I might venture to ask, what is essentially similar between this scene of the two female lizards of an asexually reproducing species (i.e. if they do not require sex to reproduce why do they have sex at all, let alone homosexual sex?) and the one entirely disconnected from it, or at least, connected only (phenomenally speaking) by the theme of genital sex, when, in thirteenth century Arabia Tifashi writes:

> The lower [grinder] lies on her back and extends one thigh and leg and embraces the other revealing her vulva, leaning to one side. And then comes the top one and hugs the elevated thigh and places one of her lips on the lips of the lower one and rubs to and fro at the length of the body. (*Nuzhat*, 237)

It is almost banal to have to state that this writer can appreciate the interspecies and intercultural differences between female lizards and female humans and more to the point that their sexual intercourse will be experienced differently and it may carry entirely different cultural significance (for example, maybe the communities of lizards are not homophobic, or are not fussy about the gender of sexual partners). But it is highly significant that in species as widely divergent as humans, lizards, penguins, birds, insects, monkeys, lions, antelopes etc. that homosexual behaviour can exist and evidently voluntarily, by choice and not simply as an opportunistic entity, and not always non-reciprocally (all these having been argued as markers of the modern queer, lesbian and gay western, white, middle-class, subject). Furthermore, it is not always possible to *effectively* bring about a study of social constructions (and categories) of sexuality. Particularly where the rest of the animal kingdom is concerned (this includes insects) this cultural constructionism is almost impossible at present, given our knowledge, technologies and communication skills.

Roughgarden notes that a "recent survey of same-sex matings in animals found ninety-four-descriptions for bird species.... [while by] 1984 male homosexual behaviour had been reported in sixty-three mammalian species" (Roughgarden, 136–137). For those scientists who are bravely attending to the existence of homosexual activity in non-human species, they do not have the luxury (technology/knowledge/perceptual faculties) to attend to the question of social constructions of homosexuality. We do not know how the Penguins in the Central Park zoo differ in their homosexual and homosocial society from those in Germany, or the ones in Japan.

In a post script to the final essay he published prior to his death, Boswell notes that "I would define 'gay persons' more simply as those whose erotic interest is predominantly directed toward their own gender ... regardless of how conscious they are of this as a distinguishing characteristic.... I would still argue that there have been 'gay persons' in most Western societies. It is not clear to me that this is an essentialist position.... I was and remain agnostic about the origins and etiology of human sexuality" (Boswell, 1989, 35–36). If I were able to speak with Boswell, I might add that his hunch, much attacked and vilified throughout (for being self-projecting), was on a right track. I might tell him that I think that there were "gay persons" in most non-western societies too, definitely in Arabia, and at least as far as medieval Arab scholars were concerned, there was a definite cultural and theoretical discourse to describe them. I wonder, in light of this new broader spectrum of discourse on homosexuality which now minimally includes the animal kingdom, and for the time being excludes the ability to study social constructions, how Boswell might have shifted his beliefs in regards to his skepticism.

In terms of the animal kingdom, the astonishing array of evidence carefully collected and documented by Bruce Bagemihl in *Biological Exuberance* argues sternly against conservative attitudes that attempt to explain away homosexuality either as "an imitation of heterosexuality, a "substitute" activity when the opposite sex is unavailable, a "mistake," or a pathological condition."[31] When on pages 398 and 399 of *Biological Exuberance* we view John Megahan's illustration of Begemihl's descriptions of various positions of sexual intercourse taking place between two female Kob Antelopes, it is astonishing and confounding to note the pornographic similarity between these sexual positions and those practiced by a great many homosexual women in their own private conferences, even if the (male-dominated) literature of pseudo-lesbian pornography fails to depict (and hence document) some of these practices.[32] What is even more astonishing is the wide range of atypical behaviour — where socially dominant lionesses "yield themselves" as "bottoms" to other lionesses after the success of a particular courtship and pursuit (Bagemihl, 433–434). The notion of diversity in nature, as argued by Joan Roughgarden, is emerging as an account which is not only essentially applicable to humans and their various cultures and historical contexts, but for numerous species for whom sexual activity was once thought to be a pure act of (mindless) reproduction. At the site of these differences in the manifestation of sexuality and sexual practice the concept denoted by Murray and Roscoe, the concept of homosexualit*ies* becomes veritably a new way of engaging with past constructionist/essentialist nomological conflict. We grant that there is not a single form of homosexuality and certainly no single uncomplicated causes (as in discourse where it is caused by childhood sexual trauma or what have you), but at the same time it becomes impossible to ignore or to delay the further search for that which makes the concept of homosexuality singular despite its multifarious manifestations.

BIOLOGICAL ESSENTIALISM

I have been arguing for a double-moded essentialism. This essentialism is not necessarily factored by biology — essentialism being evidenced in what is repeated throughout history, culture and across species (though not all); an essentialism which is not necessarily biologically but (at least) behaviorally, socially and/or emotionally fixated. Biological essentialism is a more volatile area to venture into because it acquires its origins from a deeply painful past for men and women of deviant sexualities and gender orientations. Homosexuality ceased to be listed as a biological disease in the World Health Organization's list of diseases as late as 1992. As a psychological disorder, it was removed from the American Psychiatric Association's *Diagnostic and Statistical Manual* (*DSM*) in 1973 but while the *DSM-III*, "published in 1980, was the first that did not contain an entry for "homosexuality, [it] was also the first that *did* contain a new diagnosis ... [that of] Gender Identity Disorder of Childhood."[33] Furthermore, many gay and lesbian activists, as well as their opponents on the religious right, believe that if homosexuality has genetic components then it can be eliminated through genetic engineering which is foreseeable in the not too distant future. On this point, DeCamp and Sugarman wonder "[m]ight a genetic basis [for homosexuality] ... affect social stigmatization itself, that is, might it decrease (because individuals are no longer to blame because they are "born with it") or increase (by creating an identifiable, biologically-based outcast group)?"[34] Nevertheless, the presence and prevalence of homosexuality as a sexual orientation across various cultures and historical periods and throughout a range of species from primates to insects (who are not biologically comparable in brain development, sex development and prenatal or perinatal hormonal development), does indeed render the subject itself some metaphysical essence about which we continue to wonder.

Within the field of medical enquiry "biologic theories made headway during the 1970s as neurobiologists began to unravel the genetic, hormonal, and neurodevelopmental processes involved in the sexual differentiation of neural substrates integral to the regulation of reproductive behaviors in animals."[35] However, as "the influence of experience on brain development began to be better appreciated in the 1980s, it became unfashionable to endorse either side of the nature/nurture debate, and a semblance of an interactionist approach emerged" and then "this uneasy truce was disrupted late in 1991 with the publication of LeVay's report in *Science* that provided evidence of an anatomic difference in the hypothalamus of homosexual and heterosexual men" (Byne & Parsons , n.p.). LeVay surprises us when he writes that:

> ...even the most nebulous and socially determined states of mind are a matter of genes and brain chemistry....I myself have fallen into this error [of thinking otherwise]. In 1991 I published a study in which I described a difference in brain structure between homosexual and heterosexual men. As the last sentence of the summary of the paper, I wrote: "This finding...suggests that sexual orientation has a biological substrate." By that, I was implying that there are some aspects of mental life that do not have a biological substrate — *an absurd idea...*[36]

Of course, LeVay is intuitively relying on a basic scientific premise where the material world here supervenes on the ideological and mental world — where ideas themselves (even though these are immaterial) are only made possible by material interactions (empiricisms) and de facto by neurological activity itself. In this sense constructionist claims (including interpretations of Foucault in which the world is entirely divined through ideas which are unstable, changing and *unreal*) are still implicated in the essentialism of those biological faculties which allow for thought itself. Furthermore, he notes that "believing in a biological explanation for sexual orientation is not the same thing as insisting that sexual orientation is inborn or genetically determined. Our entire mental life involves biological processes. We know that our sexual orientation, like our tastes in music and our memory of our last vacation, is engraved in some morphobiolgical or chemical substrate in the brain. It is not maintained solely by the brain's actual activity, whether electrical or metabolic" (Le Vay, 108). For LeVay it seems almost counterintuitive to claim that sexuality and sexual categories are mere social constructions and I would argue that on the basis of this indelibility of biology from behaviour that we must accept that those elements of homosexuality which constantly repeat themselves in transhistorical and cultural contexts are not merely phenomenal, but are rather embedded in similarities brought about by our constitution as a species. Therefore, in this new world of ours, and at the site of founding a new discourse for homosexual historiography where we search for nouns which require to be culturally (and temporally) impartial, we should not protest too much if thirteenth-century *tharifas* (who are referred to as Grinders by their contemporaries) are referred to as lesbians, or fifteenth-century tribades are referred to as "gay women" even though neither groups knew of Sappho or the island of Lesbos, or knew of twentieth-century political activism and the twenty-first-century political lesbian subject. In the application of the term "lesbian" to women who were eroticized by other women to the point of preference of this over heteroeroticism, the term is not intended to efface individual or intercultural or transhisrotical differences, but is rather intended to denote the lowest common denominator of homoerotic experience — that which is minimally glimpsed through the consideration of biological factors.

Laura Allen and Roger Gorski's absorbing comparison of the correlation between "sexual orientation and the size of the anterior commissure in the [male] human brain" has yielded that in "regions of the brain [which are] not directly related to reproductive sex function, differences occur in cerebral asymmetry [firstly] in the shape of the corpus callosum ... and [also] in the midsagittal area of the mass intermedia and anterior commussure (AC)."[37] The eight-year study yielded statistically significant results where it was found that the AC was proportionally larger in homosexual male subjects' brains than it was in (presumed heterosexual) women's brains whose ACs were again proportionally larger than those in heterosexual male subjects. The study also yields that "the functional differences in the area of the AC is unknown" even though a "correlation between the size of the AC, sexual orientation, and scores on tests of verbal and visuospatial abilities and cerebral lateralization [have been observed]: homosexual men and heterosexual women have larger ACs, higher scores on verbal tests, and lower scores on exams of visuo-spatial abilities ... and cerebral lateralization ... than heterosexual men" (Allen & Gorski, 7201).

Despite these findings which clearly indicate a biological essence involved in the "stereotypical" behaviours of homosexual men and heterosexual women, it was not in the capacity of this study to conclude whether these structural developments in the brain were the result of prenatal or perinatal influences — whether it was a function of environmental conditioning or genetic predisposition or both. At any rate, whether heterosexual women or homosexual men, neither of these groups appear to be in possession of a conscious choice to carry out the development of their brain structures as they feel warranted, and the specter of essentialism returns to haunt the subject once more, this time in the shape of an interactional model in which "genes or hormones do not specify sexual orientation per se, but instead bias particular personality traits and thereby influence the manner in which an individual and his or her environment interact as sexual orientation and other personality characteristics unfold developmentally" (Byne & Parsons, n.p.).

This compromise which fuses aspects of nature and nurture concepts seems to suggest that children are *born to be* gay, or *born to become* gay, as opposed to *born gay* or born and then choose to be gay or are influenced into being/becoming gay by culture, society and/or personal experiences.

So, were the *mutathakirat* discussed by al-Yemeni and al-Samaw'uli the butches of Medieval Arabia, or the tribades of Renaissance England? Windy M. Brown and colleagues write that "there have been several reports of a difference between heterosexual and homosexual women in purported markers of prenatal or neonatal androgen exposure."[38] Fetal androgen exposure in females leads to the increased "masculinization" of the brain, and as Brown and colleagues argue further, this form of exposure helps create the masculine, "butch" lesbian figure. The study was able to conclude that "women who identify themselves as either butch or femme lesbians differ in this biological marker for androgen exposure" (Brown et al., 126).[39] Similarly, Singh and colleagues noted that they "found significant differences between butch and femme lesbians in recalled childhood gender atypical behaviour, sexual style [i.e. predominantly top or bottom preferences], desire to give birth and raise children, [Waist to Hip Ratio[40]], and salivary testosterone levels."[41] These findings help reassert the notion that underlying cultural and scientific ideologies of sexuality, sex and gender, are some biological factors or markers involved in the "making" of female homosexuality, which may have been with us for much longer, and independently of, the nineteenth-century term, *homosexuality.* As Signh et al. note: "The tenacity of butch–femme roles through diverse political eras and the prevalence of such roles cross-culturally suggest they are based on stable psychobiological characteristics."

THE LIMITATIONS AND APORIAS OF THE BIOLOGICAL THEORIES

Even today, scientists who are researching into the potential developmental causes for sexual orientation are still evidently caught up in the age-old bias where male=active=masculine and where female=passive=feminine. Instead of finding the existence of homosexuals and homosexuality, as well as transgenderism and non-heteronormative heterosexuals (to name a few) as a complication of this straight forward theorem (which operates under the process of observable generalizations) many scientists still prefer to think of homosexuality and homosexuals as necessarily biologically *resembling* the sexes of their opposite gender. For example Miller writes that "[the] survival of a human predisposition for homosexuality can be explained by sexual orientation being a polygenetic trait that is influenced by a number of genes. During development these shift male brain development in the female direction."[42] What is implicit is that the male brain develops in the female direction as though the "female-like" brain of the male can only be understood as a mutation, as a subsequent development, something which comes after the original template — here a perfectly theoretical (and perhaps empirically impossible) female brain.

In geometry the concept of the perfect circle is veritably real, however there is no such shape as the perfect circle in the accidental, "natural" world, and yet we logically assume that all approximately spherical or circular shapes are in reality (which they are not) imperfect reproductions of the perfect circle. Within the scientific community it is still thought that there are perfect male templates and perfect female templates from which all other forms of maleness and femaleness are derived. The perfect female is good with languages but terrible at reading maps, she likes to play with dolls and leaves sports to the boys. Her genetic make up of two X chromosomes causes her to develop ovaries, which in turn cause the secretion of the "feminine" and female-making hormones during development.[43] As an adult, she has a nurturing, maternal impulse and hopes to procreate one day. Most importantly of all, the perfect female is heterosexually-desiring and it follows that not only is there a "perfect" gender template, like the perfect circle, but there is also an implied "perfect" sexual orientation template as well.

For example, Irina Pollard's "Preconceptual Programming and Sexual Orientation" in males, states that:

> the continuum spanning human sexuality has its etiology defined in terms of male and female-mediated forms of selective preconceptual marking .... If the prenatal environment is healthy, growth and differentiation will progress without major adjustments being made to the preconceptual potential and the resultant individual (phenotype) should be adapted to the prevailing conditions. However, if stress is sufficiently severe to cause an endocrine imbalance is experienced [sic], then newly acquired feedback adjustments at critical periods in development (the prenatal program) are made which may override the predicted setting and change the genetic potential of the individual.[44]

It is not clear why stress, in its various formations and regardless of its causes, should *cause* changes to genetic potentials, altering the phenotypes and creating offspring which will specifically develop into male homosexuals. At any rate, what is interesting here is not the question which is beyond the scope of this study to answer, but the teleology which becomes evident — where heterosexual orientation becomes the originary site from which other less popular sexual orientations follow. It might very well turn out to be true that sexual behaviour amongst primates began as heterosexual — due to the fact that this produces offspring (this is assuming Darwinism to be true) — but, nevertheless, there is not sufficient evidence to suggest that homosexuality did not coexist with heterosexuality, or that there may have been a time where these categories of behaviour were indistinguishable, i.e. where bisexuality was predominant, or perhaps were preceded by forms of asexual reproduction. Nevertheless, my project here is not to sketch another myth for the origins of human sexuality and the configurations it took up in its earliest formation, but to interrogate what is potentially the myth of what copulative relations are to biology as the perfect circle is to the study of geometrically perfect shapes: that the world began with the perfect man and the perfect woman and perfect sexual relations, from which mutations arose, giving us, through the full swing of evolution theory, the diversity that nature enjoys today. These discourses, no doubt inherited from or inspired by religious doctrines, seem to be heavily institutionalized within scientific research institutes.

Some theorists, who are clearly biased in favour of homosexuality as something which is *not* an abnormality nevertheless continue to engage in the logic where it is still a mutation (i.e. an adaptation, a subsequent development), as Edward Miller notes when he writes that a "plausible possibility for the heterosexual reproduction increasing effects of a pleitropic homosexuality producing gene would be found in the feminine traits of sensitivity, kindness, empathy, etc., that are frequently exhibited by [male] homosexuals. These traits would often make for a better father." Earlier Miller had pointed out that "It is fairly easy to imagine how asexuality could occur .... However, attraction to the same sex is harder to imagine evolving from scratch."[45]

Perhaps the worst oversight within biological theories of orientation involves the exclusion of homosexuals who are not comparable to the perfect gender template of their opposite sex. That is, feminine women and masculine men who are homosexually oriented have not been dealt with sufficiently or distinctly in any psychological or physical study. Scientists have found it easier to focus on "typical" homosexuals because they are easier to detect and because of some of the physiological similarities that they bear to members of the opposite sex, facilitating a theory of homosexuality similar to concepts of inversion. In the same vein, feminine homosexual women are equally difficult to detect and are often indistinguishable from women with bisexual orientations in both Medieval and contemporary Arabic literature on the subject. But it is critical that we do not abandon the notion that such women have also always existed, for we may be running the risk of authenticating a certain "type" of homosexual woman at the expense of others. In the following two chapters, I undertake the search for female homosexualities in Medieval Arabian literature, through which we can glimpse some of these elusive "psychobiological characteristics" involved in the making of the "typical" homosexual, even through the great gulf of space, time and intercultural differences. In demonstrating this biological continuism for one group it may be easier for us to sketch the missing history for atypical homosexuals.

Part II

The history and representation of female homosexuality in the Middle Ages

3 An overview of Medieval literature concerning female homosexuality

In the previous chapter we looked briefly at new scientific theories of natural diversity which attempt to account for the variations in actualized sexual and gender possibilities. Roughgarden, in her intuitively titled book *Evolution's Rainbow* was able to argue that sexual, gender and erotic distinctions exist for a wide variety of species, which are not comparable developmentally to mammals. But this notion of the heteroglossic universe is not new to human schools of thought, and it seems to inhabit renaissance-period thinking more often than other periods in history such as those pre-empting wars or immediately following them. In the Arabian Middle Ages, heteroglossia was a noted form of intellectual enquiry and evidence of the observation of the sexual diversity in nature can be found in the organizational structure of literature on erotology. In works by Tifashi, al-Yemeni, al-Samaw'uli, al-Asfahani, al-Jurjani and many others, we note the assignment of multiple categories to account for a wide variety of human sexual behaviour. This copia or anatomizing of sexual activity was in tune with Arab renaissance thinking: that nature is manifested heterogeneously. In his *Asl al-Åila al-Årabia* (*The Origins of the Arab Family*), Samir Saåeedi cites the following passage, which is in itself, a citation made by the medieval Muslim scholar al-Jaĥeth of a man named Muṭhana Bin Zuhair:

> I have never seen anything in man and woman that I haven't seen in the male and female pigeons....I have seen a female pigeon who mounts male pigeons and one who mounts other female ones. I have seen pigeons who mount nothing besides other female pigeons and I have seen one who mounts female ones but does not allow them to mount her. I have seen a male who mounts one who then mounts him in return. I have seen a female feign maleness and who does not allow another to mount her. I have seen all of these kinds in grinders — feminine and masculine ones and also among men who are inseparable companions and *luṯiyeen* [can be translated as male homosexuals/sodomites+sodomees].
>
> There are men who do not want women and women who do not want men.[1]

Indeed Arabic scholarly writing on the subject of sexuality (although the concept 'sexuality' in itself did not have an equivalent word for it at the time) between the ninth and thirteenth century, is heavily characterized by heteroglossic descriptions. Categories for sexual behaviour and personal traits which are not entirely dissimilar from modern concepts such as "bisexuality", "homosexuality", "sodomy", "effeminacy" (in men) "masculinity" (in women) did exist for Medieval Arab scholars. And as the above quote reveals, simply, "there are men who do not want [i.e. desire] women and women who do not want [i.e. desire] men" both masculine and feminine alike.

Furthermore it does not appear that prohibitions of either male or female homosexuality in Islamic doctrine were taken seriously prior to the mid-thirteenth century — or at least this is the picture that the remaining literary evidence yields. In the next few paragraphs I attempt to give a review of much of the material I relied on in sketching the possible social constructs and ideologies surrounding homosexuality. In the next chapter I undertake the task of focusing my reading on one very particular text, which I will resist quoting much here, but find it perfectly exemplary of this renaissance-like mode of thought.

AL-ASFAHANI (D. 1010?)[2] AND AL-JURJANI (D. 1089)[3] ON LIWAṮ AND AL-MUKHANAṬHUN

In the early years of the twelfth century, al-Raghib al-Asfahani (d. 1108) wrote *Muĥadarat al-Udaba*[4] — an encyclopedic work which acts as a mixture of adab and mujun.[5] The manuscript text was brought back into public availability by Omar Tabaå in 1999; he relied on a copy of the text which dates back to 1908. Tabaå asserts that the copy of the text he used to recreate the modern edition was at times difficult to read (being worn out) and that he did everything in his power to provide an accurate representation of the original (*Muĥadarat*, 12). He writes that al-Asfahani was "an educated man in possession of a fine balance between knowledge and intelligence and his personality as a writer was based on three founding pillars as he was both a scholar of religion, a rhetorician and a literary figure" (*Muĥadarat*,10). Though very little biographical material remains, al-Asfahani is said to have authored a number of books including "a series of monographs" on the explanation of the Quran.[6] In chapter sixteen of *Muĥadarat al-Udaba* entitled "About Mujun and Trivialities" Asfahani begins his chapter noting the Quranic verse where God wonders: "You go to males when God had created for you your spouses!" and he asserts that the prophet has condemned "the doer and the done to", and Moĥamad's request that "whomsoever is caught in such an act is to be thrown from a roof top" (*Muĥadarat*, 264). Having now performed his obligation as a Muslim scholar and cited the holy texts on these subjects, the rest of the chapter is dedicated to documenting, through anecdote, a considerable number of stories related about people who engage in activities which are supposedly forbidden. Sodomites include religious leaders caught in the act in the very mosque: "They found a Muezzin on a Nassrani boy's back in the mosque and so it was asked" "What are you doing?" and he said "Doesn't God say 'they do not commit an act to aggravate infidels or gain something from their enemy without their good deeds being recorded'? What better aggravation of the infidels is there than this?" (*Muĥadarat*, 267).

We also learn from Asfahani that sodomical relations are not organized, as it has been suggested to be the case in Greek societies, by the respective ages of the parties, but rather according to the appetites and desires of the individual beings who sought these relations. For example, after much reference to the sodomizing of young men, boys and male slaves we learn that "Abu al-Åyna said to al-Muåtasim: I walked in on Abi al-Åla' and his male slave was on his back..." (*Muĥadarat*, 275).[7] We also learn of effeminate men who enjoy being sodomized and actively seek the act:

> There was a drunkard who was crying and calling out: I wish I knew who killed Oṭhman. And so the Mukhanaṭh said to him: What would you do to them? He said: I would fuck them. So the Mukhanaṭh said: I killed him .... And so he took hold of him and he began to say: 'Vengeance for Oṭhman,' and the Mukhanaṭh says as he is under him: 'if you were in charge of avenging him and this was always your punishment then I would kill an Oṭhman every day!' (*Muĥadarat*, 275)

Although the word Mukhanaṭh was used to signify several (sometimes unrelated) sexual and gender orientations, this particular Mukhanaṭh falls under a distinct one of those meanings. We might translate him into the effeminate sissy, who is also coded as the sexual bottom — the "perfect" faggot. At the site of such similarities in the articulation of desire it is difficult to imagine essential differences as much as there are essential similarities in sexual desire and pleasure that are attributed to effeminate homosexual males in most societies, and the question of whether they individually could identify that they are different, and in what way they are so, should not seem as mystical given this consideration. While the drunkard sodomises the Mukhanaṭh (who is homosexual), the drunkard is not labeled as *luṯi* (which is often the word used for either of the male parties in a homosexual act) because his act of sodomy is not intended to be sexual but punitive. The anecdote is funny because what is considered punishment for one man is another's paradise.

In a subsection entitled "al-Mukhanaṭheen's Boasting of their arts and Excuses" we read the following:

> A Mukhanaṭh said: We are good people for if we speak we make you laugh and if we sing we enchant you and if we sleep you ride. A

> Mukhanaṭh and a luṯi met and he said: I am better than you because I am above and thus I am closer to the sky and he answers: I am more humble than you for I am closer to earth." (*Muĥadarat*, 277–278)

The Mukhanaṭheen were not looked on favorably as one poet notes (in a subsection entitled "Censure of al-Takhneeṭh"): "If a boy were pretty and fair but was Mukhanaṭh then he loses his beauty" (*Muĥadarat*, 278). The Mukhanaṭh is the effeminate male who certainly enjoys being sodomized and he is, at least to the poet above, much less desirable than an adolescent boy who is more invested in "masculine" or manly behaviour despite his androgynous appearance ("pretty and fair").

By contrast, both Greek and Roman studies of effeminate, homosexually acting males have led to different conclusions about the nature of these men's orientation. In his *Roman Homosexuality*, Craig Williams confirms Halperin's theorem in *One Hundred Years of Homosexuality* in regards to an archetypal male figure similar to (or prefigures?) the Mukhanaṭh of Asfahani's anecdotes:

> [Similarly to Halperin's point about the Greek *Kinaidos*] I am suggesting that the Roman *cinaedus* was in fact a category of person who was considered "socially deviant," but that his social identity was crucially different from that of the "homosexual," [here Craig should have been more precise and refined the "homosexual" to indicate a man who prefers to be a "bottom" or who may potentially be, though not necessarily, effeminate as well] since his desire for persons of his own sex was not a defining or even problematic feature of his makeup as a deviant: his desire to be penetrated was indeed one of his characteristics, but…men called *cinaedi* were also thought capable of being interested in penetrative sexual relations with women. Thus the deviance of the *cinaedus* is ultimately a matter of gender identity rather than sexual identity, in the sense that his predilection for playing the receptive role in penetrative acts was not the single defining feature of his identity but rather a sign of a more fundamental transgression of gender categories.[8]

There is an inconsistency in the application of the analysis which is troubling — how, on the one hand, the analysis establishes the existence of the gender-dichotomy for the ancient Romans but then moves to evacuate this dichotomy of its sexual content, on which it verily stands. On the other hand, it is possible to gather that the Medieval Arabian Mukhanaṭh, discussed earlier, was a creature whose socialization does resemble the socialization of the western "bottom faggot" of the twentieth and twenty-first centuries more so that the *Cinaedus* or the *Kinaidos*, but we can no longer attribute this difference in their socialization to the difference in cultural constructions, since there is no doubt that Arabian culture of the Middle Ages was vastly different from contemporary western culture, but despite this difference the two cultures were able to produce significantly similar articulations of sexual desire and discourses of categorization regardless of how flawed these discourses actually are in accounting for the truth of social and individual reality itself.[9]

There can be no doubt at the site of the evidence discussed above that effeminate homosexual men existed, and that they were met with considerable hostility from the larger society. Although effeminate men who enjoyed to be sodomized were given the name Mukhanaṭh, other stories indicate that there were men who were not effeminate who also enjoyed to be sodomized, and that these men were referred to as *Luṯiyeen*. Even though some relations between men involved age asymmetries, this was not a general rule. It is *interesting and important* to note that no mention of relationships or love or intimacy is made here, but that love-induced homosexual relationships are saved up for the women. Several other subsections follow in this chapter, including one on masturbation, another on what women do in the absence of their men and how they prefer to be engaged in sexual intercourse upon their partners' return. We also note that wherever possible, the author begins every subsection with a relevant prohibition from the Quran with the strange exception of the short section on female homosexual acts. Even though it is clear that Asfahani relies on al-Yemeni's 840s text, quoting at length the story of Ĥassan's Daughter and Hind, in which the prohibitory ĥadiṭh is mentioned, Asfahani does not relate that sexual love between women is prohibited by the prophet. What is possible is that Yemeni's original text may not have included this claim, which might have been inserted by scribes later on, or that al-Asfahani knew of the dubiousness of this particular ĥadiṭh (I discuss this later) and deliberately omitted its mention. Another possibility is that the ĥadiṭh in question was not coined until after Asfahani's death in the early twelfth century, which brings the ĥadiṭh's dubiousness back into question.

In the aĥadiṭh there is occasional mention of Mukhanaṭheen, although scholars have often shyly preferred to see that 'Mukhanaṭheen' here meant, specifically and only, sexually inactive castratos who were a slave class, dropping the word's other encompassments such as intersex (*khanaṭh*), and effeminate (usually homosexually acting) male. A particular ĥadiṭh related about a Mukhanaṭh named "Hayt" in *Saĥiĥ al-Bukhari* reads:

> Once, the prophet was at Um Salma's house and there was a Mukhanaṭh [effeminate man] there. The effeminate man said to Um Salma's brother, 'Abdullah bin Abi Umaiyya, "If Allah should make you conquer Ta'if tomorrow, I recommend that you take the daughter of Ghailan (in marriage) for (she is so fat) that she shows four folds of flesh when coming and eight when she's going." Then the prophet said "You should not let this Mukhanaṭh to enter upon you any longer."[10]

In another relation of the same ĥadiţh, Um Salma is alleged to have cited the prophet as saying "These (effeminate men) should never enter upon [women]."[11] The distinction in the final line is minor but remarkable, for the metanarrative of this ĥadiţh suggests that the prophet was familiar with many such men, who were effeminate and not sexually interested in women (hence allowed to dwell among them), that they had a place in society similar in rank to that of "normal" women.[12] It is very interesting that in one version of the ĥadiţh the prophet did not ban the practice of having effeminate men dwell among women, but banned *this particular man* from doing so. The prophet may have seen the man's sexualized description of the woman's body as a breach of the sexual constraint that must exist between men and women who desire each other erotically and are not married. Even though the concept of normal (*tabiåee*) had not yet entered the vernacular,[13] we do see divisions in society based on behavioral patterns: effeminacy in men, masculinity in women and various other *deviations* from the status quo.

In *al-Muntakhab Min Kinayat al-Udaba wa Isharat al-Bulagha*,[14] judge Aĥmad Jurjani (d.1089) sheds further light on the prevalence and visibility of male homosexual activity amongst men of high rank and prominence, whilst revealing scarcely anything significant about women. Jurjani relates the fact that the well-known Grand Judge of Baghdad, Yaĥya Bin Akţham[15] "was famous for Liwa<u>t</u>" (*al-Muntakhab*, 92) until he became identified with it, so much so that the writer Abi Salma wrote that "we had hoped to see justice apparent, but our implorations ended in despair, for, can the world and its people come to any good when the Grand Judge of Musļims sodomizes (*yalu<u>t</u>u*)?" (*al-Muntakhab,* 93). This is followed by two anecdotes which shed further light on the concerns and attitudes towards male homosexual preferences and their open declaration by men of prominence:

> Zidan the scribe was sitting at the hands of Yaĥya Bin Akţham writing, so he pinched his cheek. Zidan became embarrassed and his face reddened and he threw the pen from his hand, so Yaĥya said: Take this pen and write what I tell you:
>
> To any beauty[16] that I have scratched and thus angered
> Who has come to, due to his vanity, avoid me
> If you hate biting and scratching
> Then always veil yourself with a mask
> And do not show your visage to people
> And make of that above your cheeks a scorpion
> For you kill a yearner and distract a monk
> and you leave the Grand Judge of Muslims in torment. (*al-Muntakhab*, 94)

Yaĥya made advances to men (note that these are men not adolescent boys) who did not desire them, or perhaps did not know how to respond to them, however through his response to the obvious fluster he caused his scribe, we learn that he is aware of a variety of sexual differences in orientation but that his personal preference is clear. Interestingly, Bin Akṭham reprimands the "vanity" of those who are not interested in his advances and he reproaches them for the sharp "scorpion-like" looks that they would give a man making such undesirable moves. And in a flexible adherence to early Sunni religious doctrine, he reasons that such men should veil themselves, like women, if they wish to avoid the sexual advances of other men. Here is an instance of a Muslim Grand Judge whose Sunni version of Islam is unheard of today, not to mention that he is openly declaring his sexual and erotic preferences, without fear of persecution or shame. It is also possible that Yaȟya Bin al-Akṭham never authored such lines, even though he was a renowned poet, but instead these lines were attributed to him as censure or insult, since his "pederasty" (this is the term used by modern orientalist scholars, not me) was widely known. In literature of this period it was not unusual for a censure poem to be written *in the voice of* the person being censured. And in this instance, the poem appears in a "mujun" chapter — a genre of classical Arab literature where veracity was overlooked in favour of humor and crassness. The poem can nevertheless continue to be useful in informing us about the cultural discourse around homosexual activity in that period.

From discussion of Yaȟya Bin Akṭham, who was *Qadi al-Muslimeen* during the ninth century, and hence an important political and religious figure, we learn that he heavily punished fornication (intercourse between a man and a woman outside of wedlock), but it seems that he permitted relations which were outside the threat of producing illegitimate progeny or committing the sin of fornication. Reference to judge Yaȟya is made in Raghib's text who quotes a poet saying: "I live by Sheikh Yaȟya Bin Akṭham's religion and I avoid people who fornicate" (*Muȟadarat*, 265). This evidence assists us in establishing that Medieval Arabs were aware of erotic distinctions for men, and they did understand that these distinctions oftentimes involved the gender of the object choice as a vital element of erotica. Curiously, there is no mention of romantic or long-lasting affiliations among homosexually desiring men, though I would hesitate to take this omission to be evidence of absence.

ABU NASR AL-SAMAW'ULI (D.1180)[17] AND *NUZHAT AL ASĤAB*

In the twelfth century Abu Nasr al-Samaw' uli's treatment of female homosexuality oozes with a clinical/medical approach. Although the devil has not yet appeared as the cause of homosexuality, al-Samaw'uli might have known (from ninth-century sources) that some Arab cultures believed that Islam was against the practice. Nevertheless, al-Samaw'uli does not mention any religious sources on the subject, which was not unusual, given that his interests were predominantly of a clinical nature. In *Nuzhat al-Asĥab*[18] the author is in search for causes of homosexual behaviour and desires. In his chapter on female homosexuality, he provides an encyclopedia of reasons for women's sexual deviancies from heterosexual encounters. He begins by arguing that for sex to be pleasurable then there ought to be a complement between sexual partners:

> Some women prefer grinding because they are slow at cumming ... For if they had intercourse [with the male] they would be beaten to cumming and thus they rise without having fulfilled their need ... Should a woman with this trait come by a man who is slow at cumming then he would distract her from *suĥaq*. (*al-Asĥab*, 13)

Another category is an instance where the woman is quick at cumming and likewise she requires a man who is equally expedient. Furthermore:

> Some women have deficiencies or illnesses in their wombs and as a result intercourse causes them pain .... There are some women whose problem lies in wanting to kiss a mouth that is not roughened by a beard and want to press their cheeks against a soft cheek. (*al-Asĥab*, 14)

al-Samaw'uli discusses two other possible, clinical, reasons:

> There are some of them who exceed others in intelligence and deception and in their nature there is much that resembles men. Such a woman is a lover [as opposed to beloved] because she is the active partner .... It does not suit her to have to have sex at the time when her appetite is dormant. So this, together with the difficulty in cumming under the pleasures and command of the man, leads her to grinding.
>
> And some women whose womb is dominated by coldness, find pleasure in the heated friction as there is no pleasure like it in intercourse. (*al-Asĥab*,16)

al-Samaw'uli's chapter does not seem to be invested in moralism or religious condemnation, instead it seems to be descriptive of a prevalent reality. His categories do not always involve sexual orientations, but rather specific erotic preferences:

> There are some women whose problem lies in wanting to kiss a mouth that is not roughened by a beard and wanting to press their cheeks against a soft cheek. If one such woman managed to find a young unbearded man (*amrad*) then she would attain her satisfaction. Alternatively she would compensate with a girl[19] grinder where she can be choosy about her beauty. (*al-Asĥab*, 14–15)

Similarly to popular contemporary science, al-Samaw'uli's theorization of homosexuality is set within the framework that heterosexual practice, by virtue of its dominance, is the nature to which all deviant subjects must be compared, even though to which some cannot be returned. In other words, the writer operates within an ideology where heterosexual practice needn't be justified, as opposed to homosexual practice, which has origins only in shortcomings, incompatibilities and deficiencies.

ON RELIGIOUS TOLERANCE AND INTOLERANCE: THE CASE OF IBN ĤAZM (D.1064)[20] AND ABU BAKR AL-KHAFAF (D.1148)

It would seem that the dilemma facing researchers of homosexuality in Europe, from antiquity to the late nineteenth century, is that the evidence is not clear. Seldom are homosexual subjects speaking for themselves, and the evidence which remains tends to favour institutionally appointed or approved writers (such as clergy and statesmen) who were nearly always male and nearly always opposed to homosexual relations. The literature on the subject in medieval Arabia begins with a different trend. There are vivid descriptions of love and sexual intimacy between women, leaving speculation over whether this existed or not, obsolete. The Arabian literature also reveals that not all evidence points to intolerance and condemnation, as the pious Ibn Ĥazm from the eleventh century unmistakably put it in *al-Muĥalla*:[21]

> Some denominations licensed it [grinding] — as Ibn Jareeĥ has told me about al-Ĥassan al-Basri[22] who did not see that a woman inserting something as wretched — simply that she was seeking refuge from scandal (*satr*), and this way she can do without committing fornication.
>
> Others have said that it is forbidden, without exception (*al-Muĥalla*, 2232).[23]

Ibn Ĥazm, perhaps due to his piety left a vague description — "a woman inserting something," and had it not been for the context of the piece, one would have thought that Ibn Ĥazm was referring to autoeroticism.

By way of another example of this *tolerance*, which begins to dissipate in the thirteenth century, an incidental quote to be found in the most famous collection of songs and anecdotes in Arabic literature, Abu Faraj al-Asfahani's[24] (d. 897) *Kitab al-Aghani*[25] reads as follows:

> al-Ma'mun[26] was sitting with a cup in his hand when Bathal began to sing the song:
>
> I see nothing more delectable than the promise

But she sang it:

I see nothing more delectable than grinding

al-Ma'mun placed his cup down and turned to her and said: "Of course there is Bathal, fucking is better than grinding." So she became embarrassed and feared his wrath but he picked up his cup again and said: Finish the song and add the following:

I come to her when the slanderer is unaware
With a visit to a house empty of visitors but me
With a cry during the meeting and then a pause
And all these things are more delectable to me than dwelling [there][27]

(*Aghani*, 1905)

This is the peculiar story of a slave girl that al-Asfahani gives a brief biographical sketch of in the earlier pages (*Aghani*, 1903–1904). Bathal, born a slave girl, was considered to be one of the best "singers of her time" and she oversaw the teaching of some of the best court entertainers to come after her. What is intriguing is that this slave girl eventually becomes a woman of considerable wealth and power, who relied on the affections of her notable admirers to build considerable wealth. More intriguing, the story goes, is that although Bathal was sought after by numerous suitors of wealth and influence, the narrator tells us, she "refused to marry and remained this way for the rest of her life." This intriguing fact, compounded with the singer's twist of the lyrics of a known song, gives us considerable courage in assuming a homosexual inclination. What is even more fascinating is that Bathal, in the presence of Caliph al-Ma'mun Bin Harun al Rashid no less, decides to change the lyrics of a popular song to say "there is nothing more delectable than grinding." We will never know why she decided to do this but perhaps she gauged it safe to do so (perhaps because the Ma'mun was considerably drunk and she thought he wouldn't notice). The Ma'mun's reaction is also quite revealing. He disagrees with her that grinding is better, asserting his patriarchal privilege or simply his personal preference by overwriting her subjective experience, but then he asks her to proceed, authoring new lines to the song that suggest that the Ma'mun possesses insight into the subject. The final line "all these things" (of stealing into the house and so on and so forth,) "are more delectable to me than dwelling [there]" has a double meaning. The first is that this stealthy lover who is perhaps engaging with a married woman, is happy to be a visitor, she is happy not to be a dweller. Also the other meaning, which possesses sexual connotations, of course, implies that the act of surface grinding is much more delectable than dwelling; than going inside. There is an absence of the sort of violent moral condemnation we come to expect of contemporary Orthodox discourse.

There is, in Bathal's initial audacious act and the reaction of the Ma'mun, a small room in which we glimpse, if not the visibility of the homoerotic, then the relations between legislative authority (in the figure of the Ma'mun) and those who are its deviant subjects. Furthermore, it is often thought that slave girls were used sexually (consenting or otherwise) by their mistresses, but in this instance we see the "slave girl" as an active agent who seeks out the object of her affection (or lust), who steals into the empty mistress's home to engage in a sexual act she finds more delectable than the alternative.

By contrast, references proceeding from the thirteenth century onwards cease to take the shape of entire chapters and they also cease to discuss the homosexual subject either culturally or clinically – reference to homosexual relations is accompanied by reminders that it is strictly forbidden and that it is inferior, abominable, quite literally bringing the end of discussion. Somewhere in late thirteenth-century Arabia, the homosexual subject loses the privilege of speaking through citation and ventures towards a deep sepulchral closet, while the Medieval Muslim scholar loses his quest for a balanced representation. This loss of interest no doubt results in the formulaic condemnations and arguments against homosexuality that we come to see in contemporary "studies" on the subject. For example, in the fourteenth century, the belletrist Ibn Abi Ĥajala[28] (whilst not denying the practice and existence of homosexual love) refrains from seeking to cite the deviant subjects as his predecessors had done. Instead, he cites, in an attempt to persuade the reader in favour of chaste love:

> Say to she who grinds, what are you grinding for?
> Nothing satisfies your burning thirst
> Except these poor, bald, shaven saddlebags.[29]

without offering the rhetorical rebuttal which had come to be expected of anecdotal literature of this kind (I discuss these rebuttals in greater detail in the next chapter). In the same period al-Nuwayri (d.1332)[30] writes a history of the people of Rus[31] in *Nihayat al-Arb.*

> They lived a long time in their country worshiping God Almighty, the way he ought to be and then they deviated from this and worshipped statues and they began to practice sodomizing women and swapping them....This became unbearable for the women and so the devil came to them as a woman and taught them grinding and so they did it.[32]

By the fifteenth century, the devil became the cause of female homosexual desire, together with supposedly male ill-treatment. In these two contemporaneous references we can easily note the shift of the subject of female homosexuality from historical or speculative curiosity to religious and moral condemnation. Suddenly religious orthodoxy and sexual inquisitiveness, such as those we find in the work of al-Yemeni and al-Samaw'uli, become immiscible.[33] Unlike al-Samaw'uli's list of etiologies, here it is the devil who is the cause of female homosexual desire, together with supposedly male ill-treatment, the latter being even today a very popular understanding.

In the 1500s, ĥadiṭh and Quran scholar al-Hindi (d. 1567)[34] reminds us in *Kanz al-Åumal* that "women grinding each other is fornication" and that there were "at least ten reasons for Lot's people's annihilation, *to which my people add an eleventh reason: men having sex with men*" (my emphasis).[35] The initial reasons include "cutting their beards and having long moustaches ... whistling and wearing silk" (*Åumal*, 675). The erotic literature of deviant sexual practices disappears and is replaced by the strongest moral rebuke. This declivity is owed largely to a shift in the religious and political climate, where it ceased to be questionable whether Islam sanctioned homosex or not. This is in itself highly questionable given the ambiguity, or perhaps the complexity, of the Muslim holy texts. That homosexual acts are prohibited in Islam is not a matter that has always been accepted among Muslim scholars, most notable is the example of Yaĥya Bin Akṭham.

A close scrutiny of the religious rhetoric that is extremely bent on forbidding homosexuality does not seem to prevail until the fourteenth century onward. An example of this shift in religious rhetoric can be found in al-Mashtooly's sixteenth-century text on religious advisement *Salwat al-Aĥzan*.[36] *Salwat* provides a long list of evidence that homosexuality is forbidden is Islam. al-Mashtoolee writes:

> Women having sex with each other is one of the major transgressions. Waṭhila Bin al-Aqsa said: The messenger of God (p.b.u.h.) said: "Grinding is women fornicating together."
>
> He also said, p.b.u.h: "Female genitals on each other are like male genitals on female ones.... Women cannot have sex with each other without fornicating ... and thirdly God does not accept their doxology "there is no God but Allah" — the rider and the ridden upon, whether they are a male of female couple.[37]

This particular ĥadiṭh, possibly used as early as 845 A.D. by al-Yemeni is highly controversial and is thought to be a fabrication by some Muslim scholars. At any rate, I will return to this later. al-Mashtoolee continues with his reference to homosexuality:

> [Effeminacy is] of the greatest sins, which calls for damnation — not only for the man's attempt to resemble a woman but for the woman's attempt to resemble a man. Ibn Åbbas, God bless him had said: "The messenger of God (p.b.u.h) has damned effeminate men and man-acting women." And this is a true ĥadiṭh. Abu Hureira, God bless him, has said that "The messenger of God (p.b.u.h) has damned men who wear women's clothes and the women who wear men's clothes." (*Salwat*, 49)[38]

Notice that any appeal to religious texts here is not an appeal to anything said or written in the Quran, simply because the Quran makes no mention, prohibitory or otherwise, of female homosexuality. By contrast to the ĥadiţh, the Quran is considered to be infallible, to have been free from terrestrial modification. The ĥadiţh is much more difficult to authenticate and is easier to swear by or to forge.

Ibn Ĥazm, who died around 1064 A.D. and who was al-Mashtoolee's predecessor by almost seven centuries, provides one of the most significant references to female homosexuality in a discussion of the intricate legalities of Islamic doctrine on the subject. Citing himself as "Abu Moĥamad", Ibn Ĥazm tells us that some cultures prohibited female homosexuality (grinding) and made it punishable with one-hundred lashes. Abu Moĥamad traces the logic of such cultures to another thinker named al-Zuhri[39] who claimed that the prophet has said in a ĥadiţh that: "Grinding is fornication between women." al-Zuhri goes on to say that sodomy is greater in degree of sin than fornication while grinding is at the lower limits of the fornication-sin-scale. Abu Moĥamad continues that the cultures that supported al-Zuhri did so for their own purposes, supporting tradition and not searching for the true words of God, which is every Muslim's responsibility. Abu Moĥamad then offers the following refutation of these claims: The first point being that there are no such things as degrees of sin in Islam, there is no mention in the Quran or the ĥadiţh that there are degrees of fornication, fornication is fornication, plain and simple. Secondly, neither sodomy nor grinding can be seen as fornication because the prophet Moĥamad, in ĥadiţh al-Islamy, which is a highly reliable ĥadiţh, says that the definition of fornication is quite literally the presence of a penis inside a vagina between a man and a woman who are not married to each other. I would add that "anal sex" for example, by virtue of this precise definition, does not and cannot constitute fornication — it may be an unlawful act, but it is not fornication. Thirdly, Abu Moĥamad claims that the ĥadiţh relating the prophet as saying that "grinding is fornication between women" is not an authentic ĥadiţh, because not only does it contradict an authentic ĥadiţh which defines fornication in hetero-copulation terms, but because this alleged ĥadiţh itself can only be traced back so far as Makhoola and Miţhla who did not know the prophet personally or his immediate company. Therefore the ĥadiţh is unreliable and is falsified, or so he argues, it is a ĥadiţh maqtooå (a *severed* ĥadiţh).[40] Abu Moĥamad says that homosexual acts should not be seen as fornication. However, he tells us that the claim made by the renowned Iraqi Sufist al-Ĥassan al-Basri that grinding should not be seen as a sin at all, is also false. Abu Moĥamad refutes this with evidence from the Quran, which tells the believers that they are not allowed to make their bodies visible to people other than their legal spouses. He quotes a ĥadiţh in which the prophet Moĥamad says that men are not allowed to see other men's genitals and women are not allowed to make their genitals visible to other women, or for same-sex adults to cohabit in one garment (a euphemism for sexual activity?). These texts then form a clear indication that homosex, even sexual contact of any nature, is prohibited between a couple who are not married, let alone a same-sex couple (*al-Muĥalla*, 2232–2233).

Other aĥadiṭh, not discussed by Ibn Ĥazm, have indicated that the prophet was against the practice of homosexual sodomy and that he prescribed severe punishments. In *Sunan Abu-Dawud* we find:

> The Prophet (peace be upon him) said: If you find anyone doing as Lot's people did, kill the one who does it, and the one to whom it is done.[41]

And again, in the mid-fourteenth century, circa 1329 A.D., the Muslim fiqh scholar Shams Adeen al-Thahabi (d. 1347)[42] notes in *al-Kaba'er* that:

> Abi Hureira[43] has said that the prophet Moĥamad has said that "There are four who bring about the wrath of God and who are named for annihilation." And they asked, who are these, prophet of God? And he said those men who look like women and those women who emulate men and he who has intercourse with the female donkey and he who has intercourse with a male, meaning liwaṯ. It has also been said that if a male rides on another male that the throne of the Compassionate trembles for fear of the wrath of God and it is possible for the heavens to fall on the earth and so the angels hold on to the edges of the heavens and recite "God is the greatest for all eternity" until the wrath of God subsides.[44]

Even though some seemingly authentic aĥadiṭh have been seen to condemn at least male homosexual behaviour with severe punishment, we do not see this in the Quran. Although the Quran is not entirely silent about male homosexual activity, it makes hardly any reference to sodomy as a matter unrelated to the sacrilegious and criminal people of Lot. In relation to women, there is nothing to suggest that the Quran prohibited female homosexual activity. There is one verse in the Quran which has been attributed to female and male homosexuality somewhat dubiously, it reads:

> And for those of your women who commit sexual obscenities (*faĥisha*), find for them four witnesses, and if they verify then jail them in their homes until they die or until God finds another way for them. And as for those two (males) who commit this then hurt them, and should they repent and right their ways then let them go for God is compassionate. (Quran, Nisa': 15–16)

This verse in the Quran is the only one which is thought to make reference to homosexual activity without this being in relation to the people of Lot, and it is the only one which mentions women. However, this verse is unlikely to be related to homosexual activity at all due to the ambiguity of the grammar and wording. Much like the rest of the Quran, these verses have multiple meanings and possible interpretations. The primary word that I have translated as sexual obscenities (*faĥisha*) does not specifically mean sodomy or homosex, on the contrary, it means something much more general than that. It is better translated as debauchery, orgy-like activities or sex with al-maĥarem (those you are prohibited from marrying and having sex with such as your siblings, offspring, parents etc. see Quran, Nisa': 20–23) and the like. The verse may be referring to the scenario of a woman who engages with sexual activities with two men at the same time. At any rate, should the verse intend to reference homosexual activity, as it is possible to interpret (but very opaquely) it certainly does not prescribe the death penalty or even corporal punishment, as the aĥadiṭh allegedly do, and the sins committed seem to be of much less severity than those dealt with in regards to fornication in the Quran (being flogged with a hundred lashes, see Quran, Nour: 2). Should this verse be veritably about homosexual behaviours then it confounds the harshness of the aĥadiṭh and places their authenticity into question once more. In addition, the Quran requires the presence of four witnesses to the act — a very difficult circumstance to come by. This suggests that there was considerable room for evading the rule of law in early Islamic cultures where homosexual behaviour may have been prohibited, whilst in some Islamic cultures, at least in the Baghdad of the ninth century, homosexual activity was not seen as a transgression.

What is perhaps most intriguing about Ibn Ĥazm's discussion and its relevance to contemporary thought on the subject, is his attempt to undermine the interpretation of Lot's story, as it appears in the Quran, as one condemning or punishing homosexual behaviour (*al-Muĥalla*, 2225–2228). After indicating that various denominations (*Ta'efa*) set corporal and capital punishments for offenders (both insertive and receptive parties), while others permitted the act (which he asserts is against good taste but not unlawful (see *al-Muĥalla*, 2233) Ibn Ĥazm argues with evidence he selects from the Quran that:

> The stoning that hit [Lot's people] was not merely for sexual obscenities (*faĥisha*) but also because they were infidels/non-believers (*kaferoon*). [The denominations] should not stone those who have committed the act of Lot's people unless they be infidels as well, for if they do, they can no longer be supported by the Quranic verse because they would be contradicting it. In addition, God Almighty has said that Lot's wife came down with the same thing as the people of lot, and anyone with reasonable intelligence knows that she did not do what lot's people did." (*al-Muĥalla*, 2228)

The story of the people of Lot related in the Quran is often taken to mean that God condemns sodomites, but the story can be interpreted to mean that the sin of those particular people — the people of Lot, was the rejection of their prophet Lot and the only true God (for this is the predominant context in which reference to the people appears in the holy book), and their attempted sexual assault on Lot's visitor — who was an angel sent by God, no less (see Quran, Hood: 78–81). In addition, the story, while Semitic, is not Arabic but Hebraic in origin and any connotations of anti-homosexuality (or anti-omnisexuality) that it clearly entails are then the import of an earlier religion.

Homosexuality, though never laterally accepted, was also never so much of a taboo and a Ĥaram within Islamic cultures in their early formations. The Quran's permissiveness is certainly one example of this. The further Islamic cultures developed, the greater the stringencies and strictures on homosexuality became. What was once an ambiguous moral territory was re-appropriated with snippets of aĥadtih, authentic or not, and the discussion was brought to an end.

In chapters 4 and 5, we will be looking at the contemporary history and representation of female homosexuality in the Middle East. We briefly looked at the present state of anti-homosexuality rhetoric in the introduction. This rhetoric, in sharp contrast with the candid nature of Muslim scholarship from the medieval period, seems to be informed very little about the subjects it treats. In the next chapter I provide a close reading of Aĥmad ibn Yusuf's erotological work *Nuzhat al-Albab Fima La Yujad Fi Kitab* in which we gain a close view of Arab renaissance thinking in regards to sexual deviations. This chapter is then succeeded with the sharp contrast of our present times, in which we witness stringent opposition and "misrecognizing" of homosexuality and homosexuals in the Middle East.

4 A close reading of Aĥmad Ibn Yusuf Tifashi's *Nuzhat al-Albab*

Toward re-envisioning the Islamic Middle East

Since Foucault's *History of Sexuality* (Volume I)[1] introduced the idea that the sexual categories of heterosexuality and homosexuality were nineteenth-century inventions, more and more critics applied the epistemological/constructionist view of sexuality to readings of the Orient. It seemed to Foucault that the homosexual — in its strict negative/clinical sense — was an invention of European psychoanalysis, and to some critics, by means of extrapolation, that the modern gay identity was an unprecedented twentieth-century Western construct.[2] Such critics are very careful not to define their discussion of homosexual activity as anything resembling "modern" homosexuality, fearing that such a maneuver might place them at the level of a colonialist discourse that they very sensitively (and rightly) attempt to escape.[3]At first, critics claimed that in the Middle East, homosexual behaviour, the homosexual act, did not imply an identification of exclusivity, or an identification of individuals as "homosexuals." Recent counter claims to this uncompromising constructionist view of sexuality emerged in order to redress the balance. Stephen O. Murray and Will Roscoe's collection of essays *Islamic Homosexualities* (1997) was the first to take up the challenge.[4] Western perceptions of homosexual identity as a brief and recent reactionary development in the West began to be challenged, as well as the notion that no such thing existed or exists in the Middle East. This new branch of study (which has only been around since the early 1990s) is uncovering evidence contrary to the Western theory of Middle East history as one devoid of exclusively homosexual relationships. As'ad Abu Khalil has argued for the existence of exclusive homosexual identities, citing examples of widely known historical figures as early as the ninth century:

> The Abbasid Caliph al-Wathiq, for example devoted his life and poetry to his male lover Muhaj. The Caliph al-Amin....refused, despite the strenuous efforts of his mother, to have sex with women.[5]

In addition, a counterargument in Middle East studies has emerged to challenge the mainstream notion that Arab cultures were entirely anti-homosexual in the past, and that they have remained obstinately so. Abu

Khalil has also argued that "Islam did not have the same Biblical judgment about homosexuality as Christianity [and that homophobia] as an ideology of hostility towards people who are homosexual, was produced by the Christian West" (Abu Khalil, 32). In his polemic work *Sexuality in Islam*, Abdelwahab Bouhdiba has argued that Christian theology and eschatology place prohibitions on the sexual body far more greatly than Islam does. That Islam is more accommodating of the sexual urge and need in both men and women — in fact a lifestyle of celibacy is not seen as desirable in Islam, or sacred.[6] And furthermore, that Paradise is described in terms of eternal sensual/sexual reward, it is "an eternal orgasm" to use Bouhdaibba's expression, in comparison with an "unknowable" Christian heaven.[7] And if we take into account the extremist "sexual renunciation" taken up by seventh-century Christian cultures that Peter Brown expounded upon in his book *The Body and Society*,[8] we find in comparison that although the orthodox Islam of the Middle Ages prohibited sexual pleasure beyond the confines of marriage, it remained positive and encouraging of "legal" or sanctified sexual pleasure, whereas Christian orthodoxy (which was somewhat ameliorated in the Middle Ages[9] even though the practice of chaste marriages continued),[10] in opposition here to both the Judaic and Islamic traditions, would rather have it denied.

Theories of Islam account for the tension currently found in the academic literature on the subject. On the one hand, there are critics who configure Arab cultures as eternally unable to move beyond binaries of male master and female slave,[11] who also consider the notion that homosexuality, as a way of life, is a Western construct. On the other hand, there are critics who have begun to construct counter claims, well-founded on evidence, to suggest that homosexual desire is an essential phenomenon, embedded beyond pure constructionist factors. The orientalist critics who work within a blended epistemological/essentialist framework of sexuality theory tend to render Arab cultures in motion within a historical process of alluvion — of waxing and waning — of cultural peaks and lows, moving between liberal humanism (that finds its origins in Sufi philosophy and not Western enlightenment) and the more restraining ends of Orthodoxy.[12]

There are ample examples of male homoeroticism and male homosexuality in the Arab-Islamic civilization and history. And the homoerotic or at least the pederastic has a considerable history beyond the literary and beyond the Middle Ages. It is alleged that in the Egyptian Oasis of Siwa male-to-male marriage contracts were customary, and this custom, which can be traced back to the nineteenth century, did not cease until the 1940s.[13] Classical Arab poetry is pervaded by male homoeroticism, namely by the openly bisexual poet Abu Nuwas who was Caliph Harun al Rashid's personal poet in the ninth century. E.J. Haeberle cites al-Samaw'uli who suggests that a great many physicians "recommended homosexual...intercourse to their male patients for the purpose of preserving their health and youthful appearance."[14] Haeberle, a psychologist, also claimed that the "voluminous sexological literature of medieval Islamic scholars never mentions anything like modern homosexuality"(6). This claim was popular for some time but needs much revision and scrutiny due to conflicting primary historical and literary sources now emerging.[15]

While it is easy to establish a firm case for exclusive homosexual relationships in a case study of male Arab homosexualities, doing the same for women is virtually uncharted. Unlike the perceptions of the few who have dappled in this territory the field is by no means arid, and the evidence is not entirely invisible, or even scarce. In fact the period between the ninth century and the mid-thirteenth is unusually littered with references to female homosexuality. The early writings are concerned with possible causes of homosexuality while the latter ones are more invested in religious condemnation. There is a clear shift in rhetoric from tolerance and medical inquiry to an obvious disdain and prohibition in these substantial references.

Within fiction or the oral folk tales it is more difficult to locate substantial references to female homosexuality. Remke Kruk, however, has expounded upon an entire canon of oral folklore Arabic storytelling where women are very much presented as powerful, influential warriors.[16] In fact, Kruk has unearthed the trope of the warrior woman as well as identifying traces of the Amazon myth in Arab Folklore tales. In the text of *Sirat al-Amira That al-Himma*, we are told that a particular warrior princess in the Byzantium kingdom, Nura, displays no desire for men but rather quite actively prefers the pleasure and the company of women (Kruk, 1998, 102). A similar story in the *Sira* tells us that another Byzantium warrior princess quite openly desired other women and rejected men entirely (Kruk, 1993, 224). The construct of Nura's story seems to be at once textually and subtextually a story of lesbian identity. On the one hand, we are given a character who is not interested in men, but very much so in women, and on the other hand, we trace the destruction of that identity at the hands of another warrior princess who forces marriage upon Nura, whom she holds captive.

Princess Nura's story begins when she is in a monastery wrestling and defeating all of her female friends, unaware that her future husband, a Muslim warrior, is watching her. Soon after they meet, they wrestle and he is defeated on more than one occasion, and he claims that he lost to her extreme beauty and sensuality, rather than to her brute strength — a common motif in such Arab folktales (Kruk, 1993, 223). Nura then undergoes a process of being pursued by a host of unwanted and rejected Muslim and Christian suitors for the entire story. Her marriage is forced on her towards the end of the story and furthermore the consummation of that marriage is executed by force, after her counter attempt to poison her husband fails (Kruk, 1998, 113). There are many elements of resistance to the hetero-normative, together with evidence of the existence of, at least in the Arab Folklore imagination, strong warrior women, some of whom are not only subtextually but also quite frankly homosexual. These women are not typical examples of the ideal woman in the orthodox Muslim imagination that we are familiar with in Western as well as Eastern perceptions of the Middle East. It should not be ignored, however, that at the end of Nura's part of the epic, Nura is finally integrated as a happily married woman, who converts to Islam and fights alongside her new found faith. This form of conversion narrative is not at all discouraging of the theory of fixed lesbian identities, because we see this form of conversion narrative again in the 1950s and 1970s Egyptian and American cinema — where the restoration of order relies on the heterosexual happy ending of marriage and childbearing (e.g. the Egyptian films *Cat on Fire*[17] and *Pleasure and Suffering*[18] and Hollywood films such as *Queen Christina*[19]and the subtextual classic, *Calamity Jane*).[20] Mainstream cultures have very often undermined and undercut the crux of exclusive homosexual feelings by the propagation of the notion of vacillation or even curability, and if there had not been a recognized presence of a homosexual "threat" to hetero-normative social order, these narratives would not have moved so emphatically to convert the headstrong and nearly undefeated warrior princesses that they depict.

In this particular *Sira*, the conversion narrative also operates as the conversion of the Christian princess into the Muslim faith and army. The protagonist undergoes a process of renouncing her homosexuality and her Christianity — from the "disorder" and perhaps implied inferiority of both, to the "order" of the Islamic faith and the heterosexual union. The narrative may also be an allegory for the history of war between the Muslim and the Byzantine kingdoms during the crusades. The union between Nura and the Muslim fighter might be an allusion to the truce made by the (Muslim) Arabs lead by Salaĥ-Adeen and the (Christian) Byzantines who were lead by Isaac II (1187–1192).

AĤMAD TIFASHI AND *NUZHAT AL-ALBAB*

Aĥmad Ibn Yusuf al-Tifashi (d.1253) was born in the Tunisian town of Tifash in 1184 A.D. He spent a great deal of his life traveling through the Middle East, where he acted as a judge in Cairo, Tunisia and Damascus and undertook long expeditions to Iraq, where it is thought that he compiled information for his book on precious stones.[21] Aĥmad Tifashi's thirteenth-century text *Nuzhat al-Albab Fima La Yujad Fi Kitab*[22] is believed to have been composed in 1250, only three years prior to his death at age seventy. The following two paragraphs present a summary, paraphrase and translation from a thorough and original biography of Tifashi by Ĥasan and Khafajee.[23]

Tifashi came from a prominent family that was well known for making contributions to science (*åilm*). Several members of his family held highly-regarded positions either as judges or ministers and similar occupations (Ĥasan & Khafajee, 7). Born and raised in Tifash, where his father was a judge, he went to the Tunisian capital in pursuit of learning. Soon after, while still at a young age, Tifashi traveled to Cairo and studied under Åbd al-Laṯif al-Baghdadi. Later on he traveled to Damascus and worked with Taj Adeen al-Kindi. He also traveled to Armenia, Iraq [and Morocco] (Ĥasan & Khafajee, 9).

Tifashi lived in a Golden Age which was characterized by the expansion of higher learning and intellectual culture, not to mention that the political leaders of the time often relied on and sought the counsel of men of science and arts. In that particular climate, North Africa attracted Andalusian immigrants who found both peace and excellent work opportunities under a strong government (Ĥasan & Khafajee, 10).

It is important to factor these acute observations into our understanding of the cultural milieu which produced Tifashi's exemplary text. A flourishing and strong government which encourages and relies on its intellectuals; a curious, adventurous and meticulous researcher who seeks out the subjects he treats; who is also a scholar trained in scientific methodology; whose writings seek veracity as opposed to fiction or entertainment. *Nuzhat al-Albab* is not mujun literature for its own sake (it has been classified as erotology), but rather, it presents an encyclopedic study of the heteroglossia of Arab sexual behaviours and appetites. Similarly to Abu Faraj al-Asfahani and al-Raghib al-Asfahani, veracity and accuracy were important to Tifashi such that when an anecdote is being told to us, Tifashi goes through the trouble of noting down the chain of transmission (a matter that I have omitted from my citations): that is he tells us from whom he heard the story and from whom they heard it and so on. This gives us great courage in anticipating that Tifashi's intention was to provide accurate information circulating about homosexual relations/acts between women (and men) among other categories of behaviour. His work under al-Baghdadi and al-Kindi also suggests that he became open to the subject of homosexual relations early on in his intellectual career, and yet it was not until he was sixty-seven years of age that he decided to note down his experiences, discussions and research on the subject of sexual deviations. Tifashi's cool and sometimes generous handling of the subject matter is never accompanied by personal rebuke, something which characterizes nearly all of the other literature surveyed in this study, and this is a highly important distinction that critics of *Nuzhat* have missed.

Tifashi's chapter on lesbianism has received, until now, virtually no critical scrutiny whatsoever. There is a discussion of the text in the Arabic scholarly work *The History of Sexual Deviations Among the Arabs* by Ibrahim Maĥmood published in 2000, and a brief article by Fedwa Malti-Douglas published in a collection entitled *Same-Sex Love and Desire Among Women in the Middle Ages* published in 2001. Both criticisms fail to highlight the positive and engaging elements of the text (I discuss this in more detail later on). In Maĥmood's case, it seems to be a matter of an overwhelming and over-determined desire to engage the material from an orthodox Muslim stance on the matter of lesbianism as morally reprehensible, and for Malti-

Douglas it is a desire to read Tifashi's work through a feminist critique of the misogynist and patriarchal stance of orthodox Islam. The critique of Tifashi's text as one of Orthodoxy is flawed given the cultural and historical milieu out of which this text is produced and also given the candor with which the subject matter is broached, as well as the subtleties and intricacies that this text reveals about the author's attitude and the individuals and communities it implies.

THE HISTORICAL SURROUNDINGS OF *NUZHAT* AND TIFASHI'S TIMES

Tifashi's text was produced in a time immediately preceding the complete overhaul of Middle Eastern political dynamics, only a few years prior the overthrow of the Ayyubid dynasty by the Egyptian Mamluks and prior to the Mongolian conquest. In this short period in the early 1250s, the ruler of Egypt was the female Sultan Shajar al–Durr who ascended the throne following the death of the Sultan's son.[24] Fifteen years earlier, Delhi became witness to another female Sultan, Princess Radiyya who reigned from 1236–1240: during this period it was not entirely uncommon for women to take positions of political power.[25] Farhad Daftary reveals that two centuries earlier, the sister of the caliph Imam al-Ĥakim, Sitt al Muluk, ruled as regent from 1020–1024. She was followed by another female regent, Um al-Mustanzir who ruled from 1036. Daftary further observes that the "ascendancy of those [two] women to political prominence was not challenged by the Fatimid establishment."[26] Daftary then dedicates her article to the examination of the peculiar instance of one woman's appointment as a religious and political leader — a "hujja" — in Yemen in 1084. Her name was Sayyida Ĥurra, and her appointment as a religious leader of so high a rank, was and still is unprecedented in the Middle East.

Not only were women capable of occasionally holding prestigious political and religious positions of power during these crucial centuries (between the eleventh and the thirteenth), they were also capable of dispensing large sums of money, patronizing architecture, patronizing pilgrimages to Mecca and founding religious schools.[27] The works of the historians Jonathan Berkey and Michael Chamberlain have shown that throughout the Middle Ages there was a sprouting of schools, some of which were patronized by women.[28] Berkey maintains that there is no evidence that women enrolled officially in the schools, instead they very often acted as their head administrators. The education of women took place in more informal settings, such as Ĥadiṭh schools and private classes; alternatively it became a duty devolving upon fathers or husbands to educate their daughters or wives. More commonly women of scholastic prominence took it upon themselves to educate other women; however, he notes that there is no evidence that women became teachers of men. Women however were occasionally able to study alongside men in the study and transmission of ĥadiṭh. Berkey has shown that women played a significant role in the transmission of the ĥadiṭh and that in some instances women became the most revered authorities on certain aĥadiṭh. Berkey also cites an instance where a male scholar boasted of studying with a female authority (175–181). What is unquestionable and astonishing is that a considerable number of women had access to, and that they were instructed in, reading and writing. In Tifashi's chapter, we will meet women who write each other letters, and we will meet more than one poetess who makes some very clever and unconventional allusions to God and the Quran.

In light of this evidence, we have to reconsider the notion about Islamic thought and history as singularly Orthodox or homogenous. Fortunately this project is well under way, for which Edward Said's *Orientalism* was a theoretical precursor or awakening, and to his work we will continue to be indebted for some years to come. The predominant perception that homosexuality-as-lifestyle and liberal humanism, which accepts it, are both recent inventions of the West is never more obviously fallacious than at the site of an intensive reading of Tifashi's chapter on female homosexuality.

TIFASHI'S CHAPTER OF FEMALE HOMOSEXUAL RELATIONS

The title of this chapter is "Fi Adab al Saĥq Wal Musaĥiqat."[29] As I explained in the introduction to this work, a musaĥiqa (the plural of which is Musaĥiqat) means grinder (feminine noun). Grinding can be translated as "tribadism." However, the literal translation of *Saĥq* into "grinding" is imbued with cultural and political import as it forms, in Jungian terminology, an archetype in the *archetypal unconscious* related to female homosexuality. The expression "to grind", "grinding", "grinder" pervades contemporary and past lesbian English-language pornography, as well as sexually motivated cultural events. Take for example a recent advertisement for a "lesbian strip joint" that came out in Sydney in 2003. The show's slogan (it was called *Gurlesque*) invites us to participate in an "illicit bump and grind."[30]

Another example of the use of the word "grinding" is "Tofu Grinder" which is the literal Cantonese translation for "lesbian." If we take "Tofu" to be the slang word for "woman", then "Tofu Grinder" can be read as Woman Grinder.[31] It is amazing that this word — grinding — whether in English, Arabic or Cantonese, can provide a cross-cultural, cross-temporal, not to mention multilingual identification of female homosexual activity, and to a lesser extent, identity (at least identification).

In Tifashi's text *Musaĥiqat* — grinders — is not what the tribades call each other. Tifashi tells us that they called a woman *Tharifa*[32] and that grinding/tribadism among them is known as *Tharaf*. Tharaf is wit; a Tharifa is a witty woman.

> And I know that this matter is known among its masters as wit and by this name they are called, meaning, they call themselves: wits. So if they said that so and so is "witty" then it became known amongst them that she is a grinder. (*Nuzhat*, 236–237)

For a woman to be witty is itself transgression against Orthodox Muslim ideals of womanhood as well as subversion of those ideals. For example, Nafzawi writes in the 1570s, that the ideal woman should be quiet, of little mobility, even less speech, hardly any interest in her neighbors and possess much reverence and devotion to her husband. He adds that "no wonder then that some have said that if you see a woman who jokes and laughs and is playful a lot then know that she is a whore and a fornicator" (87). A witty woman, the code word for lesbian amongst women inclined to that desire, is a woman who is sexually transgressive against the licit, as well as a woman who is subversive of the Orthodox idealism of Woman, since the witty women overturn the hierarchy of popular discourse at more than one junction — i.e. sexually, culturally, socially and ideally.[33]

Tifashi reveals that a thirteenth-century Arabian bi/homo woman called herself *Tharifa* — meaning the "witty one." This reveals a more obscure possibility, that there were communities of grinder-identified women, who designated themselves a name — or a code word. Very much in the same fashion that a lesbian attends a "dyke" bar, or fully understands when her friends refer to another woman as an "embankment," these women would have needed subcommunities or subcultures through which the code word *Tharifa* can be disseminated and understood, otherwise it could not be feasible. And in this way their identities come to resemble what has been obscurely labelled as "modern" homosexual identities.

The medical discourse on the subject, Tifashi tells us, was divided: some doctors ("wise men") thought it was a natural appetite, others thought it was a disease and both groups agreed to the potential of this disease/appetite to being innate, inborn. In the thirteenth century, Arab medical discourse around sex, as it is represented here, had already engaged in the constructionist-essentialist debate. As the son of Massoyeh capitulates from his moral high ground:

> In the same way as licentiousness, as we will reveal later, whenever grinding is self-generated then it is easily soluble, easily transferable, but when it is due to physical constitution, then it is difficult to recover from and is far from accepting treatment as we have noted. (*Nuzhat*, 236)

Massoyeh tells us that wherever homosexual inclination is an acquired matter of taste, then it is easily curable.[34] Alternatively, if the subject's homosexuality is due to something amiss in her physical constitution, then her cure, rather her conversion, is much more difficult to achieve. This points to knowledge of the existence of stable homosexuals, rather, non-transient homosexuality. The medical notion that homosexuality is a disease is not the only one Tifashi presents. His attitude towards women engaged in homoerotic sex is not only tolerant, but admiring. Although he begins his chapter by describing grinding as an "illness" (*da'*), his engagement with the topic demonstrates a favourable bias when he is using his personal voice, and not reporting the sayings of others. The first time he gives the title of "wise men" (*ĥukama'*) to individuals relating information on the topic, he reports that:

> ...wise men have said:
>
> "Grinding is a natural appetite that occurs between the labia, that are concaved like an inverted boil out of which vapors are generated. These increase and consequently heat is generated as well as itchiness in the hair floccules of the labia." (*Nuzhat*, 236)

By contrast to the "doctors" who open the chapter, and by contrast to the unforgiving Son of Massoyeh — the "wise men" (as he decrees them) explain homoerotic sexual appetites in women as "natural."[35] They go on to condone homosexual activity as it brings relief to the women with this natural condition, a relief that, the wise men continue, "can only be brought about by the coming down on her from another woman." Unlike the doctors from the preceding paragraphs, the wise men do not see the matter as illness or licentiousness; in fact they seem to be veritably condoning its existence. They also seem to be in the early stages of formulating knowledge of the clitoris with its connections to the labia, which they can only comprehend as some kind of "inverted boil" that produces itchiness. I wonder if the notion of itchiness was not in itself deduced from the observation of female masturbation, or whether the word itchiness is here intended much less literally and more figuratively. The "wise men" acknowledge male impotence in satisfying the appetite of such women — their uselessness in a post-patriarchal gesture of the intellect. Tifashi consistently follows through this open approach to the subject matter.

Subsequently, Tifashi tells us in his own voice of his contacts and experiences with the communities of tribades, and since he wrote this text towards the end of his life, it would be fitting to consider the works presented therein as an accumulation of his experiences and observations made on wide-reaching expeditions. He relates that the grinders call grinding *T͟haraf* and then reveals something more astonishing that gives us a clue about the level of visibility and acceptability of same-sex relationships in some cultural circles.

> ...one of them will spend money on the other in the same way that a man does on his lover, but much more, until the spending is exaggerated to hundreds and thousands.
>
> I witnessed a woman in Morocco who had a great deal of money and a wide estate, so she dispensed a great deal of jewelry on her lover ... When she ran out of this and people began to reproach and blame her exceedingly, she warranted her lover the entire estate, which came to about five thousand dinars. (*Nuzhat*, 238)

Tifashi uses the instance he has witnessed to provide what he claims to be a typical example of romantic relationships between women — showing their generosity towards, and hyperbolic adoration for, their lovers. He chooses the word "witness" which is indelible from the visibility it implies, a visibility that becomes clearer at the end of the paragraph. The wealthy woman in this account is *seen* and reproached and blamed by the people, (presumably her neighbors and family and friends) *for her irrational spending on her lover and not at all for the gender of her love interest.*

Tifashi then continues that:

> They use a lot of fragrance, beyond what is usual, and the cleanness of their clothes is more than is characteristic and as for furniture, food and devices, of these they have better and more beautiful things than what capability can attain or for the place and time to contain. (*Nuzhat*, 238)

Fedwa Matli-Douglas interprets this section as a criticism or condemnation of these women and their practices, on the strength of a Quranic verse, of which Tifashi makes no mention, that warns women against too many adornments and vanities — against *tabaruj*.[36] Malti-Douglas however fails to mention the one critical sentence, perhaps the one *critical word*, with which Tifashi seems to be clear of preaching against the sin of *Tabaruj*. Here it is again: "as for furniture, food and devices, of these they have *better and more beautiful things* than what capability can attain or for the place and time to contain" (my emphasis). While modesty and humility are indeed highly regarded qualities in the Muslim woman (if only in the orthodox Muslim imagination), beauty and elegance are no less regarded in Muslim culture than anywhere else. Malti-Douglas removes Tifashi's text from its proper context — as a text about unspoken pleasure, as implied by the title of the book,[37] not a text of instructive erotology such as Nafzawi's fifteenth-century text al-Rawd al-Åttir or Ibn al-Jawzi's thirteenth-century text on religious rules for women (*Kitab Aȟkam al-Nisa'*). In her attempt to deconstruct and destabilize Orthodox ideology, Malti-Douglas accidentally and unnecessarily reinforces its predominance — predominance that Tifashi seems to have transcended.

In *Woman in the Muslim Unconscious*, Fatna A. Sabbah provides a highly acute definition of the perceptions of female sexuality in Orthodox Arab-Islamic cultures:

> In the discourse of legal (orthodox) Islam, the body — of women and also of men — is the field on which the writing of power, of authority, of hierarchy is inscribed with the most violence. In the erotic discourse it is a field where the only writing is that of pleasure. Pleasure is the organizing principle of the world, of beings and their relations. It is the order itself, emanating from and situated in female desire.[38]

Tifashi's text falls into the region of erotic literature "where the only writing is that of pleasure." A dynamic of inscribing "authority [and] hierarchy...with the most violence" takes place when contemporary scholar, Ibrahim Maĥmood, impresses his own religious orthodoxy in a reading of Tifashi's text; however the text itself, by its very nature, is resistant to didactic and moralistic theories of interpretation. In Maĥmood's use of aspects of Tifashi's text, we do not find analysis so much as we find a desire to eliminate or overlook the obvious elements of openness and interaction involved between these *queers* and Tifashi.[39] Instead, Maĥmood offers a traditional and patriarchal interpretation of Muslim culture, in tune with current Western and Eastern trends. Maĥmood selects from Tifashi's chapter examples that are only categorized under the heading "denunciation of grinding", without mentioning the fact of the subsection. In this way, Maĥmood coolly overlooks the positive elements that "balance" the negative ones into a rhetorical battle (and hence deludes his reader). Neither Malti-Douglas nor Maĥmood, whose intellectual and ideological backgrounds are as different as their reading purposes, could fathom that the situation in Tifashi's time might be any different from what it is today, or that Islam could exist in a cultural configuration that differs from the one Sabbah has (rightly) provided for Western intellectuals. This demonstrates the astonishingly effective stranglehold that contemporary Arab cultures have on sexuality discourse in their societies today, creating and maintaining the illusion of sanitized sexual practices, not only contemporaneously, but for all time.

While Malti-Douglas brings to light an always necessary deconstruction of patriarchal misogyny (which I will discuss later), her focus on the elements of male chauvinism in the chapter, without seeing them as elements that balance that which is said in favour of the women in question, is flawed. Women are given a voice in Tifashi's text, they are allowed to speak for themselves and about themselves through the convention of citation,[40] and they express, at times, their joy in renouncing the heteronormative modality, and at others, their joy in (re)discovering it. It is no denigration to lesbians, should some of their bisexual lovers favour men; there is simply a display of that diversity. We see this in the section entitled "Denunciation of grinding"

> [A woman] wrote to a lover of hers who had tasted a man and accompanied him: "If the Muezzin never came down from his minaret, then no one would pray in the mosque. So what is this admiration for a bucket that has been dipped in a thousand wells and then became yours, when its edges are dented and its rope is corroding? And if you return to what is fair then you will find that walking in the garden is easier than walking an arduous mountain road."
>
> She wrote a reply: "My sister I used to eat onion without knowing the taste of the damask rose and radish. So when I ate them I swore that I would eat nothing else besides. No, [I swear] by your life, you did not come into my house ever, so exit my love form your heart, because I have put, in place of your love, something that will only come out with breath [spirit]." (*Nuzhat*, 245)

The infusion of the religious with the sexual is often a trademark in Medieval Arab erotology and this literate grinder whose writing has been preserved only in the smallest proportion through citation, seems proficient in this form of allusion. The lesbian lover's argument is that sex with men does not lead to gratification, because as long as the Mu'zin (the leader of the prayer) is still in the minaret (an obvious phallic allusion) then the true prayer process, the true devotion, cannot begin. The true prayer and devotion, therefore, takes place in the lower places, in the dwelling itself. The reformed lover's reply however negates this by claiming that "you did not come into my house ever", meaning that she, the rejected lover, cannot claim to have satisfied her sexually, and must then "exit your love for me from your heart, because I have put, in place of your love, something that will only come out with the spirit."

The denunciation of lesbianism made by former grinders is a gentle one. It may cause indignation and jealousy in the former lover and it may devalue the whole concept of "same sex love among women," and yet, unlike the men in this chapter, when women denounce lesbianism they do so with less violence. They simply ask that their preferences be respected and left alone. They too find themselves in a position where they have to justify themselves for their entry into the heteronormative, as though a woman would be mad to do so. As the lesbian lover in the previous story reasons:

> My sister if everyone who saw a walking stick then started walking on it, because of whatever weakness he had, and benefited from it, then I would have excused you for not being able to walk except with a stick. But there is no admiration for your leaving what is in your nature, in order to walk in the darkness, because walking without a stick is better for your body. (*Nuzhat*, 245)

The rejected lover is confused by the woman who starts to use the "stick" simply because she comes by it, when clearly, it is better for the "nature" of the former lover's body not to use a stick — at least she does not need it. The former lover's reply is as follows:

> My sister, I used to enjoy the beating of the drum before I enjoyed the sound of the flutes. So when I heard it, something in my heart knotted up that nothing except death could resolve. So make it easy on yourself, by not making my fate your business, because it has become easier on me, because of the privilege that I now have in my hands. (*Nuzhat*, 245)

In the first half of both letters, which follow a very similar rhetorical format, the rejected lovers present themselves as individuals whose identities and persuasions are clearly biased in favour of (also implying exclusivity to) same sex love. And in both instances, the former lovers indicate a newly discovered preference for men (albeit that in the first instance presented, the rejection seems harsher). Lesbian and (certain) bisexual identities begin to take shape, and we should not be discouraged from labeling them as such, simply for fear of anachronism, because by following such a line of thought, which has a short history in itself, we are falling into another trap — that of metonyms; of confusing things in themselves with the signifiers that are allocated to them periodically. At any rate, other medieval references to the subject make a clear distinction between "women who enjoy grinding and do not reject men" and those who will only be with female lovers, demonstrating that a distinction between "bisexual" and "lesbian" women was known.[41]

In the male denunciations of lesbian sexual activity (here understood to be a process of mutual clitoral stimulation), ignorance of the female body and female eroticism is the most dominant feature. The theme that recurs tells of the narrators' (the men's) inability to comprehend how two vaginas can satisfy each other, when they do not seem to fill the "void" that is the womb (there is no clear reference to female-to-female penetrative sex). Their comprehension of sexual pleasure can only be understood in terms of what the penis can do for the female sexual organs, and they are confused about what they see as "fake" fucking, as simulation of fucking as they know it.

> God has damned the grindings of saffron stigmas[42]
> Because they have exposed the wantonness of humans
> They have aroused a war without stabbing
> Only the clanging of shield against shield (*Nuzhat*, 246)

Calling on the Almighty himself, the narrator wonders at the impiety of a war without stabbing and the impotence of a war conducted purely by the clanging of shield against shield.[43] In another instance, a similar logic follows:

> God damn you, you unfaithful whore
> How do you rub your pubis with another pubis
> When every house that is covered by a ceiling
> Must have a pillar in the middle of it? (*Nuzhat*, 246)

Again the notion of complementarity is presented here, suggesting that only physical "opposites" can engage in a proper intercourse, rather, in intercourse at all. Poetic verses which parodied both the logic and the imagery of the censure genre probably existed in abundance; however, if this was the case, the material does not appear to have survived. A short rebuttal does appear in the *Arabian Nights*; however, it gives us a hint as to what a parody genre of censure would have sounded like

> The penis smooth and round was made/with anus best to match it/Had it been made for cunnus' sake, / it had been formed like a hatchet.[44]

Unfortunately we cannot discern when this parody of the hetero-centric censure genre took place, but we do know that hetero-centric negation of homoeroticism was what pervaded most of the process of denunciation (up until the mid-thirteenth century at least). We see this again in the following poem which is much cited:

> Hey you — practitioners of grinding in the West and East
> Wake up — for fucking is better than grinding
> Wake up — because food is craved with bread
> And bread cannot be softened in the throat by bread
> If they were to patch holes in the same manner
> Then what kind of wit would patch a hole with a hole?
> And is the hammer of any use without its stick
> If it was needed one day for hammering?[45] (*Nuzhat*, 246–247)

It seems really quite a reasonable argument: "what kind of a wit would patch a hole with a hole?" However, together with the previous censure poems presented, the logic fails at the point it excludes the subjective experience of and pleasure derived from female homosexual behaviour. The violence of this exclusion might even point to jealous obfuscation of a truth known to the censurers. Their censure also fails more literally (and literarily) speaking in the above poem, because as Tifashi has described to us earlier, this act of grinding must be done at a certain angle, in which the holes do indeed fill (compliment) each other, for if:

> ... [the] lips [of one grinder are placed] atop the...lips [of the lower one], this is not useful for them nor is it pleasurable and the reason for this is because the place of pleasure remains empty of an occupant. (*Nuzhat*, 238)

The material of (male-centred) denunciation is marked with poetical elegance and persuasion that is suffused with oppression (or sheer ignorance?) of female sexuality. Denunciation of female homosexuality is marked by a wounded phallocentric machismo which reproduces and reinforces a sexual and gender hierarchy that is typical of patriarchal societies. In this instance the male voice authoritatively calls:

> Leave the grinding that has exhausted you falsely
>
> For no grinder is satisfied by grinding (*Nuzhat*, 248)

Without too hastily brushing off the obvious factual error that "no grinder is satisfied by grinding," it is best to adhere to Tifashi's text where it offers countless examples that invalidate all the male-centred claims of denunciation. The story of the Egyptian judge for example, is told, seemingly, by a highly "moral" person (the judge himself tells the story), who, coming upon the scene of the two female lovers in a luxurious Egyptian cemetery, finds them grinding their way to ecstasy. He then interrupts their activity with every intention of punishing them. He is initially alerted to their presence by overhearing the sounds of extreme sexual arousal, which both enchant and stupefy him:

> I heard, in one of the graves, a moaning and groaning and a kind of panting that strips the minds and steals the hearts. I had never heard anything like it and I didn't think anyone did it as such: with measured movements and natural rhythms and sayings of internal rhyme that cause one to forget the melody of strings and render the mistresses of the flute invisible. (*Nuzhat*, 239)

Although Tifashi provides a section for male denunciation of grinding, it seems that he also provides ample evidence of refutation of the claims made by the censurers, and the relaters of this evidence are not only women speakers and writers but, as in the story of the judge, they can also be men, who, coming upon the scene of the two unaware lovers are then educated in the sexual possibilities and pleasures available to two women.

Furthermore, in the judge's story the "moral" figure, the *judge*, is subverted: he becomes the fool as the grinders seize possession of power by humiliating him, stripping him of his mind, sanity and donkey (his only means of transport). They do this by tricking him into thinking that he is permitted to have sex with one of the women. When he enters the dwelling, interrupting their privacy, he gives the reins of his donkey to the woman whom he had every intention of replacing in the sexual act, the very woman who invited him. She waits for him to undo his trousers, to take off his pallium and badges and to draw so near his passive target that he is able to feel her warmth, then she whips the donkey and lets go of its reins. The judge has no choice but to run deliriously after it, with his "pants undone, [his] pallium tangled up and [his] member erect. Stumbling a few steps and falling on [his] face, getting up only to fall again." There is a sense of transcendent justice about the story, which the judge seems to relate without (or at least with significantly diminished) machismo. When the donkey finally comes to a halt, he has already been seen in his ridiculous condition, running back into the city, by strangers and familiar people alike. This story stands in stark contrast to a similar version of the scenario found elsewhere in the literature on grinding:

> A man entered a house and found two women grinding each other.
>
> The top one pulled him across and put him in her place, and he said: "This is a matter that requires ropes and men."[46]

The effect of the Judge's tale subverts the chapter's predominantly male-centred objections, conceptions and fantasies surrounding female homosexuality. The story challenges the belief that women cannot be truly satisfied by other women, and that in the event of the arrival of a man, two such women would be happily responsive to his advances and, thirdly, that simply through the virtue of his gender, *man* is guaranteed ascendancy to and maintenance of power in a situation involving women. Tifashi should be credited with including such a tale, the like of which we do not see anywhere else in surviving Arabic Medieval references to female homosexuality. The writing/speech of Tifashi's (male) censurers seems to be enclosed within the chapter's larger deconstructive framework, through what Derrida has termed as "double writing": the writing at once performs patriarchal supremacy at one end (as Malti-Douglas has interpreted) and provides an avenue for its deconstruction at the other.[47] Predominantly and precisely by citing women, Tifashi provides the means with which to subvert the dominant and domineering patriarchal discourse without *seeming* to transgress.

Tifashi's chapter makes no mention of penetration as a feature of female homoerotic sex; facilitating a clito-centric discussion of sexual activity. The sex that the thirteenth-century grinders enjoyed, according to Tifashi, was clitoris centred and it is significant that Tifashi dedicated a significant amount of interest in the "mating habits" of women (with other women). Tifashi tell us that sexual contact between two women was/is accompanied by the right kind of "talk" (which Tifashi, a woman poetess called Warda and the Judge, tell us is a very important part of the sexual act). The sexual process seems to be both a pleasure and an art form to be taught and learned; to be given and received beyond the binary of active-passive.

> ...the most practiced of their conditions and the most variant, which are also necessary and indispensable, are the rules of "Cuteness" and the expertise in moaning and groaning and the mastering of the trade

of sweet talk that arouses the appetite at the time. They even discuss this and teach it and expend desirables on women who are wise in it, so that they can teach it to the ones who are not good at it. (*Nuzhat*, 238)

IN PRAISE OF GRINDING

The poetry that is included here is predominantly characterized by women telling of the social advantages of female-to-female sex. They need not fear the ostracism brought about by fornication with men or the unwelcome pregnancies that can be a consequence of fornication. In these poems, the pleasure of homoerotic sex is equaled by the advantages that the practice brings socially, as one grinder capitulates:

I drank wine for love of romance
And I inclined to grinding for fear of pregnancy
So I had sex in remoteness, with my lover
And I exceeded the men in the proficiency of the work
By being satisfying (convincing) my grinding made
me no longer in need of a man. (*Nuzhat*, 244)

She begins to grind not out of a natural inclination, but for fear of pregnancy, but then discovers the work to be "convincing". This inclination to homosex is indeed different from what is termed as (Western) "modern" homosexual identity. The driving force for the grinders seems to be fear of pregnancy first and attraction to women second, this is however, not at all dissimilar from the attractions to female homosexual activity that are ubiquitous in nations where the separation of the sexes and repression of sexual desire are fanatically observed. This form of homosexual activity does indeed seem unique to a culture where even heterosexual sex is confined under an array of psychic restrictions. As such, this particular manifestation of homosexuality — where it is a practice that results from the repression of unattainable needs, seems particular to contemporaneous non-Western or third world cultures where homosexuality is largely hidden, though by no means unknown.

However, the peculiar phenomenon of homosexual activity being the result of repressed heterosexuality is not the only or even the most prominent idea of homosexuality that is advanced in Tifashi's chapter. It remains for Warda (Rose) the grinder, to tell of the joys of homosexual relationships purely in sensual terms, providing a celebration of female homosexual desire — born purely out of aesthetics. Cited by Tifashi, Warda implies the veritable presence of their communities, gives an account of their methods of seduction, courtship, praise and adoration, while men, as well as the social advantages of homoeroticism (interesting that there are any at all!) are excluded as completely irrelevant. What is of the greatest importance in Warda's poem is the female body, its multiple sensualities, and its sexual fulfillment at the hands of another woman who is simultaneously fulfilled and is clearly active in her desire for another woman's body. It is through Warda's desire that the essential elements that constitute homosexuality can be glimpsed.

> We accompany the grinders, any one of us can be joined with one who is white, soft, flirtatious, succulent, tender-skinned as though she is a bamboo stalk, with a mouth like daisies, and ringlets like dark beads and a cheek like anemone or the apples of Lebanon and breasts like pomegranates and a stomach with four folds and a vagina that conceals fire with two lips that are coarser than the Israelite's cow and a hump like that of Ṭhamood's camel and a behind as though it is the fat-tail of Ishmael's sheep. (*Nuzhat*, 242–243)

Besides the obvious aperitif aspect of the description, given that a woman of large proportions was ideal at the time, Warda also makes rather odd references to the Quran. If John Donne was ever famous for his conceits, then Warda ought to be as famous for her daring on the one hand, and her ingenuity on the other. This also suggests that she had access to Islamic education, which makes it very likely for Warda to be literate. The beloved whom Warda describes is given features of animals that are highly revered in the Quran, and this form of allusion comes close to the usual literary and poetic practice of *iqtibas* (the use of Quranic verses in one's own poetry or literary work).

Ṭhamood's camel was made by God to appear out of the side of a mountain, when his messenger Saliĥ had considerable difficulty in convincing the people of Ṭhamood that they should renounce their worship of false idols and worship Allah. The people of Ṭhamood are not convinced for long by Saliĥ, they accuse him of witchcraft and fail to heed his warning that the camel should be left unharmed. Out of irreverence they cull the animal (Quran: al-Aåraf: 73-80; Quran: Hood: 61–65). Unlike Bani Israel's Cow and Ishmael's ram, this animal is slaughtered not directly as a sacrifice but as evidence of the people's mercilessness. Its very slaughter leads to God's annihilation of the people of Ṭhamood.

The sacrificed cow of the Israelites was chosen with great difficulty: God himself, consulted by Moses, provides strict specifications — that the cow should be one that is not used for ploughing, that it should be of a young but not tender age and having not yet born any offspring, and possessing a pleasing complexion (Quran: al-Baqara: 67–71). The male sheep is sacrificed in order to save Ishmael from being sacrificed himself by his God-fearing father Abraham (Quran: al-Safat: 99–113). Two of the three animals are the females of their species, and these two animals are clearly marked in the Holy Quran as exceptional beings (i.e. they are fit for sacrifice). The very animality of this string of allusions also connotes an underlying carnal, instinctual and animal lust.

Not only are these ironic references to the Quran made in an explicitly sexual context, they may also contain, besides the obvious superlatives, a concealed comment about the beloved's social situation — she remains a sacrifice, chosen to be offered to God, in order to save peoples, nations, from the wrath of the Almighty, or perhaps chosen to provide proof of the very existence and power of God (as in the case of the camel). So it should be natural that we transfer some of these holy and magical and sacrificial qualities of the animals on to the beloved who has caused Warda to digress into these references, because ultimately this text was intended as a superlative and erotic poem. Contrary to popular religious belief which would move to defame these women, the beloved's beauty is sanctioned by God; the beauty is not hidden from His gaze but is, rather, directly an aspect of His will. Such references in such an odd context assert a kind of subversion of popular interpretations of these Judeo-Christian-Muslim stories as well as providing evidence of artistic ingenuity.

We find Warda speaking of how her "kind" steals moments to:

> isolate ourselves with them [potential lovers] with impassioned reproaches and a benevolent tone, and charming eyelids that strip the heart of its blackness. So that if our chests are superimposed upon each other and the throats embrace the throats and the lips are fitted with the lips and each of them quivers against the other, then the breathing heightens and the senses are preoccupied and the fever is raised from the head... between sucking and pinching, and going to and fro and inhalation and sighing and moaning and murmuring and groaning.... With raising and placing and winking and suggesting, and embracing and smelling and consistency and kisses and pleasure taken in the work, and the turning of sides without worry. (*Nuzhat*, 243)

The process of seduction and its consummation is a complicated multifaceted affair through which Warda demonstrates a complex conception of her desire for women and the sexual act between them. She provides a subtle response to the denunciation of homosexuality as void or emptiness, the two lips *fit* each other, both women are active during the sexual act, there is mutuality and reciprocity. Furthermore, there is "pleasure taken in the work, and the turning of sides without worry": the two lovers, uninhibited by the limited duration of the erection, can turn sides until they achieve their satisfaction and Warda will not let them do this without superlatives fit for the occasion:

> All this with royal literature and delicious moaning, so that should unloading (cumming) arrive, and the decorations decrease, it smells like the breeze of flowers in March, and the fragrance of wine in a

bottle of alcohol and you look to the shaking of the ben-oil tree branch in the rain. (*Nuzhat*, 243)

The shaking of the wet ben-oil tree announces the coming of orgasm and this is followed by wonderment: "if the philosophers look at what we are in they would be confused, while the masters of fancy and delight would fly." If by philosophers Warda is here alluding to the strict theologians of her time, then surely this incredible pleasure would stupefy them in its intensity, since it negates the hierarchical taxonomy in which Woman, always passive, is incapable of giving pleasure to herself or to another.[48] By contrast, the masters of "fancy and delight", those who invest their time less in theology or philosophy and more in sexology or erotology, would be caused a great deal of ecstasy, they would be delighted by this superlative example of a very successful, highly charged, sexual encounter.[49]

CONCLUSION

At this point one wonders what constitutes something akin to modern gay identity that I discussed in earlier chapters. The critics who take the most extreme caution *not* to define "same-sex love and desire among women in the Middle Ages" as homosexual or lesbian, create an imaginary difference, at best metonymic. The suggestion that there were no individuals who exclusively enjoyed homosexual sex is false, and this is perhaps one of the most celebrated signposts of the "modern" lesbian subject. The critics perhaps meant that the *queer* medieval subjects did not have an understanding of themselves as marginal, and did not construct their self-knowledge around and against the widely propagated understanding of homosexual practice as a shortcoming or a disease — whereas modern homosexuality does. The critics perhaps meant that a modern gay identity constitutes a political pride of which the Middle East, especially the past in that region, is deprived of. Tifashi's text however provides evidence of exclusive female homosexuality and evidence of the attitudes of these women. Their intellectual defiance of patriarchal orthodoxy and homophobia is embedded in the cultural politics reflected by their code word *Tharifa*, which means "witty woman". The grinders fuse their sexual preference with a feminist (and philogynist) *intelligence* (wit) which subverts and transcends the patriarchal taxonomy that casts women as intrinsically lower beings who must be managed by men. Warda, cited by Tifashi, also demonstrates the *Tharifat's* awareness of their erotic as well as ideological difference from the dominant practice, in a learned celebration of the multiple sensualities available between women, which (supposedly) inevitably lead to mutual gratification.

Furthermore, Tifashi reveals, through his very engagement with the subject matter, the veritable possibility that these communities experienced a period of self-awareness and interconnection within a culture that was not as hostile to or dismissive of them as previously suspected. When Sabbah observes that the "erotic discourse is an optional discourse [while the] orthodox discourse is ... compulsory, omnipresent, omniscient [,]" she is referring to a *strand* of Islam. At any rate, it is unlikely that any religion, or any cultural value system, can inflict itself so wholly and totally upon a culture that there can be no subversive subcultures or countercultures or transcendent intellectualism to counter it. After all, orthodox Islam is an ideology of Islam, it is not eternal, nor is it Islam per se.

The erotic literature and religious discourse around homosexuality that appeared between the ninth and thirteenth centuries reveals not only the openly observed existence of these deviant women (who were not *always* as totally rejected and persecuted as one might imagine), it also reveals that the ideology of contemporary Islamic orthodoxy was neither dominant nor domineering at the time. As such, our perceptions of Islam and Arab cultures as inflexible, especially in regards to the pleasures of sex, ought to come under comprehensive revision.

In the previous chapters I discussed a Medieval Islamic Orthodoxy within which deviant sexual behaviours were tolerated — provided that these deviances did not involve a direct violation of prohibitions set unambiguously in the Quran (i.e. fornication does not seem to have been tolerable to the Sunni Grand Judge Yaĥya Bin Akṭham, and yet homosexual relations were). And while, by way of another example, al-Yemeni and Jurjani tell us very clearly that homosexual relations are not permitted in Islam, the rhetoric of both scholars remains devoid of the violence and prejudicious conceptualizations that we contend with in literature from the fourteenth century onwards and in contemporary Arabo-Islamic thought. In the next two chapters, we take a look at the cultural and social status of female homosexual relations by examining literature and films from the twentieth-century Arab world. The following chapters explore the consequences of the decline of a form of Islamic orthodoxy which was somewhat more sexually permissive than its successor. This decline leaves us an annihilated (*mushooqa*) lesbian subject, whose struggle for recognition and proper comprehension is far greater than it had been in the previous millennium.

Part III

The history and representation of female homosexuality in the contemporary Middle East

5 Contemporary representations of female homosexuality in Arabic literature and criticism[1]

— Yes, they're deviant, from the norm that is, because heterosexual relationships form the general rule while homosexual ones are deviations and for this reason they're labeled as abnormal.

— Does this abnormality imply illness?

— ...That's the general opinion, but I don't see it as an illness — I see deviation from the familiar norm, that's all.[2]

So what does a contemporary novel involving modern Arab lesbians and bisexuals look like? Are there many such novels? Are they diverse in their representations? Who writes them and who reads them? And what are the prevailing societal attitudes that they necessarily imply?

It is into a cultural and social climate similar to 1950s U.S. that *Ana Hiya Anti*, the first Arabic, lesbian-centred novel, entered.[3] Lesbian pulp fiction, which dominated the 1950s in America, predominantly yielded a host of negative connotations related to women who loved women, and these negative connotations were significantly without subtlety in regards to the attitudes they sought to project. It is not very difficult to infer societal attitudes towards homosexual women from titles such as *Unnatural*, *Forbidden*, *Warped Desire*, *Killer Dyke, The Unashamed*, *The Third Sex*, *Twilight Girl*, *Her Raging Needs, Lesbian Hell* and *No Men Allowed*.[4] The titles project sensuous connotations in regards to the nature of this *deviance*. Here deviance is not a mathematical term, equalized by its relations to the central deviation on a graph. Here deviance is unsightly; it is sly, it belongs to the world of darkness and lack of decorum, dissipation and lack of moral discipline. The deviants are exclusionary and "warped," they inhabit hellish places and prey on the weak, their ends are usually torturous and dramatic, their lives twisted and highly immoral.

Admittedly, even as early as the 1950s and 1960s some pulp fiction titles were seeking to address the negative images of female homosexuality portrayed in pulp novels and cinema such as Ann Bannon's novels, beginning as early as 1957 with *Odd Girl Out*.[5] In the gay consciousness, this brought on and reflected a realisation of the importance of promoting positive public relations between sexual deviants (read: homosexuals) and the moral mass. Increasingly, depictions of homosexuality, particularly in Western societies, are becoming depictions which take into account the personal experiences of their subjects. What is accelerating in production in the West is material representing homosexuality without it being reviled. In the Middle East, discussion of sexuality in general has become heavily laden with secrecy and reticence, and depictions of homosexuality necessarily suffer from such rising conservatism.

When *Ana Hiya Anti* was published in Beirut in the year 2000, a rather temperate and calm sea of oblivion dominated, and if not oblivion, then it was the appearance of ultimate consensus on the public front: that homosexuality *is* a disease, that it *is* distasteful, unnatural, sinful and indicative of weakness of the will. A person speaking to the contrary meets staunch opposition, whereas a person supporting the negative beliefs never needs to justify them.

Ana Hiya Anti, which translates as *I Am You* (all feminine pronouns in the original language) is centred on the experiences of three main characters. Siham, the youngest of the trio, is a young woman who is coming to terms with her sexual identity and her exclusive desire for women. Layal is the (supposedly) heterosexual professor at university on whom Siham becomes transferentially fixated when Layal decides to mentor Siham and to review her poetry. Much of the novel is dedicated to Siham's adolescent writings, which easily fall in the genre of Sapphic and apostrophic love poetry. Finally, we meet Meemee, a young and attractive married woman with children, who no longer enjoys sexual relations with her husband. Meemee is also fixated on Layal (who lives in the same building) and is in the midst of extricating herself from the irritating "old hag," a widowed neighbour, with whom she has sexual relations.

Elham Mansour, the author of *Ana Hiya Anti*, was an established writer when her novel came out in the closing months of the year 2000. She had just completed the second novel of her trilogy of novels centred on her protagonist Hiba, who mirrors the author in some biographical respects as well as the protagonist Layal, in *I Am You* (the third installment of the trilogy comes shortly after the publication of *I Am You*). Mansour was born in Bålbek, Lebanon — a tourist attraction which proudly boasts ancient Roman ruins that have strangely survived fifteen years of war. Mansour went to school in Jounieh, another famous, sea-side tourist attraction constituted predominantly of Christian Lebanese families. She received her Bachelor of Psychology from L'Ecole des Lettres in Lebanon and was awarded her Doctorate of Philosophy from Sorbonne University where she completed her thesis on "the concept of liberation in contemporary political thought."[6] Doctor Mansour was the chair of the Philosophy department at the Lebanese University when *I Am You* was released, and continues to hold that position. She kindly forwarded me a collection of reviews and articles written about the novel around the time of its release. To this collection of critiques I owe considerable debt in formulating my insights into the reception of this novel and into consolidating my theory of the Arabian epistemology of homosexuality in its present configuration.

When it was published, *Ana Hiya Anti* generated a little over a dozen newspaper reviews, and yet it was considered a best seller for some time. It was distributed internationally, with a particular demand for it in the Saudi Arabian market. The reviews predominantly agreed that Mansour's novel was poor in composition, structure and logic. It is difficult to believe that the virulent attacks on structure, language and logic were not a result of reactions to the subject matter and the rhetoric deployed in the novel in regards to homosexuality. Mansour defended against the notion that her text was not artful with the assertion that every storyteller possessed their own personal techniques.[7] This onslaught of criticism appeared to be significantly motivated by hidden moral prerogatives, but of course occasionally there were ambivalent exceptions. I am not interested in defending *I Am You* against the accusations that it was "poorly written," as much as I am interested in the qualities of culture that this form of critique reveals. As such I do not intend to demonstrate or to argue that *I Am You* is *not* poorly written — in my opinion it does appear to be hastily written — it is the novel's political and rhetorical attributes, regardless of form and structure, which concern me in this article. I am interested in this text for the clusters of ideas it presents, for the societal attitudes it simultaneously implies and challenges rather than in its "literary" value.[8]

REVIEWING *I AM YOU* IN LEBANON

Writing for the prominent literary magazine *al-Naqid*, Pierre Shalhoob claimed that "despite [the characters'] level of education, the way they express their emotions and feelings is littered with superficial and clichéd sentences and words."[9] Shalhoob however, does not criticise Mansour's characters for their sexual deviations, instead, and unusually, he sympathises with the characters. "[E]ach one of them," he writes "is searching for a partner, not simply to satisfy their lust but to find a woman who can complete their beings" (Shalhoob, 15).

Qasim Nouri Åbood affirmed that the text ignored the "meaning and the form" of literary writing and added that the:

> publication of this book should not be considered an error or a "slip-up", but to the contrary it is necessary for two reasons: The first is the sensitivity involving the topic...and the second, what the story presents in excess of ambiguity of meaning and ignoring narrative skill (al-tilapia) is what distinguishes a great deal of the present Arab publications in poetry and story telling.[10]

While it might seem that Åbood did not object to the subject matter, his understanding of it is clearly inscribed in his reference to homosexual love as "*ĥub aṭhim*" ("sinful love,") whose "conflicted psychology" he wanted to see more of in the novel. For Åbood, the "lesbians" simply did not suffer enough. This attitude towards homosexuality is shared by a number of critics who reviewed the book. Yasseen Rafåyah concluded that "it is true that the subject matter is very daring, but this is not enough. We can't just write it any which way, the subject needs caution and entry into its depths, because the subject of lesbianism is the suffering of Woman, in the same way that sodomy [read as homosexuality] is the suffering of the Man and they are both a dangerous illness."[11] Rafåyah and other critics conveying this view of homosexuality are fixated upon Mansour's inability to deliver a conclusive discussion of "causes and reasons" for homosexual relations. Rafåyah was particularly fixated by the notion that Siham was sexually assaulted by her father and that Mansour should have stressed this as the cause of Siham's homosexuality. He fails to mention, as though he did not realise, that Siham later admits to having fabricated the story, partly as part of her desire to find a cause and partly to lure Layal (the unrequited object of her affection) to "fall for her."

Predominantly however, Siham's desire to find causes for her sexual orientation stems from societal claims (as exemplified by Rafåyah and other critics) that an incidental cause *must* exist. Several critics have exploited Siham's confused relations with her now-deceased father. Amina Ghusun, in a scathing review, also attributes Siham's homosexuality to rape by her father and she also fails to note that this is negated later in the story. She concludes from her moral high ground, without hesitation: "[i]t is as though the reader of *I Am You* is [presumed to be] unnerved by what is forbidden, or any taboo, and is rather irritated by Islamic teaching and morality and tastefulness."[12] She too criticizes Mansour for her "poor" literary techniques.

In Moody Biṯar's contribution, the novel is again said to be "poorly written" and the poetry (written by Siham) in it is "laughable." He too criticizes Mansour for not providing clear reasons for Siham's homosexuality. He adds: "Mansour's protagonists are invasive and sex-obsessed. They are held captive by their obsessions and their insane desires regardless of how much physical and social danger this leads them to."[13] Another reviewer writing in this vein criticizes Mansour for depicting relationships between women as being "better than the *natural* relationship between the woman and the man" (Rafåyah , 31). Maree al-Qaseefee claims that the novel is poorly written and that it resembles a short documentary interviewing two or three people "who specialize in this activity" (as though it were a sport). al-Qaseefee praises Mansour for her pioneering work and for daring to interrogate the relationship between "artistic and literary genius and sexual deviation, as well as the role that the "male plays in driving women into the arms of other women due to his selfishness, carelessness and harshness. But does this mean that the woman will definitely find compensation in a homosexual relationship? This is not what the novel concludes with any certainty."[14] al-Qaseefee's intermediate-level tolerance for this subject is admirable, even though her understanding fails to register the novel's claims about homosexuality. al-Qaseefee is quick to attribute female homosexuality to the harshness of men, whereas the novel does not exclusively discuss this point, nor does the novel at all suggest that women who have been hurt by men will be able to, or do, substitute heterosexual relations for homosexual ones.

It would seem that the majority of negative reviews rest their cases on two points: the first is that the text is poorly written, the second is that the subject of homosexuality *is* distasteful and unnatural or caused by incidents and thus it is the moral role of the narrative to reveal this.[15] Therefore, Mansour's (through the character Layal) rhetoric of conceiving homosexuality as natural is wrong, ill-conceived and irresponsible.

As is indicated by these reviews, the contemporary popular Arabian epistemology of female homosexuality seems to be based on the following assumptions:

1. Women *turn* to other women due to the "harshness" of men.
2. Women *turn* to other women due to experience of sexual trauma (with men).
3. Women *turning* to other women are immoral, deranged, and suffer mental ailments.
4. Homosexuality is caused by something whose value is unequal to the value of the presumed causes of heterosexuality (i.e. procreation/"nature"/"God's intent").
5. The cause of homosexuality is usually an aberration of upbringing.

Even though *I Am You*'s major character Siham searches for causes of her homosexuality, she finally has to reconcile herself to the fact that these causes are either non-existent or impossible to discern, a point the critics (deliberately?) failed to engage with. It is as though they were unable to grasp the concept of acausality because it was somehow a new approach to an old "problem" which was thought to be clearly understood, not only morally but also psychologically. Addressing these popular Arabian epistemes of female homosexuality, Mansour remarked in an interview with Zeina Bizzie that:

> [O]ur desire to change [the other] stems from our thinking that there is something wrong about the thing we want to change. And we presume homosexual relationships to be wrong. So what is the truth and on what basis have we founded our gauge of what is right and wrong? Everything is relative and what our societies reject, others accept, and

> what is rejected now, people will accept in the future. Therefore there are no fixed factors to be relied on.[16]

Mansour's novel was difficult for the critics to like, not only for its deliberately direct use of language,[17] but also for the ideology and rhetoric which it propagates in regards to homosexuality. The novel's rationalization of homosexual relationships seemed foreign to Arab critics, and it shocked them further because it was not achieved through preamble and circumvention, but through blatant and unambiguous declarations, such as Layal's profession that: "I am against moral evaluation when it comes to this subject — I am all for individual freedom, and as long as that freedom harms no one, then it is legitimate, in my opinion" (*I Am You*, 94). These declarations Mansour has had to re-iterate to her critics, who seem to have missed the various points she has taken up throughout her narrative. In the three interviews conducted with her shortly after the release of her novel, she stressed that homosexuality is a matter that is ignored by society and that it should be a matter returned to the arena of public discussion. In this statement, she was in fact recalling remarks she assigned her characters in the novel, as can be seen in the following:

> As for us here [homosexuality] is muffled because we are still in the magical pattern of thought. We think that being silent about a reality of some sort enables us to eliminate it. Yes, eliminate it from our thoughts, so that it nests in our bodies and our subconscious and so that it reflects itself throughout all our behaviours without our knowledge. (*I Am You, 59–60*)
>
> ....
>
> [my mother] is like the ostrich, burying her head so that she won't see. She may as well stay in her blindness or pretend blindness, the important thing is that she stays out of my affairs. (*I Am You*, 77)

In the interviews Mansour also stressed that the platonic concept of love[18] was the philosophical point she foremost wished to explore (even more so than homosexual relationships), and that it was "on this concept that the entire Greek philosophical system was based" (Jihad, 58). In Mansour's novel, Layal claims:

> I believe that the like realizes the like, meaning that a woman is looking, in her relationship with a man, for what completes her femininity, in the same way the man searches for what completes his masculinity in his relationship with a woman....If this analysis is true then it explains that in homosexual relationships, the sex of the other is not as important as the complementarity of the like. This completeness can be within the same sex, as is the case with lesbians and gays, or

between different sexes as seen in the general governing rule. (*I Am You*, 139–140)

This theoretical framework standardizes the experience of love as universal and does away with the distinction between hetero and homosexual love,[19] a distinction adamantly defended by conservative thinkers and writers who reject the nature and humanity of homosexual or bisexual inclinations. It was these ideas that she hoped to project, and it was precisely these that the critics avoided discussing, presumably because these ideas arrived on the scene suddenly and without significant precedent or preparation, and, for many readers, without the (liberationist) theoretical context they embody. Clashing with Mansour on this point, one interviewer commented to her:

> The psychological elements in this novel do not reveal the motives or the reasons behind the characters. In reality, and don't get upset with me, I found nothing except very little of this [form of revelation]. Where is the psychological analysis of your novel's characters? You say you come to the art of the novel from a philosophy and psychology background, where is the philosophy and psychology in this novel? (Jihad, 58)

While the majority of the reviews were choric in their condemnation of homosexual interests and the author's writing techniques, Ĥaneen Ghadar was of the opinion that the writing was too timid, that although sex and the penetration of taboos were promised, the language fell short of new and refreshing descriptions. She added in a review which combined several recently released novels on the subject of sex, that even women writers presented their heroines "in the traditional manner that men have depicted them" (i.e. as passive recipients of pleasure). Specifically of *I Am You* she commented that "Siham displays no sexual feelings (except through intermittent poetry between one disappointment and another)," quoting Siham's poem beginning with "I have not imagined you naked once" as evidence of her remark.[20] Later, Ghadar quotes lines which describe an orgy/party scene and comments: "three full stops [ellipsis] is what the author has left for the reader to imagine sexual activity between two women, three full stops!" (Ghadar, 7). Ghadar's review demands more woman-centred descriptions of sex and more explicit content. What Ghadar calls for is quite valid given the predominance of patriarchal rhetorical strategies involving descriptions of sex, sexuality and gender (in both literature and criticism) that position women as infinitely passive and receptive and men as virile and insatiable.

Even literary reviews themselves can engage in these traditionalist assumptions and attitudes about sex that Ghadar criticizes, including two separate reviews of *I Am You* which stand out in this regard. George Ṯrad, who singularly notes that the novel is dedicated in its entirety to the defense of homosexuality, provides what is perhaps the closest thing to a positive review of the novel. However, he concludes his review with an attitude which makes clear that women's sexual contact with other women involves the spectatorship, curiosity and sometimes participation of men, and that men in particular will find the novel erotically charged and difficult to resist.[21] Another critic, who equally feels no need to disguise his impression of female homosexuality as supplemental to heterosexuality, adds that Mansour genuinely failed to show how a woman can replace the man in the sexual act, although he indicated his comprehension of how a man can take the position of a woman in a male homosexual sex act.[22]

In their collective entirety, these reviews reflect the ongoing cultural negotiations regarding sexuality and gender taking place within a society where tensions between the religious and the secular are always highly charged, and where there is a veritable absence of radical strands of resistance on the public front. While homophobic rhetorical strategies are found in abundance, and seem for the time being immutable, the continual agitations effected by scholars, artists and filmmakers, which question social boundaries in relation to sex, gender and sexuality, should produce some positive reverberations. Eve Sedgwick once noted that an act of self-revelation (revealing oneself to be "gay" to someone of a homophobic persuasion) occasionally has the power of altering perceptions, of dispelling myths, even though she had no illusions about the extent of power that "individual revelation can exercise over scaled and institutionally embodied oppressions."[23] The sociohistorical importance of *I Am You* is certainly not in its literary methodology (though this methodology is impressive), but in its new rhetorical capacities as far as homosexuality is concerned. The reader is presented with a protagonist that s/he can at once both criticise and feel sympathetic towards, a protagonist who is at least realist, if not real.

THE CULTURAL IMPORT OF *I AM YOU*

Nuray Sakalli and Ozanser Ugurlu recently conducted an experiment in order to ascertain "whether we could observe an attitude change in heterosexual participants introduced to a lesbian person."[24] The subjects of their experiment were all undergraduate students at the Middle East Technical University in Turkey (which might render the sample socioeconomically biased). The report found that: "the study demonstrated that individuals might change their attitudes toward homosexuality in a positive way after learning about homosexuals and having [a?] positive experience with them. The study supported results of the previous study in Turkey...that people who knew a homosexual individual and homosexuality were not very uncomfortable about [it], and they increased their tolerance...even though they did not completely accept homosexuals and homosexuality" (Sakalli & Uğurlu, 117). Another study, conducted by sociologists at the University of Oklahoma "examined the impact of motion pictures about the [nontraditional] family on viewers' attitudes about family life and sexual orientation."[25] In this study, women were found to be more tolerant of sexual difference than men and that "the treatment group [asked to watch pro-gay films] experienced more favourable attitudes toward homosexuals than the control group" (Mazur and Emmers-Sommer, 157).

From the studies above we note that *how* homosexual individuals are represented in cultural discourse and literary artifacts not only reflects the predominant attitudes and beliefs of a culture but that this representation, in itself, is a key element in configuring cultural beliefs. The novel deserves readings informed by homophilia, not only homophobia, by critics whose life experiences were informed and affected by the prejudice surrounding the constitution of their sexual desires and not only by critics blissfully removed from the context and feelings of the protagonist Siham. *I Am You* was written with the intent of challenging conventional attitudes about homosexuality and it is culturally and historically important for this reason. While the critics were not at all erroneous in suggesting that there were many weaknesses in the text, none of them were willing to engage with its greatest accomplishment: its unmistakable introduction of homosexuality as a subject outside the realm of moral behaviour and thought, whilst also falling short of Western-style, pro-gay activism which may have alienated the majority of Arab readers. The novel's style remained uniquely Lebanese, and attempted to bring the reader into close intimacy with Siham, whose thoughts, feelings and self-realisation occasionally feel starkly real, hyper real.

It is true, as some critics have noted, that its characters Siham and Meemee often invite dislike, through what seems to be superficial sexual obsessions and yearnings for things which cannot be fulfilled (the love of a supposedly heterosexual woman). Their lack of self integration and fulfillment should be contextualised within the framework of prohibition which restricts these characters' ability to realise their desires. This is not a story about women who accept their desires unhesitantly or who can understand and act on them liberally. Siham, despite some growth towards self acceptance as the narrative evolves, is always trapped between excessively idolatrous love for 'Woman,' born out of pining, and a deeply ingrained, defensive kind of misogyny, born out of a cultural phenomenon wherein closeted women are unable to form stable relationships, because their natural sexual urges are competing very heavily with their urges for social acceptance, or at least social anonymity. In one of her poems Siham writes of this dividedness and disloyalty amongst those women whom she has known in a sexual manner. Earlier in her poem she has set up Layal, the unresponsive "heterosexual" object of her affection, to be in the city of Saffron, while she suffers in the city of Mint:

> Where I am in the city of Mint, the women are controlling, deprived, they talk sadness to each other and they consult each other about the preys. They leave at night and they search for the bridge of promise that ties between the two cities [in the city of saffron women "leave everything full of tenderness"], but they become hungry in the street and so they eat each other, and so I see the world, small, and I pray that the world may expand until there is a flood that erases the two cities. (*I Am You*, 193–194)

The grinding of saffron (al-Zåfaran) was once quite a common euphemism for female homosexual activity. The euphemism originates from Medieval Arabic literature, appearing in various texts as early as the ninth century as we have seen in chapters 3 and 4. Siham may be implying that the city of saffron is inhabited by women who are capable of carrying out intimate and emotionally fulfilling relations (without evacuating the deeply sexual element of these emotional relationships). In the meantime, the women in the city of Mint inhabit a hellish underworld where homosexual behaviour is either used as a convenient substitute for heterosexual encounters or where women, through fear of ostracism, are incapable of forging intimate (emotional) relations. In addition, the tragedy of this text, the mentioning of cities outside the literal war context (for the war herein described is highly figurative), completely undermines the tragedy of civil war in Lebanon or the tragedy of anything bigger than Siham being unable to live in a society that allows her to feel natural. In this way Mansour creates a fissure in mainstream intellectual thought and makes the marginal a central element in configuring the universal. Although the novel is set during the Lebanese civil war (I will discuss this in more detail later on) some time in the 1980s or 1990s, the war depicted in *I Am You* is de-centred from its literal manifestations, it is a war waged much more quietly, against the individual and the marginal in society, or rather, on a more encompassing political scale, against *heterogeneity* itself. The war depicted is a sociopolitical war in every ontological sense of the word and it suffuses the novel, its characters and their conflicted behaviours. The relationships between *deviant* women reflect not simply their own internal chaos and disorder (as some critics have noted), but also *society's* inner contradictions and conflicts. The characters' brief and unfulfilling encounters are portrayed as not simply processes of their own production since Siham's grief and alienation is owed largely to the "society [which] rejects me" (*I Am You*, 102 & 122–123).

> Where we come from in Lebanon, the lesbian is an outcast, she can't reveal what she is, she tries to hide herself, so much so that those who observe our society are incapable of finding any evidence to suggest that she exists. And if you were to find relationships of this kind, and

> they do indeed exist, you'll see that they are pursued with the utmost secrecy, without the emergence of any visible traces. (*I Am You*, 24)

WAR ON SEXUALITY, THE BODY AND THE 'FEMININE DISCOURSE'

Lebanon is a small country with a surface area of 10,400 square kilometers and a current population of 3.7 million.[26] In April 1975 the Lebanese Civil War began and continued until 1991. In the course of that history the war story unfolded, with old enemies becoming obsolete and fresh ones replacing them. What originally began as a conflict involving Palestinian militants and Lebanese Muslim militias versus the Lebanese Christian militias (joined briefly by the Israeli army), progressed into a conflict between the Lebanese Christian Militia and the Syrian army[27] and finally ended with a "war of unification" resulting from a schism within the Lebanese Christian forces themselves. The Lebanese war was brutal, controlled, and chaotic. In one instance militiamen would massacre entire villages or refugee camp populations (for example, Tal Izzåtar, Sabra and Shatila), dismembering children and adults alike, and in another instance as Miriam Cooke notes, Beirut's bank buildings, located on one street, would remain unscathed no matter how heavy the combating became.[28]

Lebanon dramatises for us a condition of war and conflicting puritanisms within which homosexuality seems to cause no more than an obscure blot of prejudice, that is (seen to be) scarcely worth dealing with, in light of the more immediate concerns and grave dangers which present themselves in this historical context. Mansour's project in this novel is to critique the obviation of the subject of sexuality and to bring it to the fore, in the hope of re-shaping, or revitalising (feminist) political activism against various social, political and military systems and means of oppression.

> Even the feminist movement in Lebanon isn't brave enough to broach the subject [of homosexuality]. It's prohibited, shameful and a sign of decadence, and illness....(*I Am You*, 24)

Within this cultural framework where sexual liberty is deemed secondary to other concerns, war features (in the novel) as a further means of exacting oppressions of all kinds.

In her relationship to war and our view of her interaction with it taking place, Layal represents one of many civilians who could scarcely understand the war's reasons or origins, *and* who were powerless because they themselves were divided confessionally (i.e. divided by various religions and denominations), and because they had no agency or infrastructure with which to act as a people united by the desire for good will among each other. Layal's powerlessness can be seen in her confessed lack of understanding as in the following:

> It's true what Meemee said, about how her husband knows [when there are] peaceful periods.... How does he know that and what is his role in the subject? I don't want to know that either, that's not the only issue I don't understand in this war, the important thing is that the situation is calm and I have to take advantage of it. (*I Am You*, 129)

Layal's ignorance of political matters is abundantly clear. She seems to inhabit a role in the conflict, a role of powerlessness and insignificance, which resembles Siham's similarly subordinate position in the moral war waged against homosexual desires. Symbolically, the war is an affair managed and *understood* by men. Interestingly, Layal is positioned in such a way as to usher in a new generation of Lebanese feminists who are preoccupied with liberating women from prohibitions and constraints, one of which includes the sexual. Evelyn Accad notes that when she attended a feminist conference in Illinois 1983:

> [m]ostly Marxist Women, speaking in the name of Third World Women, claimed that economic issues, such as food and shelter, were far more important than sex. They accused U.S. lesbians at the conference of over-emphasising sex, particularly lesbianism.... [However] sex is one of the basic needs — like food and sleep — in any culture... [and] no mention was made of the spiritual and/or psychological needs for love, affection, and tenderness, intimately connected with sexuality, felt by people in most cultures.[29]

What Accad notes is a schism prevalent within the global feminist movement. It is also a point which Mansour notes in her novel *Ĥina Kuntu Rajulan*.[30] What emerges in Mansour's rhetoric is a new third world feminism, which is now attuned to erotic desires and which sees them as equal to, if not more pressing than, issues of national liberation and women's needs in a more general sense. Mansour's rhetoric seems to have inherited the legacy of a sexually aware third world feminism which Accad notes as the necessary evolutionary step towards reconciling the schism between third world and first world feminists in her 1990 study *Sexuality and War*. What is significant in Mansour's brand of feminism is that it is a work which privileges a woman-centred discourse, what she terms as "feminine discourse,"[31] in which female sexuality, with its various formations, is a key issue at stake and where not only issues involving economic and national concerns are deemed important.

Contrary to the critics' choric assertions that *I Am You* is a work of shallow proportions, the novel seemed confounding because it was *inventing* a feminist tradition in a country where nationalist concerns blurred the core of feminist ideals and struggles.[32] Mansour's women interact with an array of prohibitions and sexual taxonomies enforced upon individuals, severely limiting their life choices. Mansour achieves this through each of her main characters: whether through Meemee, who married because "what [else] was I supposed to do?" (*I Am You*, 143), Layal — who rejects relations with men because of their misogyny and power-obsessions — or the "old hag" (who represents duplicitous "moral" women who commit the deeds but retain a superficial but applauded chastity), or whether through Siham whose moral and sexual dilemmas are more obvious and urgent. The characters' inner conflicts as well as the conflict they seem to be engaged in with society, are a result of their search for balance (between what they have, lack and need) and, as far as Layal and Siham are concerned, a search for equality (whether with men or with heterosexuals) and liberty (from social conventions) also, as Layal comments:

> I'm not married because I want to be free. I'm not against men at all, but I'm against the commitment that imposes obligations and duties. I am all for liberal relationships based on agreement and love because these continue so long as they are successful, and once they fail, every one goes his own way without ceremonies or demands.... (*I Am You*, 90–91)

Layal is proposing something quite astonishing to the society in which she lives: an end to the dominion that the institution of marriage holds over the regulation of relations in this particular society. Of course, her search for these liberties mirrors Siham's, who is equally searching for means to legitimize her desires. It is no wonder that the two characters discover a shared philosophical agreement with each other as regards the notion that love and the rules of attraction are based on similarity rather than difference (*I Am You*, 168–169). Towards the end of the narrative, and her struggle, Siham finally asserts the primacy of her feelings over forced social obligations, succeeding in establishing the new (lesbian) "feminine discourse" in its primitive form:

> Nothing arouses me except the female form, for the female body has a great effect on me and it is what awakens desire within me. What am I guilty of exactly if I can only feel the pleasure of love with a woman? It's love, and the purpose of making love is attaining pleasure and satisfaction. (*I Am You*, 170)

Here a woman harboring homosexual desires is given the opportunity of citation, which is rare. We do not hear in the contemporary Arab mainstream that homosexual relations between women are based on desire. The absence of the homosexual subject, her relegation to a closet out of which exit is hardly an option, has dominated discourse on homosexuality in this region since the late Middle Ages. The result has been the production and the reinforcement of a negative (and ill-informed) discourse, strengthening the "moral" grounds for the repression and oppression undertaken in society and by its individuals. Siham is an important character because she refreshes the discourse, allowing to enter into it a point of view for the deviant, and revealing a creature hardly in a position to cause damage to society (as any homophobic discourse suggests) and one who cannot be feared on account of her vulnerability and the injuries she endures. But, of course, a society with such deep-seated ideas about sexuality and its causes will reject this novel, as the reviews of the novel discussed earlier demonstrate. This will, however, be a superficial rejection, taking place in the newspapers and at the public front — somewhere in the privacy of consciousness, the humane representation of homosexual, bisexual and sexually ambiguous subjects will begin to affect some changes in perception.

The "feminine discourse" urged by Mansour is also to be found in discussions of sexual relations between women, who perceive each other (in this cultural context) as equals. After Siham returns from Paris, she looks retrospectively at what comforted her about being with the Parisian schoolgirl Clare, her first lover, and she writes:

> Clare, who is taintless, makes the Arabian Jasmine wonder at her purity and the sea foam asks after how she melts. (*I Am You*, 73)

I think, if only for amusement, the sentence should read "Clare who is French," for in some way her nationality renders her somewhat exotic. At any rate, Siham continues:

> Clare unveils the treasures of her body and the sun intermixes with the waves and the berries emerge deliciously and it's time to eat, Clare devours passion and finds pleasure, she knows the secrets of love and its ways and she flirts, Clare and freedom is in her dress, she undresses, she does not want to remain a prisoner, and she blows her cigarettes in a blonde cup, so who is Clare drinking and who is drinking her? (*I Am You*, 73)

Here Siham demonstrates knowledge of a sexual/love relationship which was experienced in an environment that was potentially a lot less hostile than Siham's birthplace, Beirut, and certainly less hostile religiously and ideologically to the idea of homosexual love or eroticism. Clare does not belong in the hostile city of Mint (discussed earlier), perhaps not in Layal's (idealized) city of Saffron either, but Clare takes Siham to a place where the lines between the passive and active elements of sexual practice are obscured and are made obsolete: "she blows her cigarettes in a blonde cup, so who is Clare drinking and who is drinking her?" This notion overturns patriarchal concepts wherein sexual energy converts into power, which is what seems to be the problem with the women in the city of Mint who "get hungry on their way and eat each other in the street." The novel seems to suggest that it is not only men who are engaged in a patriarchal sexual symbolic order, but also some women.[33] By doing this, the text undermines the mainstream concept of the sex act as one of power and instead conveys sexual activity pointing to the equal agency of its participants where alternative (female) masculinities and (non-heterosexual) femininities are depicted and intermixed.[34] This *queer* idea always presents itself as coming from *outside, abroad*. It is foreign (in this particular instance it is literally from Paris), it is not local but peripheral — it is always marginal and defeated (even in Paris, this idea retains a marginal status since we learn that the schoolgirls keep displays of intimacy and affection for their private concerts). However, the novel does not fall into a stereotypical depiction of this concept of sexual equality as being a strictly Western concept. For example, at Meemee's ladies'only party Layal observes women around her

> ...she attempted to observe how some of them took on a man's role and how the others took on the woman's role, as it was generally understood of these relationships — that is, in terms of what takes place between the normal woman and man. After some surveillance she noticed that the difference was only in outward appearance, because the actions were the same in the sense that whoever took on the man's role in one instant, soon took on the woman's in another. (*I Am You*, 127)

Even Layal's naïve coupling of the "man's role" to denote activity/masculinity and the "woman's role" to denote passivity/femininity is soon challenged by a guest at the party, who is shocked by Layal's suggestion that active behaviour necessarily denotes maleness (which is here conflated with masculinity). The partygoer protests that "I'm a woman and I don't want to be male, if I am doing now whatever I like with her," and she pointed at her girlfriend "that does not mean that I'm her man, we're alike and she often desires to do with me what I do with her now, we have no roles in our relationship. We're lovers and that's more important" (*I Am You*, 128). Through Layal's naivety, the reader, who is expected to be equally naïve (since the target audience was initially conceived to be a mainstream [i.e. non-queer] Arab readership), is eased into complex concepts of gender and sexuality which challenge patriarchal heteronormativity.

The novel raises further (unconventional) awareness of the issue of homosexuality among its readers through its exploitation of the transnational setting, revealing to its readership a world beyond the confines of the Lebanese nation — and how Lebanese culture treats the subject of homosexuality. For most of the critics reviewing this novel it seemed that their knowledge of homosexuality was significantly lacking in that they did not know or experience any of the communities they criticized. Through Siham's experiences in Paris and references to a Western gay civil rights movement, *I Am You* registers the cultural divide between the West and the East regarding issues of sexuality. Siham's mother discovers that her daughter's relationship with Clare, whose photograph is displayed prominently on Siham's desk, is far from the chaste one that *she*, as a child, had had with one of her girl friends. As a response to this aberration, the mother contacts Clare and hurls abuses at her over the phone. Siham's mother's reflection on making this phone call to her daughter, who (falsely) denies any sexual intimacy in her relationship with Clare, is as follows:

> Yes, she is free [to do whatever she likes] and we have nothing to do with her. If you continue to be her friend she will influence you...We can go back to Lebanon together...and you can continue your university education there — we can endure the war just like everybody else. If you want to know the truth I prefer war and its dangers to the cesspools of Paris and its depraved world. I don't want to lose you and I don't want you to befriend people of this perverted kind. We still preserve in Lebanon, a certain degree of morals and good behaviour. I don't want your education, regardless of its importance, to deprive you of these high morals that we have inherited from our forefathers and predecessors. (*I Am You*, 27)

Clare, being French, is to a great extent free to be a lesbian, while Siham, who is Lebanese, is not as free. Clare, under the traditional Arab mother's gaze, exists in a "depraved world" which acts easily as a potential contagion for our upright protagonist Siham. It is a world that is far more dangerous than the Lebanese Civil War and is less favourable to live in — a thought that is in itself indicative of the degree of refusal in question and the mother's insensitivity to the carnage produced by the war. In lieu of Clare's liberal unclosetedness there was, until recently, in Lebanon, a physical and literal necessity for closetedness as means of survival, and Clare genuinely fails to show any sensitivity to the cultural realities separating her activism from Siham's denial:

> Are you that backward in Lebanon? You say that your mother is educated and mature; what kind of maturity and education is this? I can accept her calling me a lesbian but for her to describe me as diseased and dirty, to accuse me of contaminating her daughter — I can't accept that at all! (*I Am You*, 23)

Clare, who must encounter a daily dose of diluted homophobia in France cannot comprehend that heavy dose of it that she will encounter under the heteronormative Middle Eastern gaze, be it either Muslim, Christian or Jewish. Nor can she begin to comprehend Siham's desire to continue to deceive her mother about her sexuality. For Clare this self-denial is precisely what gives society power over the individual. For Clare self-denial is also defeat, though the novel in itself fails to clearly articulate the Frenchwoman's motivations behind her political stance. In the meantime, Siham wants to deceive her mother because, so early in the development of her sexual identity she "always suffered a guilty conscience, swinging between her inclination and desire and her upbringing and all the moralism she received at home from her mother and at the nuns' school in Lebanon" (*I Am You*, 33).

In the conflict which arises between the two school girls we glimpse a microcosm of the conflict between feminists denying the importance of a sexual revolution, championing the rights of third world women who are deprived of (what they see as) more important and more basic needs and other feminists, often from privileged first world countries, who champion the sexual liberation of woman in a way that suggests that this can be done *before* or even without dealing with economic and political inequities from which both men and women suffer in third world nations. While Clare's uncompromising activism is necessary in shifting negative attitudes towards homosexuality, she fails to deal maturely or realistically with the difficulties and dangers Siham faces in doing this. The depiction of their relationship is not a simple and superficial treatment of a "cultural clash," but is allegorical of the conflicted relationship between the two nations. After all, it was the French who founded Lebanon by separating it from Syria after World War I. In addition, perhaps without intending it, the author demonstrates the dangers inherent in the calls for a replication of the Western gay and lesbian rights movement in the Middle East. What is needed is a new strategy, better suited to different cultural and social conditions, one which Siham fails to discover or even realise the need for throughout the novel — deception, self-denial and invisibility remain her only recourse.

The French, inseparable from their history of colonisation of the Middle East, have left a lasting impression on the nation that is now Lebanon. Siham attended one of the nuns' schools and it is in these schools that we note the colonial influence of the French, particularly on the Christian Lebanese. Etel Adnan observes that the nuns' schools "created in Lebanon and imposed on it, a system of education totally conforming to their schools in France, an education which had nothing to do with the history and the geography of the children involved."[35]

One could even say that the cultural rift created in Lebanon by French influence obscurely led to the sixteen year civil war. The Lebanese, mostly the Christians residing in East Beirut and the Northern parts of Lebanon, began to exhibit inclinations to Frenchness and Westernisation that were less apparent in their Muslim counterparts and they took on an identity that allied them (the Lebanese Forces and later the Lebanese Militia of Eastern Beirut — Kata'eb) with what is considered to be the nemesis of the Arab nationalist — Israel. And yet, within the novel and in society more generally, the Frenchised Christians seem to have learnt nothing more than fashion, language, perfume and music from the French — when the clash of cultural ideologies on sexuality occurs the Lebanese Christians of the early to late twentieth century period, represented by Siham's mother, are not happy to emulate the French. Since the end of the civil war in 1991 there would have undoubtedly been some cultural changes (the growing influence of English and English speaking media and the decline in French influence being the most noted change, as well as an increase in secularity as a result of the end of confessional warfare), but the period in which the novel is set and the period it reflects is pertaining to a time where factions within Christian Lebanese communities/groups attempted to forge, in the same manner that the Turkish government has, an identity that identifies with the Western (European) 'other' more so that with the Arab 'other,' albeit that this identification is ornamental at best.

But I do not wish to delve too deeply into the speculative context in which this fascinating text was produced because, all in all, it is a very specific story and about specific individuals. The author communicated to me that she wrote this as a result of life experience, she wrote about people she met and people she knew. Through Siham, Mansour explores how a homosexual individual who is lacking any formal acknowledgement of her existence comes to comprehend, realise and accept her sexuality against a backdrop of prejudice and refusal.

THE INDIGENOUS DEVIANT

The novel presents Siham as a masculine lesbian figure. Growing up in a society where the topic is not only forbidden but consequently unknown, Siham begins to conceptualize herself as the male-woman because her desire for women at this stage can only be understood within the concepts and ideas available and sanctioned in the wider culture.[36] The author writes about Siham's pubescent period:

> She used to express her protest [about getting her period] by rejecting all forms of feminine attire, by always wearing pants and button-up shirts and could not be comfortable in anything other than boys' shoes. Her mother was at pains to witness this. (*I Am You*, 11)

Siham, who from a very early age exhibits erotic feelings for women including her own mother and her primary school teacher, can only initially conceive this kind of love at the expense of her own femininity and femaleness because of the conceptual anorexia surrounding representations of the sexes and sexual orientations. On the other hand, Siham's exhibition of masculinity might be confused for a desire to be male, whereas it might stem from motivations which are entirely different from those presumed by patriarchal cultural configurations.

Siham only ever feels truly at ease when she is in Paris completing her final school year. For her and other Middle Easterners like her, the West offers a democratic safe haven for sexual liberty, even though the West itself is not necessarily safe.

> Siham began her Parisian life with the utmost excitement. She was an intelligent girl; fearless, invasive of every unknown in order to learn its secrets. She was overwhelmed by this magical city and decided to discover its landmarks and worlds and in Paris there are many landmarks and many more worlds, but what designates entry into a particular world are the human's specific inclinations that draw them into walking through open doors; and in this magical city doors are flung wide open for the purposes of fulfilling desires and inclinations of all kind. (*I Am You*, 12)

A girl who is intelligent and fearless may pursue her natural inclinations in a location such as Paris, but when she returns to Lebanon her relationships are limited to meaningless sexual encounters with uncaring women, two unrequited love situations (only one of which was consummated) and finally settling in a relationship with a married woman who is generally represented to be "as dumb as a brick."

And yet, even though *I Am You* is easily a transgressive text, it is still nevertheless restrained by the very forces of culture and society that it attempts to stretch. The local hero, Layal, understands the degree of ostracism homosexuals in Arab cultures face and does not want to instigate a revolution counter to the religious revolution. Layal is very practical in her thoughts as "[s]he very well knew the extent of the danger caused by this subject in our society, for, those people are scorned and no one understands them" (76). After embracing Siham, Layal says:

> ...I advise you, as you have done before, even if the matter is difficult at first, to socialize with young men. You might get attached to one of them and that will be the end of that. Think of marriage and childbearing, forget yourself and follow suit from the other girls. Try, even if this requires that you lie to yourself in the beginning. (*I Am You*, 77)

Layal implies that if a woman is capable of resisting being with another woman and is also capable of carrying out an intimate relationship with a man then she is heterosexual enough. And it is better that a woman save herself from the social difficulties that present themselves in the event that one chooses to live out one's erotic urges, than to complicate her life by gratifying her senses. In the novel Layal's resistance of the sexual advances of Meemee presents itself as a little too difficult, minutely too difficult, for us not to suspect that there is a kind of heterosexuality which manifests itself as a discipline, where the heterosexuality is the result of repression, or denial of erotic feelings towards women. The text itself provides us with ample reasons for the ambiguity surrounding Layal's sexuality. We learn from her that her male partner is overseas and that she misses him occasionally, however, she also displays active repression of her homoerotic feelings. For instance, when Meemee attempts to seduce Layal over dinner by wearing a "transparent dress underneath which she wore very small briefs" (*I Am You*, 110). When Meemee rubs herself against Layal we are told that "Layal's body quivered at this contact but she kindly pushed Meemee away from her" (*I Am You*, 112). Afterwards, when Layal is invited into the lounge room for coffee after the dinner is over, she briefly soliloquises: "God, I hope we get through this night in peace. Meemee is very beautiful" (*I Am You*, 113). At the evening's end Meemee requests an embrace and the following description is to be found in the text:

> They adhered to each other in this fashion for some time. Layal felt the warmth of Meemee's body, her senses awakened and she almost…But she withdrew from Meemee's arms and said: "Let's get some sleep." (*I Am You*, 114)

Later in the novel Layal is invited to one of Meemee's ladies' only parties, and she arrives in true Cinderella fashion with everyone becoming quiet at her entrance. As the evening progresses, the following event takes place (after Meemee's girlfriend makes a great many protestations against Meemee's ostentatious advances on Layal):

> She drew near Layal, took her by the hand and pressed her body against hers and they began to dance. Layal's body awakened and she embraced Meemee intensely and kissed her. Meemee had begun to relax in her arms when the old hag came to drag her to herself. Layal returned to her seat indignantly but when she sat down she began to observe the scene before her: kisses and performances that were quite arousing. (*I Am You*, 128)

After this Layal leaves, having demonstrated some signs of indignation (one would think for having been interrupted), and she remarks:

> "I don't want to understand." She removed from her head and memory everything that she saw moments earlier and attempted to return to her writing and work. She missed her boyfriend… "Should I call him? He's abroad and won't satisfy my alert body. No I won't call anyone." (*I Am You*, 129)

A paragraph later, she decides that she will call someone, her friend Raya who teaches psychology at university and we learn shortly after this that she and Raya share an ambiguous mutual "admiration" for each other that never once "crossed that boundary" (*I Am You*, 130) of mutual admiration. The most significant reference to Layal's possible process of repression takes place when she is driving Meemee to a restaurant towards the end of the narrative. She was, of course, cornered by Meemee into doing this and wonders whether it was "her curiosity that dragged her into this kind of behaviour [... or whether] there was a Don Juanian inclination that spurred her on into doing what she was doing?" (*I Am You*, 149). Unfortunately for us, and quite characteristically for Layal, she stops short of the ultimate discovery. "She did not complete these thoughts because they arrived at the restaurant" (*I Am You*, 149). It is peculiar that Layal fails to continue these thoughts at a later point in the novel, and yet it is also intriguing. Her sexuality is left in a position of fluidity, escaping categorisation through its instability. The character's sexuality is never fully revealed to her and neither is it to the reader.

Interestingly, while the narrative relies on omissions to relate Layal's erotic interactions with Meemee, her relationship with Siham is not at all ambiguous. The important distinction between Meemee and Siham is that the latter is a young and impressionable undergraduate whilst the other is a voluptuous woman well into her adulthood and in full possession of skills of seduction.

While *I Am You* might *seem* like a superficial novel, which is ill-written, as the scathing reviews have claimed, it is invested in various academic discourses at once; the philosophical and the psychological, the literary as well as the (culturally) historical. Mansour's novel is the first of its kind, as a novel about a lesbian protagonist, whose suffering might initially appear incidental, trivial and unworthy in light of the atrocities of war which surround it. But Siham's pain is shared by numerable beings, whose desire for inclusion in society competes heavily with their desire to live out fulfilling romantic and erotic lives. As psychological studies have shown, contact with individuals who identify as homosexual (whether in real life or through film and literature) have a tendency to greatly reduce hostile feelings towards homosexuality as a malignant entity. In addition, the proliferation of positive, or at least realistic, representations of individuals of deviant sexuality and gender, assists those individuals in *coming to terms* with their own sexual identities. *I Am You*'s triumph is to be found in its audacity to name the nameless and to heavy-handedly dismiss centuries of orthodox traditions and cultural complacency as regards variant sexual orientations.

Lebanon is presently the only Arab-speaking country within which a Gay, Lesbian, Bisexual and Transgendered civil rights organisation was formed. The Lebanese GLBT group Ĥelem (which means *Dream*) has been recently created. Although, to my knowledge, no actual activism has yet taken place, their web site now documents the Gay and Lesbian underworld, which homosexual men and women frequent in the form of nightclubs, restaurants, bathhouses, cinemas and cruises.[37] The first Arabic-language Gay and Lesbian magazine, *Barra* (which means *Outside*), is now being printed and distributed in Lebanon, among university students in particular.[38] The situation remains far from ideal for homosexual and transgendered individuals living in Lebanon, but those individuals who share much of their adolescent and young adult despair with Siham, eventually outgrow the social mythology drilled into them by society and they learn to accept themselves and to find happiness within the limitations of their environment. Not all of them, of course.

I Am You does not present us with a happy, well-adjusted lesbian heroine, instead, it presents a young woman's struggle to understand herself and it bespeaks of her torment and her poetic catharsis in the form of a near psychotic obsession with an unattainable (and unsuitable) woman. But this is not a failing on the part of Mansour, as the novel resists becoming another (stereotypical) instance of a literary, tormented homosexual anti-hero — because the torment the author inscribes does indeed exist and it reflects a reality shared by beings who are unnecessarily oppressed in their societies. A happy, well-adjusted heroine will emerge in time, and her politics will be better articulated because she will be writing *for* herself and *about* herself, and, who knows, this very heroine might be the project (or producer) of the second Arabic lesbian-centred novel ever written. A novel which we still await, six years on from *I Am You*'s publication.

BEFORE *I AM YOU*

Other contemporary literature on the subject of homosexuality has been outstanding in its penetration of cultural reticence, but such literature predominantly involves male homosexuality. Ṭhani al-Suwaydee's novella *Diesel*[39] is a rare literary achievement in contemporary Arab literature, unveiling a postcolonial *queer* ideology of gender and sexuality, carefully hidden beneath the façade of traditional views. *Diesel* is a lyrical, magical-realist, even Baroque, "oral" composition of an effeminate protagonist, who is sexually interested in men. Diesel, our protagonist, who also becomes a widely reputed entertainer who sings and dances with unmatched finesse, and maintains a poetically convoluted and highly symbolic monologue, addressed to his (male) "friend," who is possibly his lover or a figment of his imagination. The story transcends the questions of "good" and "evil" surrounding homosexual inclinations and at no point does it unambiguously deliver a unified sexuality that can be easily categorized as "homosexual," since Diesel may possibly be read as a transgendered individual. However, Diesel is coded predominantly as an effeminate homosexual male. During his professional visit, as a much sought-after entertainer, at the governor's daughter's wedding, an anonymous woman makes the following remark to Diesel:

> It's been said that you tie the earth and the sky together; you're the middle-ground-solution (*Ĥal Wasat*) to all the groans of desire. Forbidden [from having] men, we have nothing but tree braches to play

> on top of....we who worship the virgin and pray abashedly in the face of religions. (*Diesel*, 85, this and subsequent quotes are my own translations)

This rather peculiar and ambiguous speech is perhaps referring to the prevalence of homosexual relations in Gulf countries as a direct result of the segregation of the sexes (homosexual acts can be seen as the middle-ground-solution to erotic desire, since heterosex is banned outside the confines of marriage, given that "we...worship the virgin"). Diesel's answer does not engage the woman directly on this point; instead his reply thwarts conservative attitudes towards the human sexes and human sexuality, which are widely prevalent in (Judaic, Christian and Islamic) religious discourse.

> The male, my dear is a model within which you can find a small sea that murmurs (*Yuṭharṭhir*) in his body and which teaches him that femininity is continuity, and that woman is our original formation...for you are what you are, a woman fragrances this day with her breathing and accepts the males' daily prayers in order to return them to their true nature, to their origin, to woman. (*Diesel*, 85–86)

In a rather profound moment within a predominantly fragmented and disconnected text, Diesel overturns patriarchal and traditional, even theological, discourse on the human sexes and their sexualities. Instead he presents woman as the "original formation"[40] from which "man" came, clearly contradicting the story of creation, told in the three Abrahamaic religious texts. This does not, however, imply Diesel's alienation from religious life, because the religious is a daily part of life, as the closing sentence of the novella makes clear: "Come, come my mute friend, dawn is nearing, get up and pray" (*Diesel*, 63). Despite its stylistic and poetic convolutions it is not possible to read this novel without registering notes on the homoerotic, which Suwaydee makes, without naming homoeroticism as homosexual. The narrator tells us that at age fifteen he decided to spend a night at the mosque, after his father expelled him from the house for being late in coming home after the evening prayer. He alludes to his first sexual encounter in this way:

> [al-Mu'thin]: If you want to sleep here [in the mosque] tonight you have to pay your dues to one of the travelers who are sleeping in one of the corners of the mosque.
>
> I said: I don't have any money.
>
> He said: There must be some favour you can provide to *that* traveler that will please him.
>
> And then he went to that traveler, spoke to him and sat in his place while the traveler came and patted my head. He placed his hand on my neck and then on my chest and asked: "have you ever heard of virtue?"

I said "yes."
He said: And the smell of virtue?
"I don't know," I said.
And here was where it all began, my friend. (*Diesel*, 22)

Later we learn that the traveler was invited by the narrator's father to spend several days with them in their house. The traveler shared the narrator's bedroom, and presumably also his bed. Diesel reminisces, "how wonderful was that traveler. He showed me more fatherly tenderness in one week than what my father did throughout my whole life with him" (*Diesel*, 24). Even though there is no explicit reference to homosexuality, Diesel is coded as an effeminate man, who enjoys the company of women in the non-traditional manner. As he tells us, "[w]hen I was eighteen I began to meet up with widowed and divorced women who came to visit my sister. Between them and I a family life grew despite that they were of a different sex, which was only different in its physical make-up. And there was a woman who, every time I saw her, would get up to leave and I used to feel that my masculine craving steered my body to another instinct, which reminded me of that traveler who suddenly disappeared from my life" (*Diesel*, 25). Shortly after this Diesel discovers a way to express his sense of being, when at the wedding for one of the widows he finds himself dancing sensually. "I felt as though I genuinely possessed the body of a woman for the first time. I was no longer able to resist the violence of femininity; my whole body began to move as though my sudden awareness veered in the direction of limitless expression" (*Diesel*, 26). It is proclamations such as these that obscure Diesel's gender identity, but out of them emerges what may be the character's conveying of his awareness that he is sexually different from the norm. Diesel does not rebel against rigid notions of gender and sexuality, as the queer Western theories have done, but rather incorporates himself, voluntarily, within a gender and a sexual orientation which are both deemed inferior by patriarchal standards, that is, he declares himself, a womanly man. With this incorporation, we do not see Diesel's defeat or humiliation but rather we witness his celebration, his release and return to the "true form" of which he speaks in a highly symbolic language.

The author of this novella, Thani al-Suwaydee, a United Arab Emirates citizen, received little acclaim for his only poetic novel when it was first published.

> At first everyone wanted to avoid writing about it, because it dealt with issues considered sacred in society, but in the last two years people began to open up to this story, suddenly everyone wanted to write about it, they all wanted it to be the most important novel. After ten years of its publication the critics began to discover a novel called *Diesel* coming out of the Emirates.[41]

It would seem that even though Arab cultures are in possession of seemingly immutable cultural codes as regards sexual behaviour (men=male=active, women=female=passive, and all heterosexually desiring), it would seem that the converse of this phenomenon is a continual literary pressure placed by writers, filmmakers and some publishing houses on maintaining an open dialogic discourse on sex. It is no wonder that *Diesel* has been dubbed a "shock value" novel.[42] These constant movements and tensions within culture, between blind conservatism and the need for moral prerogatives, seem to be in a constant process of negotiation.

Suwaydee's novel seems to indicate a revolution in the audacity of the Arabian novel to present anti-patriarchal views, to celebrate effeminacy in men and to indicate that homosexual relations in Islamic cultures abound. Suwaydee's novel received some publicity when the author was interviewed for al-Jazeera's literary-review program, "Awraq Ṭhakafeeya."

In a similar fashion, the much more famous Egyptian writer, Yusuf Idris, was able to publish his short story in the widely read Egyptian magazine *October* in 1987.[43] Idris's story explores the mind of a man's transformation into a homosexual ("latent homosexual").[44] *Abu al-Rijal*, or as Saad Elkhadem has translated it, *A Leader of Men*, also ambivalently situates its homosexual protagonist. Instead of Suwaydee's first person narrative, we have an omniscient third person narrator who is less sympathetic with Sultan (the main protagonist) than Diesel is sympathetic towards himself. Instead of a great entertainer, *Abu al-Rijal* is the story of a man who once was a thug. The short story constitutes Sultan's transformation from a virile leader of men, a chief, to an elderly, feeble and balding man giving in to his (recently realised) desires to be sodomized.

Similarly to Suwaydee's novella, Idris resists projecting onto the reader any moral evaluation of his subject, leaving his readers to either pity or loathe the process of a man's humiliation. This humiliation seems to be epitomized at the moment he makes a request of one of his underlings — the request surprises his subordinate when he discovers that he is being asked to play the role of sodomite. Opinions on the meaning of *Abu al-Rijal* differ, but the general consensus is that the piece obviates quite skillfully any obvious endorsement of negative evaluations of homosexuality itself. That is, although homosexuality features in this story, it is not situated anywhere within a dichotomy of good and evil. Elkhadem writes that:

> Remembering that Egypt...has been lately pressured into conservatism by the new Fundamentalists, one realizes the risk Mr. Idris has taken by depicting the emotions and the sexual desires of a homosexual without condemning or even reprehending them. On the contrary, he even lets his protagonist voice his dissatisfaction: .... "...indeed, why is it wrong for a human being to be a [homosexual]."[45]

Ramzi Salti was quick to point out, however, that although Idris features a homosexual protagonist in a morally ambiguous light, he did not attempt "to dispel existing negative stereotypes of the homosexual in Egyptian society."[46] Indeed Idris does not critique the social and cultural ideology which codifies sodomites in the ranks of "men" as powerful and active agents, while sodomees are relegated to the ranks of "women," who are weak and passive receptors. And while the text yields a more complex handling of the subject of homosexual desire than simple sermonizing or revelation, the short story must to some extent subsume predominant cultural preconceptions of homosexuality if it clearly avoids addressing these directly. This is exemplified in what Sultan reveals about his attitude toward men who find pleasure in being sodomized by other men:

> His [Sultan's] masculinity was never doubted, ridiculed, or abused, which is quite the opposite of what their neighbor, Umm 'Id, used to scream...in the face of her son when he came home late; she would accuse him of being taken by the other boys into the corn fields...she would yell with certain words that would make Sultan boil with anger and hate for this woman, and pity for her son, his friend.[47]

While Idris's story registers for us the existence and nature of very local homosexualities (in the Egyptian rural areas of the early twentieth century perhaps), it also reiterates an essence about how identification comes about. The son of Umm 'Id and the Western "faggot" share, at least, a social experience.

It should be noted that Idris, Suwaydee and Mansour all attend to the issue of homosexuality in their literature rather openly — with Idris, an already prominent writer, staking his reputation on it. al-Suwaydee and Idris demonstrate an artistic ingenuity in attempting to transcend both negative societal attitudes and direct engagement (affirmative or disputative) with them, while Mansour sets her narrative on a collision course with conservatives (as we saw in the reviews). The three works introduced and discussed above tend to present the phenomenon of homosexuality within larger humanist concerns and thus, in this respect, they are successful in being revolutionary and enlightening. They demonstrate that no culture is capable of being homological, that fissures which disrupt mainstream thought always surface, no matter how minutely and no matter how hostile the prevailing cultural environment may be to them. In the next chapter we will look at Egyptian attitudes to homosexuality in the twentieth century through a close study of gay-themed films. Films from the decades preceding the mid-1970s tend to be engaged in a rather open and positive dialogue with its audience as regards sexual deviation. Egyptian cinema has had a profound impact on much of the Arab world (being the equivalent of Hollywood or Bollywood for the Arab world), like any national cinema — through its ubiquity and prevalence — its productions are bound to reveal much about the cultural dialectics that produce them.

6 Some like it luke-warm

A brief history of the representation of (homo)sexuality in Egyptian film

In her comprehensive English-language study of *Arab Cinema,* Viola Shafik contends that "the Egyptian law of censorship issued in 1976" demonstrated that the "most important taboo areas [such as religion, sex and politics, were to be] kept under state surveillance."[1] She rightly observes that "criticism of Islam was not allowed" (Shafik, 34) and this certainly continues to be the case today. However, it would seem that other aspects of the code were able to be subverted or ignored, particularly those concerning the portrayal of deviant sexualities (though not the portrayal of any erotic or sex act in itself) which would have fallen under the rubric of "immoral actions." Though banned by the code, alcohol consumption and the use of drugs (Shafik, 34) also appear throughout the history of Egyptian film. The decade of the 1970s witnessed a particular freedom of representation for the Egyptian film industry, which has yet to be revisited today. The representation of homosexuality on the Egyptian silver screen yields a rather parallel picture to the one traced in Vito Russo's monumental history of the Hollywood *Celluloid Closet.*[2] Russo's book and the eponymous documentary which ensued, demonstrate that the representation of the homosexual is present in silent and early black and white (Hollywood) film, and that this changed with the advent of the Motion Picture Production Code in 1930, authored by Will Hays at the commission of the Motion Picture Producers and Distributors of America (Russo, 31). The code continues in its influence until the mid-1960s. During the three decades consumed by the code, the representation of homosexuality takes on the shape of the monstrous and the heavily subtextual.[3] By contrast, in Egyptian film, the homosexual is seldom coded as monster, but similarly, with the advent of the Egyptian version of the Hays code in 1976, the homosexual is relegated to a dark closet and her/his representation becomes only possible through clandestine symbology.

By the end of the 1970s, textual and subtextual references to homosexuality become rare and only in the films of Youssef Chahine do they appear at all after the mid-1980s. Chahine is the youngest of three prominent Egyptian film directors who have featured openly homosexual characters as well as elaborate plotlines with significant homoerotic subtext.

The others, Niazi Mustafa and Salaĥ Abu Seif both launched their careers at the very time that Egyptian cinema was developing into an industry (in the 1930s).[4] Mustafa and Abu Seif often collaborated and they both seemed to be on good terms with Chahine.[5] All three shared their unique interest in representing both textual and subtextual homosexual characters, who were very often portrayed in an unusually sympathetic light. However, it seems that this interest is limited to their films of the 1960s and 1970s. During these decades Egyptian cinema is characterized by a certain freedom of representation that dissipates significantly as the censorship code begins to take effect.

A good way of documenting or illustrating this shift in the cinema industry (which no doubt also reflects religious and cultural attitudes) would be in taking a close look at the 2003 Egyptian remake of the 1959 Hollywood film *Some Like It Hot*.[6] In *Firqat Banat Wa Bass* (*Girls Only Band*, circa 2003)[7] the director Shareef Shåban has gone to great lengths to make the remake of the 1959 Hollywood film less radical in its representations of sex, and the subtext of homosexuality. For example, in *Some Like it Hot*, Sugar (played by Marilyn Monroe) is caught out by the band manager when she drops an alcohol flask on the floor. The band manager prohibited alcohol consumption, which was illegal in the timeline of the American film. What Sugar drops in the Egyptian version are cigarettes (even though alcohol is not illegal in Egypt and has certainly featured in many a film by this point), for the pure and uncorrupted Egyptian Sugar (Sukara, played by Amira Fatĥi) must not be associated with alcoholic consumption.[8] Not only is Sukara transformed into a smoker rather than an alcoholic in this film, she also appears without possession of the sexual agency or even desire which is characteristic of the original Sugar. The scene where Joe (Tony Curtis) romances Sugar as he impersonates a wealthy businessman on a yacht he pretends to be his own, is radically altered in the Egyptian version. In *Some Like It Hot* Joe uses a form of reverse psychology on Sugar to lure her into having sex with him, telling her of his impotence when faced with women (also perhaps implied homosexuality). Although we do not see representations of the actual act of sex, if only for the reason of censorship if not good taste, the implication that their relationship is consummated is as clear as the filmmakers of the time were able to make it.

In *Girls Only Band* the scenario set up by Joe is not shown to be an elaborate ploy on his part to lure Sukara into a night-long session of "kissing." The scene, cut short, shorlty after Joe declares his impotence, suggests that the couple do not engage in any sexual activity at all, since in the following scene Sukara plants chaste kisses on Joe's lips — standing in sharp contrast to the 1959 version of the long, lingering and passionate kiss goodnight. In this way audiences are not offended that the young woman is having premarital sex even though the motivation behind Joe's elaborate deception and his luring her to the yacht no longer makes any sense. What is interesting is that the filmmakers who have gone to great lengthens to sanitize (an already sanitized) the 1959 Hollywood film and continue to participate in sexually symbolic jokes, such as the number 69 appearing prominently on the Band's tour bus, which has a long pink stripe running across the side of it, being reminiscent of the tour bus used in the landmark gay film *Priscilla Queen of the Desert*.[9] What is even more interesting is that this timid remake of *Some Like it Hot* more than forty years later, not only pales in comparison with the audacity of the original but also pales in comparison with a 1960 Egyptian film inspired in some respects by the release of *Some Like It Hot* a year earlier. Garay Menicucci points out that the Egyptian film *Sukkar Hanim*[10] (*Miss Sugar*)

> makes the statement that to be modern is to replace traditional arranged marriages with unions based on romantic love ... the film replaces the de-eroticized image of [an earlier transvestism film] *al-Anissa Ĥanafi* with a provocative and overtly sexual drag .... The film has a gay ending reminiscent of *Some Like It Hot*. In the last scene of the American film, when Lemmon pulls off his wig and declares he is a man, his intended fiancé remarks, "Nobody's perfect!" In *Sukkar Hanim*, when Layla's father is about to be wedded to Sukkar in drag and the real gender of the bride is disclosed, Layla's father is undeterred by the revelation that his intended marriage partner is a man and cries out, "I want to marry."[11]

In the 2003 remake of *Some Like It Hot*, the comment "Nobody's perfect!" is replaced by an opposite reaction: speechlessness and a look of disgust by Osmond's counterpart, implying that in Egypt there are no homosexuals, or at the very least, the narrative de-queers this character.

It is highly significant to note the evident regression in Egyptian cinema's representation of sexuality on screen. What was permissible in the early 1960s and to the end of the 1970s eventually became undesirable, while certain markers of sexual liberty came to be seen as Western imports, which were also undesirable. However, despite the restrictions, perhaps even precisely because of them, some contemporary Egyptian filmmakers and screenwriters have struggled to represent sexuality and sexual taboos on screen — but this sexuality is always (at least phenomenally) heterosexual. For even though contemporary audiences might accept a heterosexually transgressive film, no filmmaker of recent times has either been able or willing to present homosexuality on screen in the style of 1970s filmmaking.

When female director/producer/screenwriter Inas Degheidi brought us *Muthakarat Muraheeqa* (*Diary of a Teenage Girl*)[12] in 2001, she caused much commotion amongst the film critics, and was labelled a pornographic filmmaker.[13] The sex scenes of the *Diary of a Teenage Girl* are modest by Western standards and hardly warrant the label "pornographic" in any standards as they involve a fully shielded Gamila running her fingers over the bare chest of her lover Raouf — who has, anyway, just married her unofficially (i.e. without the presence of witnesses or a Sheik) so that they can consummate their urgent passions without shame and to ease Gamila's sensible fears of social ostracism. Gamila soon discovers that without the presence of witnesses her elopement-style marriage counts for nothing as she is subsequently subjected to rape, the loss of the family honour and the fears of being an outcast as an unwed, pregnant teenager. Degheidi is renowned for her feminist film-making; applauded by most audiences and reviled by others (in Egypt and abroad), her films portray strong female leads who are unconventional and unruly, who embody sexual prowess to which Egyptian-movie goers are not accustomed. Degheidi's male protagonists are always depicted as insensitive to the subordinate place of women in Arab society and as inherently selfish. (In *Diary*, Gamila refuses to marry Raouf when he finally returns, having left just after their unofficial marriage, saying "you abandoned me...you can't know what I've been through.") Degheidi received death threats and was taken to court by an Alexandrian lawyer charging her with obscenity. Therefore it would seem to be fitting that a discussion of the representation of homosexuality on the Egyptian screen should begin with Inas Degheidi's 1993 film *Dentelle*,[14] in which the homoerotic acts as barely a suggestion, a whim, which may or may not be present subtextually, in the style of Hollywood films such as *Calamity Jane*[15] and *Queen Christina* (Russo, 63–65). The means with which the subject of female homosexuality is broached (if it is at all) only further delineates the filmmaker's attempts at making the picture able to pass the Ministry of Information's censorship department,[16] without suspicion and without rousing conservative audiences against her.

In *Dentelle*, Degheidi borders on portraying a homoerotic relationship between two life-long friends: Saĥar (the circus performer turned cabaret dancer, turned popular entertainer, played by Egyptian cinema veteran Youssra) and Mariam (another cinema veteran Elham Chahine), her much more docile best friend who sets up a law practice in Alexandria and lives with Saĥar. The two women, who at first seem inseparable and share a close intimacy, are torn apart by their love for one man who wants (and does) have them both, Ĥussam (well-known actor, Maĥmood Ĥameeda). When Saĥar is arrested for drink driving and assault of a police officer (in a comic scene), she is taken to Abu Sharki police station. There she meets Ĥussam, senior detective at the police station, and drunk, she promises to give him a "night you will never forget." She then proceeds to call Mariam who hurries to collect her friend. When Mariam enters Ĥussam's office it is an instance of love at first sight for the two characters. For Ĥussam, Mariam represents the kind of woman a traditional Arab man will want to marry — she is quiet, from a respectable family, holds a "decent" profession and is respectably dressed. This contrasts rather sharply with Saĥar, who represents the kind of woman who is desirable only for erotic purposes, her drunkenness (which goes against the dictates of Islam) and her overt sexuality disqualify her from public respectability. As Ĥussam comments shortly after their first meeting to a friend of his:

What bothers me Fatĥi is that the two are so mismatched, one's a tramp, the other is well-bred and elegant...

Fatĥi: You should have called me to come to see the tramp.

Mariam eventually learns that Saĥar has fallen for Ĥussam who becomes a close friend of the pair (by finding Mariam a suitable place for her law practice and by helping Saĥar receive front page attention from the press, thus making her career). When we see the women alone they are usually in bed at night talking before going to sleep. It is peculiar that two women might need to share the same bed, but economic reasons might be the pretext under which these scenes operate. In addition, during such scenes Saĥar and Mariam are always depicted as discussing Saĥar's romantic interest in Ĥussam, while we also see Mariam's growing distress as she struggles to keep her affections (supposedly) for Ĥussam secret from Saĥar. On one such occasion, as the two women share the close quarters of the double bed, Saĥar asks:

Why would a man like Ĥussam be so interested in me?
Mariam: You don't know your own worth. If he searched the world over he'd never find a girl like you.
Saĥar: You're just saying that because you're my friend and you love me.
Mariam: Believe me you have the kindest heart. I've never met a person with your generosity... Ĥussam couldn't find a better girl.
Saĥar: Do you know what I wish for? ...I wish we could get married together and live in the same house.
Mariam: Our husbands wouldn't like it; they'd try to separate us.
Saĥar: No way! We'd cut them up and throw them in the sea.

When Saĥar, who is now convinced that Ĥussam loves her, learns that he intends to marry Mariam, she gracefully bows out of the contest leaving Mariam for Ĥussam. Even though Mariam has fallen in love with Ĥussam, she decides that she cannot betray her friend Saĥar and in order to honour the wishes of her ailing father she rushes herself into an unhappy marriage with an older man. Together with her new husband, Mariam immigrates to Canada, which is depicted (in the tradition of pathetic fallacy) as a cold and isolating place as the characters are surrounded by mountainously white snow. Unable to bear her estrangement from Egypt, Ĥussam and Saĥar, Mariam divorces her husband and returns to Egypt with the intention of marrying Ĥussam. In the meantime, Ĥussam and Saĥar are now married due to events which were initiated on Miriam's wedding night. In their mutual sadness at losing the woman they both love (Saĥar declares that the reason none of them are happy is because "the three of us love each other"); Ĥussam and Saĥar find solace in each other. Eventually they marry after at least one pre-martial sexual encounter (which significantly takes place on Mariam's wedding night). When Mariam returns, war breaks out between the two women. Mariam feels betrayed by Saĥar who thinks that Mariam is being irrational. Exercising his legal right to marry more than one woman, Ĥussam and Mariam marry. After numerous comic scenes where the two women are engaged in a battle to secure Ĥussam's time to themselves, the resolution to the dramatic conflict comes after Saĥar has a near fatal car accident. Lying in her hospital bed, Saĥar realizes the fragility of her existence and the extent of her love for Mariam (who is now pregnant with Ĥussam's child), which has been compromised by Ĥussam's arrival on the scene. Saĥar asks Ĥussam for a divorce and then Mariam follows suit and divorces Ĥussam also. In the scene following the divorce requests, Saĥar opens the door to her apartment to find Mariam gleefully proclaiming: "We're together again. I'm divorced." This is followed by laughter, a passionate embrace and much twirling.

The way the two characters express their love for each other always borders on the homoerotic, however, in the tradition of the subtextual, their love can also be seen in the vein of "intimate friendship," (which can be passionate but devoid of sexual intent) which is not very different from the kinds of friendships we see in Emma Donoghue's study of *Passions Between Women*[17] and Lilian Faderman's readings of "Boston Marriages,"[18] and other forms of female bonding ("woman-identified woman") suggested by Adrienne Rich, which exist within and along a "lesbian continuum."[19] No doubt, any homoerotic content in *Dentelle* is but subtext and a pretextual criticism seems to be levelled at men's relations with women as well as their interference with the relationships women forge with each other. It is also clear as one closely scrutinizes the screen text that the screenwriter, producer and director, Inas El Degheidi, has gone to considerable lengths in ensuring that the suggestion of a sexual relation between the two women is not evident even in the slightest look or touch (although much caressing and tender touches take place as the women lie together in bed), but rather that the possibility remains strictly in the realm of intimation (not dissimilar from the screen text of *Calamity Jane*). It is left for the imagination of a gay audience, or a conservative yet sex-obsessed audience, to plot a different course for the story line and to read between the lines. Upon the release of this film it was not the "gay-friendly" groups who heralded its masked potential but rather the conservative Islamist groups who called Degheidi a lesbian, making a lesbian film, something which she has repeatedly denied in television and newspaper interviews.[20]

Precisely because the film is born in a climate which is increasingly leaning toward orthodox religiosity, it should not be robbed of its homoerotic subtext even though Degheidi has denied that this was her intention. Her denial should be read as recourse to better survival in the mainstream than a reflection of the true potential of the film. The last scene of *Dentelle* features the two women raising Mariam's infant child in the air, after the toddler innocently looks up at her two "mothers" and the trio seem to indicate a happy unconventional family; a family which has rejected the patriarchal model and is rather founded on intimacy and understanding, which is implied to be exclusive to women. It is hard not to herald this narrative as at least queer given the fact that it ends with divorce and the destruction of heterosexual coupling at the same time that it portrays a union, or rather a re-union, of a homosocial, if not homosexual, nature. I will not be surprised if the final frame of *Dentelle*, with the two doting mothers entertaining their little girl along the beach, will become somewhat emblematic of a gay and lesbian human rights movement which will arise in that country, given the opportunity in the near future. Such is the only representation of what is potentially female homosexuality (or rather, bisexuality) that I was able to unearth in recent Egyptian cinema — the love, though, if it exists, dare not speak its own name, it merely implies itself, if that.

Such an anorexia of images of homosexuality (to paraphrase Jan Oxenberg's expression in the documentary film *The Celluloid Closet*) was not always the case in terms of the representation of homosexuality on the Egyptian silver screen. In fact, homosexual and bisexual characters have made several appearances in Egyptian film. The number of male homosexual characters, however, far exceeds the number of women, and, in this respect, the scarcity of images representing female homosexuality speak of the general oppression of women in patriarchal societies. In these scarce representations, women and men of deviant sexualities have a tendency to share similar tragic fates or else have their deviance corrected by the end of the narrative (through heterosexual union). Their sexualities are often depicted as transient in order to please the moral mass and in order to reflect a social reality where a great deal of homosexual behaviour is indeed a form of transience. In this way the homosexual subject, qua inherently desiring subject, is rarely depicted on screen. Instead a mutant, transient homosexual is most often what is depicted, particularly where women are concerned.

Homosexuality is a renowned "sin" that Arab cultures have had a tendency to indulge in for various sociocultural reasons, oftentimes the least of which is an innate inclination within the desiring subject toward same-gender eroticism. In fact the recourse to homosexual behaviour is commonly found transhistorically and transculturally in the event where heterosexual unions are hard to come by due to religious ideals of female chastity and the bonds of marriage. Due to the ubiquity of this practice of homosexual behaviour, voluntary or naturally-occurring instances of homosexuality have been overlooked for the purposes of keeping the subject under the sway of taboo and abnormality. In addition, this suppression maintains the widely held ideology that heterosex is natural and superior to homosex which is unnatural and born of abnormality or circumstantial strain. The roots of this biased appraisal cease to mystify us considering the fact that most homosexual behaviours in such cultures do involve some kind of compensation for the true object of desire — a member of the opposite sex. In this case this homosexuality, if not unnatural, then, at least, is not in conformity with the nature of most of those who practice it. In this chapter, as throughout the rest of this work, the homosexual subject is not an individual who practices sex with members of their gender; it is an individual who *desires* some of those members. Sexuality here is attended to in its purest psychical form (i.e. the erotic imagination). From the perspectives of the late twentieth and early twenty-first centuries, this distinction between practice and innate desires should be clearer to us, and it certainly is clear to, at least some, genuinely homosexual men and women who continue to inhabit societies which disavow the idea (and the fact) of naturally occurring homosexuality. As one of the characters in Remi Lange's Algerian ficto-documentary *The Road to Love* comments:

> They say homosexuality is a sin — a "ĥaram" that leads to hell. I found it very difficult to live with my homosexuality until I was 18. It was like a hell living in my village. I was always hiding. The most difficult thing for me was convincing the guy I loved that it wasn't a sin, that it was totally normal. But that guy was a hypocrite, he was not with me out of loving care, he wasn't in love: he couldn't have sex with girls because of the taboo of losing your virginity. Because of religion and of the lack of money to get married, men couldn't have girls, so they swept down on homosexual men … They were all hypocritical.[21]

We learn from Aĥmad, who is Algerian, twenty-seven and "gay" that his society observes strict religious rituals of pre-marital chastity, which is applicable to men and women almost equally. We also learn that homosexual men and women fall prey within this society to individuals seeking homosexual acts for purposes which are predominantly culturally imposed rather than personally chosen.

Of course, no society is without exceptions and those who do not abide by the laws of compulsory heterosexuality are usually among the ranks of infidels, prostitutes or individuals of considerable wealth and influence to whom laws do not apply — at least this is how the popular imagination tends to represent them in film and literature. And it is within this cultural context of understanding homosexuality that *Ĥamam al-Malaṯily* (*Malaṯily Bathhouse*)[22] is presented, whilst its male homosexual character, Raouf, subverts popular understanding of homosexuality by being unable to be brought back into the norm of heterosexual desires.

The title of Salaĥ Abu Seif's 1973 film *Malaṯily Bathhouse* is strangely translated as "An Egyptian Tragedy" on the opening credits of the film, even though the title of the film can be easily translated as I have done. There appears to be a sensitive awareness that foreign viewers of this film should not regard its content as conspiring with or approving of the morally loose behaviour of the libertines it depicts. Starring Shams El Baroudy and Yusuf Shåban and based on a novel by Ismåeel Walieddin, the film opens with a long scenic tribute to the city in general and to Cairo in particular. Depicting congestion and dense populations, Abu Seif visually implies the polymorphous vagaries of the city in which an immoral underworld is bound to flourish. So long is the opening scene of Cairo's traffic, interspersed with various shots of traffic signs which are not being obeyed and traffic wardens' instructions which are not being heeded, one cannot help but take this scene to be emblematic of the state of disarray which the film suggests is facing Egyptian society (in what is likely to be during the Egyptian-Israeli war of 1956). Even though a highly organized urban life appears on the surface of things, if one looks closely at the picture, one will see much contradiction. Cars parked under "No Parking" signs, pedestrians walking on the street rather than on the pavement and crossing the road when the traffic light tells them not to cross, cars driving the wrong way down a one way street, etc. A city vibrant with life, which appears to be regulated by hundreds of permissions and prohibitions enforced by the rule of law, whilst, in the meantime, an underworld ruled by whim and individual desires begins to emerge: those people who do not follow the rule of law, who deliberately disobey it to fulfil their own purposes. This opening scene is very suited to the overall theme of the film as we follow the story of the innocent country boy, Aĥmad, who leaves his family back in the rural regions of the Egyptian eastern province. He dreams of financial independence, a rented apartment for him to put up his mother and father in, and the ability to pursue a law degree at university. Soon his noble quest is forgotten, partly due to lack of employment opportunities and partly because he falls into the underworld of Malaṯily's bath, which is visited by men of importance and prominence. Added to this is his preoccupation with Naåeema, a poor girl who has resorted to prostitution for livelihood, whom he happens to meet on his first day in the big city.

Desperate to find a place to stay, Aĥmad comes upon Ĥamam al-Malaṯily where the owner Ali greets him and generously offers him free accommodation (and later employs him as his accountant). Here we learn that Aĥmad and his family are refugees from the Ismaåilia (which was then occupied by the Israeli army) and here too we first meet the homosexual character Raouf who makes many clear advances on Aĥmad who is too innocent to quite comprehend them. Ali and Raouf are good friends, Ali provides young male prostitutes for Raouf's pleasure and for the pleasure of other men of prominence who appear periodically on the set. Although the male prostitutes, Samir, Kamal and Fatĥi, share some screen time in which we learn that they come from a background of poverty and desperation, they are incidental to the main plot.

Although the implication that homosexual practices are taking place is evident and textual, the representation of sex, both hetero and homosexual, continues to take the form of highly coded and symbolic frames. For example, when Aĥmad and Naåeema have sex for the second time we simply see them laughing as they go under the dinner table, which begins to shake and on which a bottle of red wine is spilled on a white table cloth. This is ironic, of course, because we know that Naåeema is not a virgin since she works as a prostitute and the wine here stands as a depiction of mirth, recklessness or even Naåeema's loss of her psychical virginity — that her relationship with Aĥmad would be the first time she engages in a romantic (rather than a mercantile) sex act. The representation of homosex, however, is much more discreet, in the sense that although it is much more discussed, it is much less overtly represented or implied. The scenes shot inside the bath indicate that there is a "back room" in which special activities take place, although we do not see what these activities are. In addition, numerous men are being massaged by other men but this, of course, falls under the pretext that this is part of the bathing service that the bathhouse provides. A scene, which begins with a close up of Raouf Bey's face as he moans and groans for no immediately discernible reason, soon reveals, as the camera pans out, that Raouf is receiving a massage from one of the underlings at the bath — Moĥsin. Raouf Bey says: "You're amazing Åmi Moĥsin, your hands are like the kicking of mules. Cigarette?" and he offers him a cigarette. In this short scene, Raouf is possibly coded as a bottom and the homosexual act is associated with images of bestiality — an association which is not without precedent.[23] In this same scene Aĥmad is sitting barely a meter away from this action; he is, significantly, the only man in the shot who is fully clothed, and he is talking to one of the male prostitutes, Samir. Grabbing Samir's leg Aĥmad leans closely over to Samir and tells him that he must find work in his own trade, to think of his future since his current vocation is not stable, respectable nor reliable. Despairingly, Samir points out that poor men like him do not have the luxury to think of the future but have to live every day as it comes. A nearly identical conversation ensues between Aĥmad and a semi-naked Fatĥi, after Samir walks away in frustration from Aĥmad's innocent implorations.

When Muålim Åli is taken into custody after one of his former employees (Kamal) commits murder (the murder of his new employer, a prominent and anonymous director of a casino who is implied to be a "sugar daddy" figure), Raouf takes Aĥmad with him to his house. It is during this exchange that we get a glimpse, not only of the voluntarily homosexual character Raouf but of the filmmaker's biases and intentions in his depiction of Raouf. Through the characters of Samir, Kamal and Fatĥi, the archetype of the male whore has already been explored, whilst the homosexual who volunteers and seeks this act is the dissipated aristocrat. The use of male slaves for the pleasure of their male masters has a long and well-documented history within the ancient Arabian empire.[24] The implication here is that this situation has not changed — Raouf Bey, the wealthy master still continues to exploit young, innocent and impoverished men who rely on him as means of livelihood, but who do not engage in these behaviours for any pleasure of their own. In this respect, Raouf is an unsympathetic character whose sexuality initially appears as entirely physical and devoid of any emotional sentiment. In the scene following Aĥmad's implorations of Fatĥi and Samir, the implication that Raouf intends to prostitute Aĥmad for his pleasure becomes clear, although we learn shortly afterwards, that Raouf (exploring another stereotype) is really looking for love, which he cannot find.

Aĥmad has learned through earlier conversation with Samir and Fatĥi that selling oneself, prostituting oneself, is oftentimes the only recourse that the poor are able to resort to in order to make a living. In addition, he is learning that high ideals of self-education and diligence and perseverance do not always work and are not always a viable option. The scene in which Raouf attempts to seduce Aĥmad in his mansion is intercut with scenes of Naåeema being visited by a male client. She is now in love and she feels unable to fulfil her task as a prostitute. Soon enough she realizes that she has no option but to subjugate herself to the desires of the client (who is the Mayor, no less) and the mistress of the brothel who employs her. In the meantime Aĥmad is topless (for the first time in a homosocial context) and is posing for Raouf as he sketches his sitter. There is no doubt of Raouf's intention although it would seem that Aĥmad is still oblivious at this point.

Raouf begins to dance to James Brown's *Like a Sex Machine*, takes off his robe and attempts to dance with Aĥmad who coyly sits down on the couch. Both bare-chested and sitting beside each other, we see Aĥmad smoking his first on-screen cigarette (he has always declined them until this point; I wonder if the cigarette is indicative of his "moral" corruption), he soon realizes what Raouf's intentions are. Raouf runs a hand across Aĥmad's face (something which he has done a number of times at this point) and says: "Know what Aĥmad? Even though perdition is a very painful feeling, when it brings two people together it can be a very pleasurable experience." As Raouf further solicits Aĥmad, the seduction scene climaxes in his making his intentions clear. Raouf says:

> One thing that always confuses me when I read it is the work of al-Jabarti. There used to be respect and freedom for the individual. [Placing his fingers on Aĥmad's bare chest] why can't a person do what he wants, wear what he likes, grow his hair without anyone picking on him, why don't we [dialogue unclear] our roles in life, shatter this tedium in which we live....

This speech is cut with a rather peculiar sequence of shots, showing Raouf with long plaited hair, parted in a pony tail, wearing a hippie-like hemp shirt and walking down the streets of downtown Cairo. Menicucci provides the following useful analysis of this scene:

> In the seduction scene as the artist reflects on his life as a homosexual, he tells the youth that it is evident from reading the chronicles of the 18th–19th century historian Jabarti that there was unrestricted freedom in the past. In the modern period there is none. The artist

begins to imagine what a tolerant society would look like and the camera cuts to the artist in the Tal'at Harb district of Cairo — a traditional cruising place for gay men (Menicucci, n.p.).

The camera throughout this piece operates as though it is hidden, acting as a surveillance tool to a social experiment — letting a queer looking man out on the unsuspecting streets of Cairo and filming the natural reaction of the people. It would be interesting to learn whether this scene was filmed in a controlled environment, or whether it veritably played the role of documentary footage it implies itself to be.

The seduction scene shortly reaches its anti-climax when Raouf breaks down, realizing that Aĥmad is not interested in him sexually. After he asks Aĥmad if he has "tried love," he moves to touch him again. Aĥmad draws back and this recoil signals Raouf's break down in the form of revealing his autobiography:

> When my father found out, he ran away, he couldn't bear seeing me like this. The psychologist told my mother that there is no use, that we have to accept the matter of fact and she, she turned to drugs. When she became certain that indeed there was no use she ran away, she emigrated, emigrated and left me far away from her, she abandoned me, she abandoned me. I can't forgive them ...O ... Rest, suffering, suffering, suffering.

Raouf begins to sob, predominantly because of the tortured loneliness he lives, both as an orphan rejected by his family and a man incapable of finding or carrying out romantic relationships, which he clearly craves (if not more than, then) as much as physical intimacy. Menicucci erroneously interprets this scene as "an unfortunate case of pop psychologising [where] Abu Seif explains the artist's homosexuality as stemming from a love/hate relationship with his mother" (Menicucci, n.p.), whereas it is clear that Raouf's hatred for his mother stems from her rejection of him *because of* his homosexuality *and not* that his homosexuality came about because his mother rejected him. This scene, the last time we see Raouf in the film, resounds with a sympathetic portrayal of a homosexual character and it is interesting that Raouf Bey (in fact, the entire narrative of the film) never mentions the word "luṯi" (or its equivalent), although at no point is his identity deemed transient or a matter of the will, since it would seem that even the doctor has advised that Raouf's situation is permanent or incurable. Interesting also is the sympathetic light in which his story is cast: his parents' abandonment over a matter he cannot help does seem to break away from the stereotypical depictions involving demonization, but at the same time reinforces the stereotype of the unhappy and loveless homosexual.

Seldom does the homosexual subject achieve the opportunity to speak for her or himself in the fiction of Egyptian cinema and virtually not at all in the present context. Therefore, these rare instances in Egyptian cinema's past illuminate the way for understanding cultural attitudes about the subject and the presence of a marginal gay epistemology: Raouf understands that restrictions of sexual freedoms arose recently and he is attuned to the cultural heritage of the past in which homosexual relations were more widely accepted than in their present context.

In many ways *Malaṯily Bathhouse* was a prophetic film, in that it depicted an Egyptian society which still enjoyed sexual freedoms inherited from past social configurations. Through the character of the nameless story teller, the film predicted the rise of religious zeal, which is indelible from the new political crises which were awaiting the Arab world by the close of the 1970s. Without a doubt the nameless "Fool" of the *Malaṯily Bathhouse* undergoes his own transformation. From a teller of religious folktales and historical chronicles of great leaders and brave men, he eventually becomes the voice of "moral" conscience. At one point, he reminisces to his immediate company that the prophet and his companions won entire conquests "with their swords and with rocks, not with perdition." (The word Dayaå here translated as 'perdition' is also uttered by Raouf Bey during his seduction scene). For the Fool, there is a connection between the moral laxness enjoyed within the Egyptian underworld and the crisis of control and sovereignty faced by the Arab world and Egypt in particular. While the heroes and heroines of the tale pursue the fulfillment of their erotic desires, the Fool recounts how their country is being dominated and robbed by the Egyptian upper classes (whose capitalist interests are allied with imperialist nations) as well as the foreign powers. Suddenly the film's interest in social issues of sensuality and eroticism becomes indelible from the political and military threats faced by the Arab world and the Egyptians in particular. The Fool's character eventually develops into the moral voice of the film, a voice which seeks to curb lust and desire in favour of a military fervour to protect the nation and its sovereignty. The Fool's moral warnings, which seemed to coexist with the debauchery of the underworld, bring a clear message, as his final words in the final scene of the film make clear:

> Every crisis has its resolution, but only the strong can resolve problems. It is the strong who write history. There is no time for crying, tears and wailing. Wake up. Wake up .... Wake up Egypt. History waits for no one. Wake up Egypt. Wake up.

It is interesting that a certain brand of religious orthodoxy, in its infancy, has a tendency, like the character of the Fool who frequents the bath house, to be able to intermix, to coexist, with elements of society and individual behaviours it ultimately seeks to eliminate. We have seen this in the works of Aĥmad al-Yemeni and in Ibn Hazm's opinions on homosexual activities.

Malaṯily Bathhouse is unusual in its simultaneous depiction of religious ideology and bodily pleasures. The film tends to portray both as elements of life, while other films discussing the subject of homoeroticism do not tend to discuss religion at all, which is in itself unexpected. Rather, what these films do is assume a certain degree of cultural knowledge and agreement that the subject is forbidden in religion and that it is not approved of by society at large. For example, in the delightful comedy of *Bint Ismaha Maĥmood* (*A Girl Named Maĥmood*),[25] directed by Niasi Mus̱tafa in 1975, the question of religion does not surface so much as the issues of cultural belief, perhaps because the two can sometimes be interchangeable.

A Girl Named MMaĥmood exploits the genre of transvestism as comedy. Through a woman's identity being mistaken for a man's (as she impersonates one) several homoerotic images can be presented safely and innocently to mainstream audiences. The film revolves around al-Ĥag Firghalee who is a simple, illiterate and traditional man who has an only daughter, Ĥamida (played by Suhair Ramzi). Firghalee, a widow, runs a furniture shop and is very protective over his daughter who has recently graduated from high school and was accepted for university. Ĥamida loves Ĥassan, a young man in his final year as a medical student, and he encourages her to pursue a university degree, but alas, Firghalee has other ideas about the place of women in society. When Firghalee finds out that Ĥamida has enrolled at university, he gets angry and places her under indefinite house arrest, forbidding her to go to university. In true comic fashion Ĥamida continues her studies, with Ĥassan, who conveniently lives in the same building, supplying her with the course readers and the books she needs. Firghalee discovers this and bans all the books from the house.

It is not until Firghalee reveals his plan to marry his daughter off to a man she dislikes intensely, named Waĥeed, that Ĥassan comes up with an ingenious plan to save her from her troubles. This plan is inspired by a class he has just attended on transexuality and transsexual surgeries. Ĥassan lures Firghalee to the hospital where he and his colleagues study and he convinces him that they are a group of doctors who have just performed gender reassignment surgery on his daughter Ĥamida who is now Maĥmood. The simple, illiterate Firghalee believes this and laments the loss of his daughter who is now a handsome young Maĥmood. Firghalee who had always wished for a son accepts his new son and loves him. As he cannot tell the others the truth, he instead tells them that his estranged son Maĥmood has now come to live with him. When they first meet in her new (performed)[26] gender, Ĥamida/Maĥmood remarks: "I always knew I was going to be a boy." Her father faints.

In addition to the scenes where Ĥamida's transvestism is used as an excuse to bring the entire female cast of *A Girl Named Maĥmood i*nto sexual contact with Maĥmood, who is really the female actress Suhair Ramzi, we are also presented with a number of scenes where Ĥassan kisses Ĥamida (dressed as Maĥmood) in public places, where dumbfounded onlookers express their horror. At one point, Ĥassan remarks to a distressed Ĥamida, "don't worry, men kiss like this when they meet." He is, of course, referring to the commonly accepted show of affection that Arab men are accustomed and permitted to display for each other, but peculiarly he refers to Ĥamida as Maĥmood on two occasions and she resorts to correcting him, as though he had forgotten (or does not wish to remember), that her name is Ĥamida and that she is really a woman.

The effeminate son, Maĥmood, attracts both the male and female workers at Firghalee's furniture shop. The women are particularly attracted to Ĥamida in her Maĥmood garb for reasons which are not entirely clear. One male worker thinks that Maĥmood might be a member of "the third sex" which is, as he explains to his colleagues, "someone who is neither ... nor ..." (i.e. an intersexed individual). Eventually however, the workers come to understand his effeminacy as indicative of his homosexuality — although the term (or its equivalent) is never uttered.

At one point in the narrative, "Maĥmood" and Ĥassan are seen kissing by Waĥeed and are also suspected of being intimate by Maĥmood's father, in whose mentality it is one thing for Ĥamida to become Maĥmood, but it is quite another should his son be homosexual. Becoming disenchanted with his employees' jokes about the "sissy-ness" of Maĥmood and fearing for his son's "masculinity" and heterosexuality when Waĥeed catches him in the act of intimate kissing with Ĥassan, Firghalee decides to send him to a "morally loose" woman to make a man out of him. What ensues is perhaps one of the greatest subtextually homoerotic scenes to ever grace conservative cinema screens anywhere.

Maĥmood is asked to meet with the cabaret entertainer Lawaĥith, who greets him with a bottle of whiskey in her home. Maĥmood thinks that he is there in order to clinch a deal for the furniture shop from this important client. Maĥmood soon realizes that Lawaĥith has other ideas. Maĥmood (who, we must remember, is the actress Suhair Ramzi) is lured into the bedroom where Lawaĥith lunges at him/her, throws him/her on the bed and kisses him forcibly. Being an upright, heterosexual heroine, Ĥamida, of course, resists these advances and is in effect frightened by them and in this way no perceived homosexuality takes place — since the cabaret entertainer thinks that she is seducing a man, while the man who does not desire her is actually a woman. On the other hand, the elaborate plot and Maĥmood's transvestism seem to be the pretext under which two actresses can perform something of a sexual scene and where two "men" can be seen kissing on screen. Nevertheless, despite the film's daring flirtation with the subject, the cultural attitude towards Maĥmood's (seemingly homosexual) disinterest in Lawaĥith is registered and is unmistakable. When Lawaĥith realizes that Maĥmood wants no part in her call to "liberate yourself man, liberate yourself!" she realizes that "it's true after all! I have to call Mr. Waĥeed so that he can tell your father."

Maĥmood: Tell my father what?

Lawaĥith: You mean to tell me you don't know? You have to go see a doctor, don't you dare ignore this in yourself kid, don't you dare!

Furthermore, the film also makes a point about the freedoms granted to men and forbidden to women. Like *Dentelle*, the pretext for the film, from which mass audiences emerge clueless of the subtext, is that the film is exploring the freedom permitted to men and forbidden to women. In one scene where Ĥamida is dressed in her swimming costume at the local pool, revealing her female body, she comments to Ĥassan "I've fallen in love with Maĥmood, with the freedom he grants me. I can go anywhere and do anything I want." This is reminiscent of another film *Lil-Rijal Faqat* (*For Men Only*, 1964)[27] in which two women dress as men in order to gain employment as engineers in a prominent oil company. The film also exploits their transvestism in order to create scenarios where two female actresses as well as men and male-looking-women can come into intimate contact.[28]

By the end of *A Girl Named Maĥmood*, Maĥmood finds himself forcibly engaged to two women, with a third woman claiming that she is carrying his child, not to mention Lawaĥith's claims that Maĥmood was a wild lover (because s/he paid her). All this leads Maĥmood to have to reveal her true identity but only after her father is told by the "doctors" that his son Maĥmood is pregnant (this is due to a simple mix up, Maĥmood/Ĥamida is not pregnant). Ĥassan brings Firghalee back to consciousness, who recognizes him to be the man Maĥmood had been kissing earlier on in the narrative. He proceeds to strangle him, exclaiming: "you're the one who spoiled my son's good upbringing!" to which Ĥassan replies "I'm willing to correct my mistake, I'm willing to marry *him*" (emphasis mine). In the final scene the sheik who is going to perform the marriage ritual asks Waĥeed "what is the name of the bride?" to which Waĥeed retorts "Maĥmood Firghalee al-Said." The sheik is evidently confused and remarks: "this is a masculine name, is the bride male?" to which Waĥeed retorts "yes, and pregnant too." Eventually Ĥamida appears in her white wedding dress and all is revealed. The final line of the film has Waĥeed saying to a guest who has arrived a little too late to witness the resolution and the revelation (that Maĥmood is Ĥamida): "Mr. Maĥmood is marrying Doctor Ĥassan, any objections?!" at this, the guest Souåd (who has been pursuing Maĥmood), faints, but Waĥeed's powerful and clear line stands out in its reinforcement of the "disguised" theme of the film, which is about homosexual romantic unions — about "marriages" which are neither sanctioned nor acceptable in society or in present configurations of Islam.

What is also interesting about this film is its pseudo-scientific impartiality towards the phenomenon of transexuality, which was only becoming known within the worldwide scientific community in general during the decade *A Girl Named Maĥmood* was released. The following is a paraphrase of "Dr" Ĥassan's explanation of why Ĥamida has turned into

Maĥmood: every child, when he is a fetus, has the potential to develop as either a boy or a girl and when he develops into a boy, the female aspects remain present inside him. Since Firghalee's daughter was born a girl, then there was always a boy inside her. In every cell there are 46 chromosomes, two of which are related to gender and the egg contains the X chromosome. The sperm carries either an X or a Y chromosome and if an egg met with an X-carrying sperm then the result is a girl and if the sperm carries the Y chromosome then the result is a boy. "But with your daughter there was a union between two X chromosomes and a Y chromosome, meaning woah!" exclaims Ĥassan.

Simple, illiterate Firghalee cannot really follow all of this and he asks "so what made the boy inside her spring up today?" to which Ĥassan answers pointing his finger at the ceiling "His infinite wisdom." There seems to be a subtle evocation of a theory of sexuality and gender which acknowledges the multiplicity and diversity prevalent in nature. At the same time the audience is placed at ease through dramatic irony; their conventional beliefs needn't be heavily challenged: Ĥamida is still Ĥamida, she is not really Maĥmood, there are no homosexually desiring characters (or at least they are not aware of this). Although the film appears to be dealing with the issue of transgenderism, it also exploits Ĥamida's transvestism to explore concepts of homosexuality. Through this the film attempts to rationalize homosexuality as a form of transgenderism (women who desire other women must be essentially men) and fails to provide a significantly thorough examination of homoerotic desire.

Niazi Mus<u>t</u>afa, who directed *A Girl Named Maĥmood* and who was a friend and mentor to Salaĥ Abu Seif who directed *Ĥamam al Mala<u>t</u>ily* in 1973, also brought us the much more explicit depiction of homosexual relations in the drama *al-Mutåt wal Åzab* (*Pleasure and Suffering*), circa 1971.[29] Starring Shams al-Baroudy and Nour al-Sherif (both of whom have had a role in films depicting openly gay characters: Baroudy later starred in *Ĥamam al Mala<u>t</u>ily*, while Sherif later played the tormented gay character Amin, in the 1977 film *Cat on Fire*[30]).

Pleasure and Suffering follows the story of a group of four girl friends headed by the ice-queen Nana (Baroudy) who is a fashion designer. The rest of the main cast consists of Nana's lover Salwa (played by Safa' Abu Såoud) and her other friends, Fifi and Elham (played by Suhair Ramzi who claimed the starring role in *A Girl Named Maĥmood*). Elham is a compulsive thief who finds sexual pleasure in petty theft. We soon meet Ådel (Nour Sherif) who we do not learn until later, is a con-man, who becomes interested in Nana — but is warned by her friend Fifi that "she does not like men, she has a complex." Soon we learn more about Nana's fear of men from her directly. When Salwa informs Nana that her father is thinking of arranging a marriage for his daughter to a work colleague (of his), Nana protests, as she tenderly touches Salwa's face:

> I object to this. Men are trouble ... they think they're masters and we're slaves. I hate them all, the first of them is my father. Can you imagine that I hate my own father? He used to beat up my mother in front of me ... They're all like that, believe me my darling, you're not cut out for this sort of thing. I worry about you.

The representation of female homosexuality in this film thus tends towards the popular understanding that homosexual inclination in women is born out of trauma or a hatred for men, which can be corrected if the right man comes along. And this is precisely what happens. Ådel falls in love with Nana, who falls in love in return. However, the film does not provide signals fit only for this simplistic popular interpretation. Similarly to *A Girl Named Mahmood*, there is both heteronormative, mass-audience cliché of the "genre film," and the room for subtle intimations that invite alternative or subversive readings. But on the other hand, in its centralization of the first onscreen lesbian relationship as being secondary in its nature and primacy to heterosexual union, the film manages to obviate transgression against popular belief and opinion and, in a way, the film helps to inscribe further misconception and misunderstanding of innate homosexuality.

Despite this dominant reading, there are still elements which undermine it. For example, in order to seduce Nana, Ådel not only gets her drunk, but resorts to slapping and beating her.[31] The resemblance of this to her mother's situation with her father does not escape her and yet this beating seems to prepare her for accepting Ådel's sexual advances and his declaration of love. In this way Nana's love for Ådel is no more than the displaced Elektra-like love she has for her father. The "love-making" scenes which follow the beating are interspersed with images of running water; Nana dressed in a red garb strolling gaily through a wheat field; images of sunflowers; more flowers; more running water; a screen shot of the couple in bed with suggested nudity, embracing, kissing; more nature scenery. The suggestion seems to be that "nature is running its course," Nana is "flooded" with pleasure and release; and the beauty of the heterosexual union is marked by its relegation to the natural order of the world. The suggestion seems to be that homosexual unions on the other hand are devoid, firstly, of emotional fulfillment, and secondly of endorsement from the natural order of the human cosmos.

After her sexual encounter with Ådel, we see Nana now dressed much more femininely. Her hair, which was once dark coloured and tied up, is now light coloured and flows freely down her face. About this instant transformation (literally overnight) she comments: "I can't believe that I've changed and so quickly. I have been afraid of men all my life, but you, you're something else. Ådel, I love you." The implication is clear, the suggestion regarding the transience of female homosexuality is transparent. And yet the film, whilst presenting this popular cultural belief about homosexuality, nevertheless complicates the picture through the character of Salwa, whose representation might be more akin, though much more discreet, to that of Raouf in *Malaṯily*.

Salwa's devotion to Nana is carefully coded through the looks she gives her and the yearning and hurt that the actress intimates when Salwa loses Nana. Her general relegation to the margins of the film (as a supporting role), suggests that Salwa is representative of a more authentically homosexual character. For example, in the early scenes of the film, Nana claims that "love is empty talk," clearly indicating that she does not perceive what is between her and Salwa as love. At this point Salwa stares painfully at Nana who is not aware of her longing and these looks appear discreetly, without emphasis, as though the filmmakers were attempting to obviate the disapproval of the mass audience, whilst also appeasing their "gay" viewership.[32] In addition, Salwa and Nana's relationship does seem to be marked by eroticism and longing for physical pleasure. That is, although their relationship is not emotionally fulfilling, it is at least sexually so. In one of the early scenes of the film the "sexual chemistry" is depicted through a rather obvious lustful look that Nana gives Salwa as they dance at a night club, while Salwa gives a more coy, though desirous, look in return. We note Nana's lips open partially and discreetly and the ever so slight movement of her tongue, as she intimates strong erotic desire which must be repressed for the benefit of representation on the silver screen, however the lust coded in that look is unmistakable, to Shams al-Baroudy's credit as an actress.

Ådel and Nana's relationship is complicated by the fact that he is part of a trio of conmen who are blackmailing Nana, Elham, Fifi and Salwa. Nana discovers that Ådel only pretended to want to help them retrieve photographs (which implicated Nana and Salwa in theft carried out by Fifi and Elham), and that he is part of a larger scheme to involve the girls in the robbery of the cigarette factory safe (in exchange for the damning photos), where he works. This rather complex and dramatic discovery brings Nana much distress. After the robbery the girls decide to flee to Alexandria for a little while. During this trip we learn the "roots" of Elham's kleptomania: her father, who clearly favors his other daughter, once taunted her for stealing her sister's doll. From this memory she awakens calling out: "I'm no thief, I love you papa, I love you." The resemblance of this childhood trauma to Nana's conflict with her violent father is evident and the implication that Nana's homosexuality is generated by similar traumatic dis/attachment from/to the father, is made even more clear through Elham's subplot, whose (equally deviant) sexual exhilaration is derived from theft.

It is during the girls' time in Alexandria, when Nana believes that Ådel has abandoned her, that she attempts to resume her sexual relationship with Salwa. Salwa, of course, is furious. When Nana comes to her bedroom she places her hand on her leg, whilst sitting beside Salwa on the bed. At this moment Salwa registers her first dismay, firstly by pulling down her night dress to cover her thighs and secondly by pushing Nana's hand away. Nana then implores: "Please Salwa, forget everything that has happened" placing her hand once more on Salwa's knee. Salwa again removes Nana's hand and replies: "It's my fault that I believed you. You're free to do what you want. [mimicking Nana] 'I hate men, they're trouble ... They think they're the masters and we're the slaves' and when I started to hate them you fell in love with them."

Salwa leaves and declares that she will sleep in the lounge room. Following this scene, we see a man by the side of the pool at the resort (who is later revealed to be an undercover detective) making advances on Salwa. Salwa is evidently not interested in him, but when she sees Nana approaching, she quickly befriends him in order to arouse Nana's jealousy. Nana is evidently jealous but Salwa's victory is short-lived, for Ådel returns to right his wrong and to propose marriage to Nana, who accepts in an instant. Ådel's return follows the scene where Nana attempts to resume her sexual relationship with Salwa for the last time in the narrative. In the final scene, when everyone is arrested by the undercover detective and placed in the police van, Salwa, eyes welling up with tears, looks painfully at her lost love, Nana, because she realizes, with Ådel's return, that their relationship has truly ended. Nana never returns the look, Ådel now consumes her attention.

Depictions of homosexuals in Egyptian film, though rare, do not possess the quality of demonization for which Hollywood films of the mid-twentieth century were renowned.[33] However, these films propagate misconceptions of their own. Peculiarly, whenever homosexuals are depicted, they appear as victims, either of childhood trauma or the prison of their social lives. Ultimately, male homosexuals are seen as predators while female ones are generally presented as women burnt by traumatic experiences with men. We saw above how the homosexual character can be presented safely to mass Egyptian audiences – so long as the homosexuality is corrected in the end, or it is not victorious or triumphant, and seldom is it depicted as desired independently of strenuous social and personal circumstances. We also do not see overtly successful homosexual relationships, homosexuality is about sex, unless perhaps if we were to consider the subtext of *Dentelle* as an exception. We saw that in *A Girl Named Maĥmood* the subject had to continue to be skirted, we also saw the misery in which Raouf lives in *Malaṯily Bathhouse*. In addition we saw the heavily coded nature in which the potentially homoerotic relationship in *Dentelle* was presented. In *Pleasure and Suffering* Nana was returned to the rightful path through her heterosexual union with Ådel.

In the 1979 film *al-Suåood Ila al-Hawiya* (*The Rise to the Downfall*)[34] lesbian relationships are again depicted as transitory. Although the homosexual content is very brief and does not contribute greatly to the storyline of the film which is about Israeli espionage and Egyptian counter espionage, the Egyptian anti-heroine Åbla (who becomes a spy for the Mossad, played by Madeeĥa Kamel) is explicitly depicted as having sexual relations with the Frenchwoman Madeline (played by Imam) who secretly recruits her as a spy. This relationship wanes and becomes secondary to Åbla's new primary interest, Ramon, who is a Mossad secret agent posing as an Egyptian media correspondent. It is interesting that by the end of the 1970s homosexuality came to be depicted as the result of Western influence and in addition as something to be coupled with the betrayal of one's nation, one's culture and core values. In one of this film's substantial allusions to sexual activity, we see Åbla and Madeleine in bed together, with a mid-range shot of Åbla's sweaty face after she has moved into the frame to answer the ringing telephone. Her homosexual activity can be seen as further proof of her descent into degeneracy and wayward ways. This film will mark the last explicit reference to female homosexual activity in Egyptian film.

This film is followed by *Genoun al Shabab* (*Mad Youths*) in 1980.[35] The only information I can here present is from memory and from a web site advertising the sale of an original poster for the movie and as such I cannot engage in a close reading of the film, which left a lasting impression on me of societal perceptions of homosexuality. The film stars Aĥmad Ramzi and Mervat Amin and was directed by Khalil Shawqi. It centred on a group of wayward college students who become involved in various immoral acts including the use of marijuana. The film's protagonist (Amin) is a tragic figure who is corrupted by the immoral "hippie-like" conduct of her university colleagues. She initiates a sexual relationship (which is implied clearly, but whose activities we see nothing substantial of) with another female student and dies at the end of the film, no doubt in the film's effort to warn wayward youth and to demonstrate to them that such are the consequences of homosexuality and/or drug use.

A year prior to the release of *Genoun al-Shabab*, Youssef Chahine, who had previously hinted at his own sexual preference in his film *Alexandria Again and Again* (Menicucci, n.p.), completed *Alexandria Why?*[36] In this film Chahine's explicitly homosexual character, the Egyptian aristocrat Ådel (whose mannerism and appearance are reminiscent of Rock Hudson), is presented (ironically) as a patriotic figure whose intense hatred for the British occupation of Egypt during World War II leads him to the murder of drunken soldiers, procured for him by paid thugs, as a form of psycho-political release. When he is brought a young and impressionable British soldier named Tommy Friskin, he finds himself unable to kill him. Perhaps because Tommy's unassuming innocence attracts Ådel, who at one point explains: "I should never have asked you your name, never offered you my bed, never spent the whole night looking at you." Youssef Chahine has been singularly responsible for most depictions of homosexuality on the Egyptian silver screen (albeit representations of exclusively male homosexuality), but these depictions, humanist as they are, remain marginal to (and discreetly presented in) the main plot of his films.[37] Chahine himself never openly or unambiguously declared his sexual preference even though he has hinted at it. A biography of his life written by Ibrahim Fawal and published in 2001 peculiarly shuns any mention of the theme of sexuality dealt with in Chahine's films,[38] nor does the biography broach the subject of the director's own sexuality, except right at the onset on page one where Fawal informs us coyly that Chahine has been married to the same woman for forty years. In the usual tradition of reticence, homosexuality remains hidden, more so in this day and age than thirty or forty years prior; it is the love that dare not speak its name, even though, it seems, everyone knows about it.

With the end of the 1970s also came the end of depictions of homosexuality, whether textual or subtextual. A new agenda in dealing with sexuality now seemed to be occupying the filmmaking industry — the question of sex could be raised (much to the consternation of a mass audience becoming increasingly more conservative), so long as this sex involved a man and a woman and preferably within the sanctioned confines of marriage. Inas Degheidi's films[39] have acted as somewhat revolutionary in the feminist insights they throw into the mainstream, and in their depiction of "illicit" heterosex, however, it is apparent that even Degheidi, who is honest in all respects concerning Egyptian society and sex, cannot bear to broach the subject of homosexuality directly as is evident in her film *Dentelle.*

Looking more broadly at filmmaking in the Middle East in general, we perceive that the revolution of humanist insight into sexuality has not come to a halt. Remi Lange's Algerian film *The Road to Love* (2004) deals with extreme openness with the problems facing Algerian homosexual men, who share a crisis of identification because their culture suppresses homosexual behaviour as acts of love or born of innate desire. Maryam Shahriar's Iranian film *Daughters of the Sun* (2000)[40] braved a long battle with Iranian censors and eventually was allowed for international release, where the entire film content (which was edited for the showing in Iran) was restored. Turkish filmmaker Ferzan Ozpetek's sexual chronicles *Ĥamam* (2000)[41] and *His Secret Life* (2002)[42] deal with (male) homosexuality in modern Turkish society with a realism of which Middle Eastern films on the subject have been deprived. In addition to this, the short film genre is now proving to be an effective means within which homosexuality can be depicted by homosexuals themselves. The Palestinian short film *Diary of Male Whore*[43] deals candidly with the question of sexuality in a world where it is indelible from politics — where the individual body is an erotic landscape, which can be occupied and exploited. The short Lebanese film *Shou Baĥibak* (a.k.a. *Crazy of You*, 1997)[44] by writer/director Akram Zâtari flaunts the sexuality of its male protagonists and their cruising methods. Added to this is the growing awareness within gay and lesbian Middle Eastern communities living abroad that some form of organized resistance to homophobia is needed in their home countries, as exemplified in the two recent documentaries *I Exist* (2003)[45] and *Dangerous Living: Coming Out in the Developing World* (2005).

Although, as we will see more clearly in the conclusion, this organizing for gay rights is still in its infancy, and mostly thus far ineffectual, these years mark the beginning of the Arabic Stonewall. In time, as the religious fervour wanes and collective self-awareness amongst homosexuals in the Middle East increases, a new cinema will eventually develop. In this cinema the homosexual subject will cease to be invisible and will make a return to the Egyptian silver screen. What form will this return take? One only wonders. And how many more years will it be before the first deviant heroine or hero appears in the mainstream? This is a question which will be answered eventually, in time.

Part IV

Conclusion and references

7 Homosexuals, the people of Lot and the future of Arabic homosexuality[1]

In the last chapter I concluded with something which might at first glance appear as wishful thinking. There are so many barriers, cultural, political and religious, to the actualization of dignity for homeland Arabs with a homosexual orientation. We saw earlier how transgendered individuals are quickly earning legal rights in the strictest Islamic environments, even though these people continue to be outcasts culturally and socially speaking. Despite the fact that homosexuals in the Middle East face a dire situation in light of popular religious mythologies surrounding them and the rhetoric intended to "misrecognize them," there is an extremely logical and thorough Islamic religious argument *against* the tradition of prohibiting homosexuality as the most evil of sins or sad of disorders. The theological and scriptural material studied in chapter 3 posits a serious challenge to the rulings on homosexuality that recent cultures (and nation-states) of Islam have adopted. As this new scripture-based view of homosexuality gains more attention worldwide, more and more Muslims will have to question the cultural and social mythologies they had been taught about homosexuals. For example, the revered Muslim scholar Dr Qardawi states that:

> The rule goes that opposites attract and that Allah the Almighty created man and woman to propagate the human species. For one to be sexually attracted to someone of the same sex is a deviation from this rule.
>
> ....
>
> The People of Lot in the Quran are thus depicted with all kinds of corruption and sin: transgression, ignorance, sin and crime, and mischief. Again, describing the People of Lot, Allah says, "Verily, *by thy life (O Prophet), in their wild intoxication, they wander in distraction, to and fro.*" [al-Ĥajar: 72]. Their actions are described as a wild intoxication, which can be, by no means, an explanation of something one is naturally born with.[2]

I hope that I have sufficiently demonstrated the logical and evidential fallacies of this form of thinking: one which sees sexuality purely as an exchange of (economic) reproduction, whereas it would appear that sexuality and sexual behaviour have far more complicated outputs and drives operating within them for this to be the simple fact of the human universe. Furthermore, we must not ignore the fact that homosexuality is something that one is indeed "naturally born with," regardless of whether this is a bad or good political strategy. It seems plausible that at least some homosexuals are born homosexual, while others are born to become so.

In the Middle Ages the kind of ill-logic deployed by Qaradawi was present, but it was in no way as prevalent, as exacting and entrenched culturally as it is in the present time. Even in the earlier decades of the twentieth century, as we saw in the previous chapter, this anti-homosexual rhetoric was being drowned out by other political movements geared towards democratization, republicanism and nationalism. Further, it was not until the twentieth century that Arabian homophobic rhetoric began to see both homosexuality and its acceptance as Western imports. Indeed, this is the logic which prevails whenever the suggestion that homosexual rights are human rights, as Qardawi puts it:

> All divine messages spoke of the People of Lot and denounced their ill-doings. The West, however, wishes to turn homosexuality into something acceptable by society. Not only that, but laws and regulations are being construed to legalize this sin and many of the issues surrounding it (Qardawi, n.p.).

This rhetoric, aimed at rousing nationalist (now Islamist) sentiments against the subject by allying it with the West, neglects to mention that those factions in the West, with whom Islam is at war, i.e. fundamentalist Christians and right wing Zionists, think almost identically about homosexuality as Qardawi and his cohorts do. In fact, Islam in this instance and in this mode of interpretation is peculiarly at war with an *ally*.

THE POLITICS OF LGBTIQ ACTIVISM AND THE POLITICS OF THE MIDDLE EAST

Prior to the Qaåeda's icon-canonization of the struggle, Palestinians were fighting a predominantly secular war. But this changed when Osama Bin Laden released his first tape after the successful destruction of the World Trade Center in New York, in 2001;[3] he maintained that the war to free Palestine was a religious war — a Muslim holy war to be exact, of global proportions, intended to drive out Western economic and political interference in the Middle East. There can be no doubt that Palestine and its nemesis, the state of Israel, are very important in the Islamist imagination, and that this war symbolizes all that is unequal between subjugated Eastern lands, oil reserves and Western imperialism. And in this way, it is peculiar to note that objections to the exploitation of Islamic countries are not all sounded in those countries alone, but that *queer* activism is very often in agreement with these objections. For example, there is a significant faction of the Israeli queer collective that is openly against Western imperialism and Israeli occupation and mistreatment of Palestinians. These rebels and renegades form a minority group within LGBT and feminist organizations in Israel, but they nevertheless create an unusual yet powerful alliance.

The Women in Black is a feminist organization that holds protests on a weekly basis against illegal settlements, occupation of the West Bank and Gaza, and the treatment of Arab Israelis as second-class citizens. It has since become a worldwide "loose" network of women protesting against any military aggression.[4] Kvisa Sh'chora is part of a Queer collective in Israel, which protests against the oppression of Palestinians; they see this as a parallel to the oppression of sexual minorities.[5] During the first Israeli Pride Parade of 2001 (held in Tel Aviv), a group of gay activists naming themselves the "Gays in Black" marched under the banner "There is No Pride in Occupation" (Waltzer, n.p.). Hagai El Ad's article, entitled "Gay Israel: No Pride in Occupation" articulated the political sentiment of the action, although he is not affiliated with either Kvisa Sh'chora or the Gays in Black. He writes:

> Jerusalem, Feb. 21, 2002. It appears that a meeting of gays and lesbians with Israel's Prime Minister, Ariel Sharon, will finally take place. Is this an achievement for our community, or an example of a lack of feeling, callousness and loss of direction?
>
> ....
>
> It would be unbearable to simply sit with the Prime Minister and on behalf of our minority ignore the human rights of others, including what's been happening here in relation to Palestine for the past year — roadblocks, prevention of access to medical care, assassinations, and implementation of an apartheid policy in the territories and in Israel.
>
> The struggle for our rights is worthless if it's indifferent to what's happening to people a kilometer from here.[6]

Similarly, in the United States, a group of "queers" naming themselves QUIT (Queers Against Israeli Terrorism) descended on a Starbucks Restaurant in Berkeley, California, and claimed that it was now Queerkeley. A web site dedicated to the event explains:

> About 25 queer settlers descended on a downtown Berkeley Starbucks on Saturday, August 17, claiming Berkeley as "a city without people for

people without a city." The group, organized by Queers Undermining Israeli Terrorism (QUIT!), posted a banner proclaiming the reclaimed café "Queerkeley — A Prophecy Fulfilled."

They also erected homes (transformed "Palestinian civilian homes reclaimed from another street theatre action), lawn furniture, and signs reading, "It Works In Palestine, Why Not Here?" and "It's Ours Because We Say So." They erected plastic palm trees to "make the concrete bloom," and gave patrons a tract explaining their religious claim to the land as follows:

> "Land of fruits and nuts ...
>
> "And the Lord saw that the queer people were harried in this land. And the Lord spake onto the prophet Harvey, "You will lead your people across the wide waters unto a new land." Harvey was fearful, and he cried to the Lord, "How will we cross the wide waters? For they are cold, and they are filled with all manner of hazardous substances and raw sewage and other pollutants." And the Lord responded, "fear not, Harvey, for a great bridge will be built, and the people will cross into this land. And this land will be called Berkeley. I say, Lo, I have promised the land of Berkeley to the lesbians and to the gays, and to the bisexuals, and to the transgenders and to the intersexed, and to all of the gender variant peoples. And this land shall be blessed with fruits and nuts, unto 50 genderations."[7]

Mocking the Zionist phantasm of "a city without people for people without a city" and the mythologies which accompany racial and religious continuities, the rhetoric of the organizers of QUIT clearly falls in the region of liberal politics. The situation yields a great deal of complexity and irony, since it is hardly a secret that Arabic cultures are rampantly anti-homosexual and deeply patriarchal and oftentimes misogynist. In nation states where Islamic law is the law of the state, homosexuality has been known to receive corporal and capital punishments. And while Palestine is neither a state nor an observer of strict Islamic laws, because of the integration of Christian Palestinians among other factors, it is also no secret that homosexuals are outcasts there, as they are in most of the Arab world. But for the Palestinians it has long been apparent that any ally is a good ally, particularly Israeli ones. So the Palestinian — and by extension the Muslim Jihadist, who has been culturally and religiously (let us say, ideologically) trained to inhibit the sexual body (not only the homo or bi or trans bodies) finds herself at an awkward point of self-rereading. I do not doubt that the great bulk of any nation on earth are either incapable of performing or unwilling to perform self-re-reading and will not fantasise that the Palestinian mass is an exception to the rampant rule. However, the Israeli Queer and feminist alliance that is voiced with and to them, puts them at conflict with their own cultural ideology. They have an important and necessary Israeli ally — a macropolitical ally that is constitutionally more radical than themselves in terms of liberating the body — not only the Palestinian body but also the homosexual and transgendered and the female body and the male body — liberating, then, not only the political but the sexual self.[8] One wonders what impact these exchanges and unusual alliances will have in the long term, particularly at a revisionist point in history, on relations between homosexuals and their homelands.

As we have seen throughout this work, agitations of mainstream beliefs about homosexuality occur on a regular basis in the Middle East, but it remains unclear whether these agitations are sufficient for ushering in a return to a more sexually permissive Islam, such as the one we note in the Middle Ages. There's a rich literature devoted to the description of sexual behaviours and implied desires in which Islamic faith and jurisprudence were not at odds with speaking candidly about the body and a variety of sexual activity. But whether popular Islam can begin to shift in this new (and old) direction may not ultimately be a matter which depends on what the scriptures say, but rather, as Ibn Ĥazm (in the twelfth century) and As'ad Abu Khalil (in the twenty-first century) suggest, "religion ... is much more than a holy text. Religion is a holy text plus interpretations, plus local culture, plus tribal conditions."[9] Ibn Ĥazm also notes that (in his time) different Muslim cultures *Islamicised* their beliefs about homosexual acts — i.e. found scriptural support, which he doubted.

> The people are not good at assessment and do not know how to find supportive scriptures and they do not interrogate their beliefs ... As for us, we consider their assessment to be false, and the sayings of others should not be attributed to the prophet. Grinding and thighing are not fornication, and since they are not fornication they do not have the same punishment, and no one is entitled to set punishments according to his opinion, and so he can swear by this punishment all he desires, for this is a violation of the punishments set by God Almighty.

Those who believe that the doings of Lot's people are the greatest degree of fornication should be aware that [fornication is only possible between a man and a woman and only when the male member is in the womb], for they do not have a supportive text to begin with, but should they find something similar then they would tyrannise and oppress. (*al-Muĥalla*, 2233)

In this day and age, it appears as though this Islamification of the prohibition of homosexuality that Ibn Ĥazm criticizes as early as 1100 is shared unanimously in the Muslim (and Christian) Arab/Persian world, and this is due to the loudness with which homophobic rhetoric is projected and perpetuated in Arab/Persian cultures. However, since Islam qua scripture is inherently much more flexible than its monotheistic predecessors in regards to sex and homosexual behaviour, as Bouhdiba has argued, the "queer jihad"[10] has only begun.

ON THE INTERNET

In recent years, devout Muslims who consider themselves as gay/queer or transgendered have begun to collect themselves in the only possible international space they have — cinema and the Internet. al-Fatiha.org is a Queer-Muslim site that challenges the widely accepted notion that homosexuals are enemies of Islam. Based in New York and founded in 1998 by Faisal Alam, the web site's mission statement declares that its aim is to provide "a supportive and understanding environment for LGBTIQ Muslims who seek to reconcile their sexual orientation or gender identity with Islam."[11] The founders of this organisation have chosen a highly sensitive name "al-Fatiha" which is the "Opening prayer," recited at the beginning of each daily prayer, five times daily. On their web site the organisation initially used the token opening remark before the beginning of their main text "Bism Allah al Ruĥman al Raĥeem" (In the Name of Allah, the Most Gracious, Most Merciful") in accordance with Islamic tradition and scholarship. The new revamped web site has omitted this cultural identifier which has had an ironically secularizing effect on the site. Since *al-Fatiha.org* was conceived in the late 1990s, together with its strongest likeness, *GayEgypt.com* (in its promotion of Muslim homosexuality), literally a dozen of other sites catering for LGBT Arabs, or Muslims or Iranians or Arab/Muslim/Middle Eastern gay/trans men or women, or any combination of the above, began to surface. In fact, the years between 2003 and 2006 saw a dramatic increase in the number of homophilic Arab/Middle Eastern/Muslim-gay-lesbian-trans web sites — but significantly all of these seem to be operated from Western countries, predominantly due to the dangers encountered in homeland-based web sites.[12]

The recent introduction of live journals, web blogs and other forms of Internet journaling has also seen an explosion in the presence of the issue of Arabic (including Iranian) and Muslim homosexualities on the Internet. The queerarab.blogspot.com for example, playfully claimed in February 2006 that it is dedicated to the "rantings of angry sarcastic bitchy queer Arab Americans," but so far the blog has managed to attract only two regular contributors. While a new site named "Eye on Gay Muslims" is presently set up by an anonymous founder who also uses the site as a web blog.[13] These Internet presences do appear to have had an impact by raising awareness around the subject of homosexuality in Islam, and the treatment of homosexuals in Muslim countries, and this has spilled into a global queer jihad, or a queer jihad in exile. For example, in Canada, a grassroots movement named the Muslim Canadian Congress (which "provides a voice to Muslims who are not represented by existing organizations") openly issued support for Canada's same-sex marriage policies.[14] While Abdel Nour Brado, Secretary of the Islamic Commission of Spain, asked that the subject be debated further (among Spanish Muslims), while the Spanish government contemplated the introduction of "full access marriage" to same-sex couples.[15]

Furthermore, in January 2006, Australian LGBT newspaper *Sydney Star Observer* reported the unsuccessful efforts of a Gay Muslim group to "hold an event about the lives of [Muslim] gay men and lesbians" during the 2006 Festival of Muslim Cultures, which was intended to "celebrate Islam's 'diversity and plurality' across Britain."[16] Shortly after, the Muslim Council of Britain's (MCB) policy advisor Mohamad Åziz "revealed a five-year plan against homophobia in an interview with PinkNews.co.uk" while the MCB's spokeswoman, Inayat Bunglawala, categorically denied their commitment to such a policy. And while such vacillation may seem discouraging at first, the fact that homophobic ideologies are being contested at all within certain Islamic institutions (even though these are West-based ones) demonstrates that the minor agitations of the few dissidents have begun to have some effect on social and cultural policy.

At the site of these very real problems and negative ideologies of human sexuality, where does the academic discourse on gay historiography fit in? I have concentrated my efforts to contest the conclusions arrived at within Western discourses of "gay historiography." The argument in nearly all readings of female homosexuality in the (both Western and European) past have included some kind of apology or preface that analysts should not too hastily apply their own cultural experience to the evidence from past times. This is because in the West there is a lesbian presence on the discursive, social and legislative levels which is unequaled in the modern Middle East. However, what is one to do with literature on, and evidence of, female homosexual relations and eroticism in the past, when today hardly any form of visible culture as it is known in the West exists? And yet, the literature on medieval grinders and their grindings depicts dozens of facets that do repeat in the modern Western world. In this vast litter on the subject of female homosexuality we glimpse literature on the "masculine man-hating" ones and the feminine, bisexually inclined ones (taken at face value for once), literature which also proves that they existed in communities and subcultures and that at times they avoided public attention (i.e. were closeted) and at others did not fear the reproach of the public. It is difficult to believe that the grinders somehow vanished for an entire period between the thirteenth century and the twenty-first. But what is more engaging is that Arabian Medieval female homosexuality resembles postmodern Western female homosexualities more closely than modern and premodern female homosexualities in the West do. What we have here, at the site of this medieval literature, is an inversion of the dilemma faced by Western lesbian/gay historiography. It is not the contemporary present which needs to be guarded against injecting itself into images and ideas from the past;

rather, here it is the past which shows us its own epistemology — but one which strangely resembles our own "present" frame of reference.

Ultimately, it is this peculiarity of similarity-despite-difference which causes us to turn once more to a revision of essentialism, one which takes into account all the lessons learnt from postmodern theories of grand narratives and post structural theories of concept-formation. That is, humans do invent the world in which they live, through ideological constructs and concepts of the things that our minds encounter. This is an important concept which surfaced forcefully with chapter 2 of Michel Foucault's *The History of Sexuality* and one upon which many critics and theorists have built. But the inverse of this acute observation of epistemology and ontology should not be neglected either.

I hope that throughout this work I have paved the way for this simple conclusion: that homosexuality is not simply a human concept or a human construct and it is possible that there is nothing specifically human about homosexuality at all. In addition, even though concepts of homosexuality exist this does not render homosexuality immaterial, on the contrary homosexuality has numerous (both known and unknown) physical components. I hope that in light of this argument, certain Western theorists might think more carefully about the care they took in making homosexuality a Western construct — separate or discontinuous from homosexual behaviour. I think that in doing this, such theorists have given postmodern Western civilization too much credit and have set the West as the originator of a fact of physical/organic life that seems to me to be beyond human control. In addition, in light of this new research, Boswell's seemingly outrageous assertions require serious reconsideration. Firstly, it seems now that religious orthodoxy is not necessarily immiscible with tolerance of sexual conduct, for the religious orthodoxies of the Arabian Middle Ages (observed in the person of Yaĥya Bin Akţham and the writings of al-Yemeni most notably) were not sexually-closed as contemporary orthodoxies of the same religion are today. Secondly, Boswell's assertion that there may have been homosexual marriages and unions which predate the civil rights movement in the 1970s, no longer seems unlikely or implausible, if we consider what Brooten has uncovered; what medieval scholars have written about long-term relationships between women; and the fact that although it is not widely known and unexpected, homosexual marriages presently take place in the Middle East — in the midst of repressive and hateful cultures.

By denying the possibility that there are gays and lesbians in both past and present Middle Eastern societies, because "gay" and "lesbian" are culturally specific identities, we unwittingly collaborate with the conservatives in those homelands where exclusively homosexual persons are unlikely to encounter anything but ignorance and monstrosification of her/his inner most private being. It is both unsettling and significant that the homophobic rhetoricians in the Middle East often rely on the common recourse that homosexuality is a Western decadence, rather, a Western concept.

What we need to overcome the most in the Middle East, is that lingering and domineering sensation that pervades almost every Arab household (certainly every one that I have been into) — that homosexuality was always a taboo; always ĥaram; illicit; illness; disease; Western decadence; affluent decadence; psychological twistedness; hormonal imbalance; due to trauma or the segregation of the sexes. But the questions which interrogate these fallacies have already begun to be asked, even though these questions need a few more decades of sustained development for us to be able to fully gauge their impact and potential.

Notes

1 INTRODUCTION: CONTEMPORARY VIEWS OF FEMALE HOMOSEXUALITY IN THE MIDDLE EAST

1. Arabic examples of book-length studies include Ibrahim Maĥmood's *The Forbidden Pleasure: Homosexuality: Sex in Arab History* and *Talal Adeen al-Munajjid's al-Ĥayat al-Jinsiya åind al-Årab*. English examples include J.W. Wright Jr. and Everett K. Rowson, eds. *Homoeroticism in Classical Arabic Literature*; Stephen O. Murray and Will Roscoe, eds. *Islamic Homosexualities: Culture, History and Literature* (this collection includes a brief article on female homosexuality entitled "Woman-Woman Love in Islamic Societies," 97–106); Arno Schmitt and Jehoeda Sofer, eds. *Sexuality and Eroticism Among Males in Moslem Societies*; and the most recent (2005) and exciting monograph by Khaled El-Rouayheb *Before Homosexuality in the Arab-Islamic World, 1500–1800*. French examples include Abdelwahab Bouhdaiba's *La Sexualité en Islam* and René Khawam's contributions to French letters by translating various medieval Arabic texts invested in homoeroticism and pederasty such as his *Les fleurs éclatantes dans les baisers et l'accolement* by Ali al-Baghdadi; *La Prairie des gazelles : éloge des beaux adolescents* by Moĥammad al-Nawdji and *Les délices des coeurs, ou, Ce que l'on ne trouve en aucun livre* by Aĥmad Tifashi. See bibliography for complete references.
2. For a discussion of the classification of the texts as "literary" or "historical" please refer to the introduction to chapter 4.
3. Eve K. Sedgwick, *The Epistemology of the Closet* (Berkeley: University of California Press, 1990).
4. Elham Mansour, *I Am You* (Beirut, Riad El-Rayyes, 2000). Hereafter cited in text as *I Am You*.
5. Salaĥ Adeen al-Munajjid, *al-Ĥayat al-Jinsiya Åind al-Årab* (Beirut: Dar al Kutub, 1958).
6. Shehab Adeen Aĥmad Ibn Yusuf al-Tifashi, *Nuzhat al-Albab Fima La Yujad Fi Kitab*, ed. Jamal Jomåt (London: Riad El Rayyes, 1992). Hereafter cited in text as *Nuzhat*.
7. al-Sheik al-Nafzawi, *al-Rawd al-Åttir fi Nuzhat al-Khatir*, ed. Jamal Jomåt (London: Riad El Rayess, 1993); al-Sheik al-Nafzawi, *The Perfumed Garden*, ed. and intro. Alan Hull Walton. Translated by Richard Burton (London: Book Club Association, 1982).
8. Abu Nuwas, *The Forbidden Texts*, ed. Jamal Jomåt (London: Riad El-Rayyes, 1994).

9. Muntasir Muthhir, *al-Mutåt al-Muĥarama: al-Liwat Wa al-Suĥaq fi al-Tareekh al-Årabi* (n.p.: al-Dar al-Ålamiya lil Kutub Wal Nashr, 2001). Hereafter cited in text as "Muthhir."
10. Khatib Ådnani, *al-Zina Wal-Shuthooth Fi al-Tarikh al-Årabi* (Beirut: al-Intishar al-Årabi, 1999). Hereafter cited in text as "Ådnani."
11. Such works and compilations include the works of both ancient and contemporary scholars, including Jamal Jomåt, Salaĥ Adeen al-Munajjid, Ibn Ĥazm's discussions of homosexual acts in *al-Muĥalla*, Tifashi's erotological compendium *Nuzhat al-Albab* and Bouhdaibba's work *Sexualité En Islam.*
12. Ibrahim Maĥmood, *al-Mutåt al-Maĥthoora/The Forbidden Pleasure: Homosexuality: Sex in Arab History* (Beirut: Riad El-Rayyes, 2000). Hereafter cited in text as "Maĥmood."
13. It is interesting to note that in Ådnani's version of the genesis of homosexual activity, the devil appeared as an adolescent man who seduced male villagers one by one.
14. For example see Alauddin Shabazz, *Homosexuality 911: Whence Came this Perversion?* (n.p: n.p., c. 1993), 20. Hereafter cited in text as "Shabazz."
15. Two notable works on the subject are Joan Roughgarden's *Evolution's Rainbow: Diversity, Gender and Sexuality in Nature and People* (Berkeley: University of California Press, 2004); and Bruce Bagemihl's *Biological Exuberance: Animal Homosexuality and Natural Diversity* (New York: St Martin's Press, 1999).
16. In this vein Edward M. Miller argues that the presence of diverse traits and interests (including those which may produce homosexual inclinations in individuals) "serves to provide a high degree of variability among the personalities of offspring, providing the genotype with diversification and reducing competition among offspring for the same niches." See Edward M. Miller's "Homosexuality, Birth Order, and Evolution: Toward an Equilibrium Reproductive Economics of Homosexuality," *Archives of Sexual Behaviour* 29, (2000): n.p.
17. I mean this here in its most general sense. Sexual deviants constitute not only homosexuals but individuals who fail to restrict themselves to what is considered licit acts of sex by the ever-changing hermeneutics of religious doctrine.
18. See Scott L Hershberger, "A twin registry study of male and female sexual orientation" *The Journal of Sex Research* 34, no. 2 (Spring 1997): 212–223; and Michael J. Bailey et al. "Heritable Factors Influence Sexual Orientation in Women" *General Psychiatry* 50, no. 3 (March 1993): 217–223.
19. Simon LeVay, *The Sexual Brain* (Cambridge: MIT Press, 1993).
20. Simon LeVay, *Queer Science* (Cambridge: MIT Press, 1996).
21. *The Last Supper* Dir. Stacy Title. Screen. Dan Rosen. Sony Pictures. 1995.
22. Although the majority of HIV infections known in the United States have been thought to be transmitted through male-to-male sex, transmission through heterosexual intercourse is the most common cause worldwide. See for example, *HIV and AIDS: The Global Inter-Connection* ed. Elizabeth Reid West Hartford (CT: Kumarian Press, 1995). This collection focuses on the atrocities the disease has caused in poorer African countries. More specifically to view how HIV/AIDS now affects a worldwide population of which a small minority is homosexual men see Janneke Van De Wijgert and Nancy S. Padian's "Heterosexual Transmission of HIV," in *AIDS and the Heterosexual Population,* ed. Lorraine Sherr (Poststrasse: Harwood Academic Publishers, 1993), 1–9; and Lawrence O. Gostin's "AIDS in Africa Among Women and Infants: A Human Rights Framework" *The Hastings Center Report* 32 (2002): n.p.

23. Two interesting studies which recover an archaeology of the criminalizing and pathologizing of homosexuality include Thomas Stephen Szasz's *The Manufacture of Madness : a Comparative Study of the Inquisition and the Mental Health Movement* 190–207, 272–288; and Francis Mark Mondimore's *A Natural History of Homosexuality*, in particular see "Perversion and Inversion," 34–51 and "From the Inquisition to the Holocaust," 197–218. See bibliography for full publication details.
24. Ålia Shuåyb, *Kalam al-Jasad: Dirasa Ikhlaqiya* ([Kuwait]: Dar Åliya lil-Nashr wa al-Tawzeeå, 2001). Hereafter cited in text as "Shuåyb."
25. John Boswell, *The Marriage of Likeness: Same-Sex Unions in Pre-Modern Europe* (London: Fontana Press, 1996).
26. For examples of same-sex marriages in the Middle East see Brian Whitaker's "Arrests at Saudi 'Gay Wedding'" in *The Guardian*, March 18, 2005, http://www.guardian.co.uk/saudi/story/0,11599,1440618,00.html 01/01/2006; Åliya Shuåyb cites an article in *al-Ra'ee al-'Åm*, November 2, 2001, in which two Lebanese women are incarcerated for marrying each other (by wearing wedding bands and living together, see Shuåyb, 24); and also see the Associated Press' "Arab gays face hormone treatment, prison: UAE mulls punishment against dozens arrested at mass gay wedding," 26 November, 2005, http://msnbc.msn.com/id/10218234/ 01/01/2006.
27. See Noura El-Ĥakeem's "Not First But Welcome!" *Hurriyah: A Magazine for Queer Muslims*, Fall 2005, http://huriyahmag.com/fall/features.marriages.htm 01/01/2006.
28. Paula Sanders discusses a similar situation in which this logic operates within the context of medieval jurisprudence. Before transexualism and transgenderism came to be known and understood, the phenomenon of intersex was more readily visible and hence regulated by the jurists. Hermaphrodites were assigned a place of gender indeterminacy where they were higher in rank than *women* but lower in rank than men. "It should stand behind the men and in front of the women as a precaution, because if it is a man standing among the rows of women, his own prayer is invalid; and if it is a woman standing among the rows of men, then the prayers of those men on her right, her left, and behind her will be invalid." Cited in Paula Sanders' "Gendering the Ungendered Body: Hermaphrodites in Medieval Islamic Law," in *Women in Middle Eastern History*, ed. Nikki R. Keddie and Beth Baron (New Haven, CT: Yale University Press, 1991), 80.
29. Mohammed Mahdi Kariminia quoted in Megan K. Stack's "Changing Their Sex in Iran" *Los Angeles Times*, January 25, 2005, A1.
30. Robert Tait, "A Fatwa for Freedom," *The Guardian*, July 27, 2005. http://www.guardian.co.uk/g2/story/0,,1536658,00.html 01/01/2006.
31. See Åbd al-Waĥed Marsee, *al-Shuthooth al-Jinsy wa Jara'im al Qatl/Sexual Deviations and Homicides* (n.p: Dar al-Fikr al-Jamiåee, 1998). In addition Muntasir Munthhir's chapter "Mashahir Wa Jara'im Fi Dunya al-Suĥaq Wal Liwaṯ" (translates as "Famous People and Crimes in the World of Female and Male Homosexuals") recounts crimes committed by homosexuals in such a way as to suggest that this behaviour is typical of homosexuals (particularly men) and that the crimes committed are caused by the sexual orientation of the perpetrators.
32. See Amnesty International's *Breaking the Silence: Human Rights Violations Based on Sexual Orientation* (London: Amnesty International U.K., 1997) for a list of violent and oftentimes fatal crimes committed against homosexuals due to their sexual orientation.

33. Vasu Reddy "Perverts and Sodomites: Homophobia as Hate Speech in Africa," *Southern African Linguistics and Applied Language Studies* 20, no. 3 (2002): 165. Hereafter cited in text as "Reddy."
34. I agree with El-Rouayheb who notes that "Islamic religious scholars of the [Ottoman] period were committed to the precept that sodomy (*liwaṯ*) was one of the most abominable sins a man could commit. However, many of them clearly did not believe that falling in love with a boy or expressing his love in verse was therefore illicit." See Khaled El-Rouayheb's *Before Homosexuality in the Arab-Islamic World, 1500–1800* (Chicago: University of Chicago Press, 2005), 3. El-Rouayheb rightly limits this analysis to the period of his study which dates from 1500 to 1800 A.D. and deals with the Ottoman Empire, however there is ample evidence which supports that this is the general moral stance that Islam has often taken on male homosexual activity: i.e. it is the action of sodomy, rather than the feelings of admiration or desire for other men which is seen to be objectionable. It was precisely this doctrinal distinction which lead one anonymous twenty-first century essayist (and anonymous for a good reason) to note that the prophet himself may have been at least "queer". The essay entitled "Islamic Scholars Ignore Evidence that the Holy Prophet Muhammad (peace be upon him) was "Gay"!" appeared briefly on the radical website GayEgypt.com but had to be removed due to a number of serious death threats. At any rate, although the essay in itself offers some rather insubstantial evidence to support its weighty claim, it remains a curiosity as to why Paradise will be filled with young virgins as well as young men who would be at the disposal of the now deceased devout (male) Muslims for infinity (see *Quran*: al-Insan, 19–21). In addition why should repenting for committing the act of sodomy suffice, according to the Quran, to excuse the parties from punishment (see *Quran*: Nisa', 16)? Also see Jim Wafer's "Muhammad and Male Homosexuality" *in Islamic Homosexualities*, eds. Stephen O. Murray and Will Roscoe (New York: New York University Press, 1997), 87–96.
35. *Dangerous Living: Coming Out in the Developing World*, dir. John Scagliotti, First Run Features, 2005, DVD.
36. For example of this claim see Joseph Massad "Re-Orienting Desire: The Gay International and the Arab World," *Public Culture* 14, no. 2 (2002): 372.
37. Mubarak Dahir "Is Beheading Really the Punishment for Sodomy in Saudi Arabia?" *Sodomy Laws* (December 2002), http://www.sodomylaws.org/world/saudi_arabia/saudinews19.htm 22/08/2006.
38. See *Sifat Saĥib al-Thawq al-Saleem wa Masloob al-Thawq al-La'eem*. Hypertext to be found at the (Arabic) classical literature library (al-Maktaba al-Turaṭhiya), accessible at http://www.alwaraq.com or see bibliography for details of a printed edition. Subsequent references to alwaraq and the classical literature library will be abbreviated as MT. Jalal Adeen al-Suyuṯi (d.1505) was an orthodox Muslim scholar whose most serious works came in the form of ĥadiṭh transmission and explanation. E.M. Sartain demonstrates that al-Suyuṯi rejected the study of classical logic and "scholastic theology" on the strength that this was forbidden by God (32–33). Instead he adhered to strict observance of the Shariåt and the Sunna and was a strong advocate of early Islamic Mysticism (Tawasuf). R. Irwin asserts that "quite a number of erotica have been ascribed to him but the attributions seem doubtful and none of the pornographic books are listed in his autobiography" (746). See bibliography for complete publication details.
39. Abu Nasr al-Samaw'uli notes that a certain type of grinder may take a passive male for a lover by rubbing herself against his backside. See Abu Nasr al-Samaw'uli, *Kitab Nuzhat al-Asĥab fi Muåsharat al-Aĥbab*, ed. and comp.

from original manuscripts by Taher Ĥaddad (PhD. Diss., Fredrich Aleksander University, n.d), 13–17.

40. For more information on the "Mukhanaṭhun" see Everett K. Rowson's "The Effeminates of Early Medina," *Journal of the American Oriental Society* 111 (1991): 671–693. This article is by far the most authoritative on the subject. Rowson notes that: "according to Abu 'Ubayd (d. 224/838), the *mukhanathun* were so called on account of their languidness (*takasur* ...), while a languid woman was called *knunuth* .... Later lexicographers define the *Mukhanath* as a man who resembles or imitates a woman in the languidness of his limbs or the softness (*lin*) of his voice" (672–376). Also see Rowson's "The Categorization of Gender and Sexual Irregularity in Medieval Arabic Vice Lists" in *Body Guards: The Cultural Politics of Gender Ambiguity*, eds. Julia Epstein and Kristina Straub (New York: Routlegde, 1991), 50–79.
41. David Greenberg notes that it is "beliefs that homosexuality is evil, sick, or undesirable — and the corresponding efforts to punish, cure or prevent it – that make homosexuality deviant." See David Greenberg, *The Construction of Sexuality* (Chicago: Chicago University Press, 1988), 2. Hereafter cited in text as "Greenberg."
42. Edward Stein, *Forms of Desire* (New York: Routledge, 1992), 330. Hereafter cited in text as "Stein."
43. David Halperin, *How to Do the History of Homosexuality* (Chicago: Chicago University Press, 2002), 10. Hereafter cited in text as "Halperin, 2002."
44. For more on the intense rejection of essentialism see Diana Fuss, *Essentially Speaking Feminism, Nature and Difference* (New York: Routledge, 1989).
45. As David Halperin notes: "I set up a monograph series entitled Ideologies of Desire at Oxford University Press, established a Greek and Latin translation series called The New Classical Canon at Routledge, and co-founded (with Carolyn Dinshaw) *GLQ: A Journal of Lesbian and Gay Studies*." Halperin, 2002, 1.
46. David Halperin, "Lesbian Historiography Before the Name," *GLQ* 4, no. 4 (1998): 563.
47. For Sedgwick's critique see *The Epistemology of the Closet*, 45–47.
48. See John Hawley ed., *Postcolonial, Queer* (Albany: State of New York University Press 2001) and also his *Postcolonial and Queer Theories* (Westport, CT and London: Greenwood Press, 2001); Eithne Luibhéid and Lionel Cantú Jr. eds. *Queer Migrations* (Minneapolis: University of Minnesota Press, 2005); and Cindy Patton and Benigno Sánchez-Eppler eds. *Queer Diasporas* (Durham, NC and London: Duke University Press, 2000); Arnaldo Cruz-Malavé and Martin F. Manalansan IV, eds. *Queer Globalizations* (New York: New York University Press, 2002).
49. For examples of this poststructuralist tendency (which pervades most of the literature listed above) see Dennis Altman's "Rupture or Continuity?" in *Postcolonial, Queer* ed. John C. Hawley, 19-41; also see Terry Goldie's Introduction to *Ariel* 30, no. 2 (1999), 9–26. This issue is dedicated entirely to "Postcolonial and Queer Theory and Praxis."

2 CONSTRUCTING AND DECONSTRUCTING SEXUALITY: NEW PARADIGMS FOR GAY HISTORIOGRAPHY

1. Ĥafe<u>th</u> was and continues to be, long after his death, one of the most celebrated singers in the Arab world. His life was cut short by disease, but he was able to leave behind a considerable trail of leading roles in romantic films

and a number of highly regarded, orchestral songs. He has been nicknamed "the nightingale" (al-Åndaleeb) for the smooth and deep texture which characterizes his singing voice. The Beiruti publisher Dar al-Åwda has published his autobiographical writings entitled *Qusat Ĥayati: Åbd al-Ĥalim Ĥafeth̲* (*The Story of My Life*) and *Muthakarat Åbd al-Ĥalim Ĥafeth̲ Kama Sajaluha Bisawtuhu* (*The Diaries of Åbd al Ĥalim Ĥafeth̲ as Recorded in his Own Voice*). There has been several books written about "the nightingale" by writers such as Moĥamad Riffâtt al-Moĥamy, George Ibrahim Khoury, al-Sayed al-Shurbijie and Majid T̲rad. See bibliography for complete publication details.

2. For more information on homoeroticism in Andalusian love poetry see James T. Monroe's "The Striptease that was Blamed on Abu Bakr's Naughty Son" in *Homoeroticism in Classical Arabic Literature*, eds. Everett K. Rowson and J.W. Wright Jnr. (Columbia University Press, New York, 1997). It should be noted that Monroe argued for an asexualized interpretation of the poems he treated. That is, he saw that the poets' suggestions of homosexual behaviours and/or relations were only intended as figuratively transgressive, not literally. Also see James T. Monroe's *Hispano-Arabic Poetry: A Student Anthology* (Piscataway, NJ: Gorgias Press, 2004).

3. John Boswell, *Christianity, Social Tolerance, and Homosexuality: Gay People in Western Europe From the Beginning of the Christian Era to the Fourteenth Century* (Chicago: Chicago University Press, 1980). Hereafter cited in text as "Boswell, 1980."

4. John Boswell, (1994), *The Marriage of Likeness: Same-Sex Unions in Pre-Modern Europe* (London: Fontana Press, 1996).

5. Warren Johansson and William A. Percy, "Homosexuality," *Handbook of Medieval Sexuality* ed. Vern L. Bullough and James A. Brundage (New York: Garland Press, 1996), 155–189; Richard J. Hoffman "Vices, Gods, and Virtues: Cosmology as a Mediating Factor in Attitudes toward Male Homosexuality." *Journal of Homosexuality* 9, no. 2/3, (Winter 1983/Spring 1984): 27–44; John Lauritsen, "Culpa Ecclesiae: Boswell's Dilemma" in *Homosexuality, Intolerance and Christianity: A Critical Examination* (New York: Scholarship Committee, Gay Academic Union, 1981); Wayne R. Dynes, Christianity and the Politics of Sex in *Homosexuality, Intolerance and Christianity: A Critical Examination* (New York: Scholarship Committee, Gay Academic Union, 1981); also see Warren Johansson's article "Ex Parte Themis: The Historical Guilt of the Christian Church," in the same collection.

6. For example see Brent D. Shaw "A Groom of One's Own" New Republic (July 18, 1994): 33–41; or David Wright's "Homosexuals or Prostitutes? The Meaning of Arsenokoitai," *Vigiliae Christianae* 38 (1984): 125-53 as well as his "Do You Take this Man — Same Sex Unions in Premodern Europe," *National Review* 46, no 16 (1994): 59–60; also see William L. Petersen "On the Study of 'Homosexuality' in Patristic Sources," *Studia Patristica* 20 (1989): 283–288.

7. As is widely known, this emphasis on the world of ideas and concepts is triggered by Foucault's seminal *History of Sexuality*, Vol. 1, in which he argues that the invention of categories, i.e. categorization in itself is an act based on arbitrary decisions. As such it may be possible to create a "category" which pathologizes left-handedness or which groups individuals with a singular similar characteristic (this can be choice of sexual partner or facial freckles etc.), this, Foucault argues, creates in turn "a species of individual" in popular or "major" ideologies. Foucault, writing at and from the very limits of

ontological thinking, wanted to demonstrate the intersections of mind with the material world on which, he implies, it supervenes. It is precisely this notion: that the mental supervenes on the physical (creates it or interprets it as a concept in language or ideology) which I find myself most critical of and it is precisely this point which allows Foucault to initiate a historiography of sexuality which is invested in social constructions of sexuality, suggesting that sexuality per se, the binding characteristic itself, cannot be known or fathomed except *qua* constructions. This is a highly persuasive argument which provides a great deal of benefit to intellectual pursuits, but the point I find myself constantly asserting is that this stratagem for reality, through which our modes and systems of thought can come to be "understood" or known, is not *proven* and is certainly no more persuasive or logical than theories embedded in the assumption of the essential and universal constants.

8. Warren Johansson, "Ex Parte Themis: The Historical Guilt of the Christian Church," *Homosexuality, Intolerance and Christianity: A Critical Examination* (New York: Scholarship Committee, Gay Academic Union, 1981).
9. There are no references to Ĥassan al-Yemeni in English studies, and only very minor references to him are included in Arabic. As such, he is both a historically and literarily obscure figure, even though it appears that portions of this chapter are repeated in later works (such as al-Samaw'uli's, Tifashi's and Raghib Asfahani's) on the same subject. The modern edition of *Rashd al-Labeeb* does not come with a critical introduction, and the only source I have found for the author's date of death is in Haji Khalifa's reliable biographical encyclopedia *Kashif al-Thunoon* (c. 1651), MT. See page 454.
10. Aĥmad Bin Moĥamad Bin Åli al-Yemeni, *Rashd al-Labeeb Ila Muåsharat al-Ĥabib* (n.p: Thala Lil Tibaåt Wal Nashr, 2002), 125. Translation and emphasis mine. Hereafter cited in text as *Rashd*.
11. David Halperin, "Lesbian Historiography Before the Name," *GLQ* 4, no. 4 (1998): 561. Hereafter cited in text as "Halperin, 1998."
12. al-Bukhari, in *Sahih al-Bukhari*'s "Kitab al-Libas," ĥadiṭh no 5435, *Ĥadiṭh Encyclopedia* Ver. 2.1, Ĥarf, Cairo and Riyadh.
13. For more information refer to Elizabeth L. Kennedy and Madeline D. Davis, *Boots of Leather, Slippers of Gold* (New York: Penguin, 1993); also see Joan Nestle, "The Fem Question," in *Pleasure and Danger: Exploring Female Sexuality* ed. Carole S. Vance (London: Routledge & Kegan Paul Books, 1984), 232–241.
14. John Boswell "Revolutions, Universals and Sexual Categories," in *Hidden from History:Reclaiming the Gay and Lesbian Past*, ed. and intro. Martin Duberman, Martha Vicinus, and George Chauncey, Jr. (New York: Penguin, 1989), 26. Hereafter cited in text as "Boswell, 1989."
15. Bernadette J. Brooten, *Love Between Women: Early Christian Responses to Female Homosexuality* (Chicago: University of Chicago Press, 1996), 76. Hereafter cited in text as "Brooten."
16. In *Christianity, Social Tolerance, and Homosexuality* (Chicago: Chicago University Press, 1980). John Boswell writes: "During the 200 years from 1150 to 1350, homosexual behaviour appears to have changed, in the eyes of the public, from the personal preference of a prosperous minority, satirized and celebrated in popular verse, to a dangerous, antisocial and severely sinful aberration" 295.
17. For alas, we note that in his opening chapter on *suĥaq*, al-Yemeni declares that "He [i.e. Prophet Moĥamad] peace be upon him said: "women grinding each other is fornication."

18. As one critic of Boswell's points out: "consciously or unconsciously, the author, qua church apologist, rejects at the very beginning the idea that the source of intolerance may well lie within the very nature of Christianity itself" see Richard J. Hoffman "Vices, Gods, and Virtues: Cosmology as a Mediating Factor in Attitudes toward Male Homosexuality" *Journal of Homosexuality* 9, no. 2/3 (1983/1984): 28.
19. See Abu Nasr al-Samaw'uli, *Kitab Nuzhat al-Asĥab fi Muåsharat al-Aĥbab*, chapters 6–8, ed. & comp. Taher Ĥaddad (PhD. Diss., Fredrich Aleksander University, n.d.), 16.
20. There is considerable confusion over the identity of the King and the Queen in question, for although Yemeni tells us that Hind was the wife of *Nuåman al-Mu<u>th</u>hir* (presumably Nuåman al-Mu<u>th</u>hir the first, who reigned circa 400–418), *Tarikh al-<u>T</u>abari*, by al-<u>T</u>abari, tells us that Hind was the wife of *al-Mu<u>th</u>hir* the Third (c. 504–554). In the meantime, the modern scholar Jamal Jomåt seems to be of the opinion that Hind was *the daughter of*, not the wife of, the Lakhimid King Nuåman al-Mu<u>th</u>hir, and that she was in love with a woman named Zarqa' al-Yamama (*Nuzhat*, 32). If Joumåt is correct then our protagonist is Hind Bint al-Khuss, that T. Bauer describes as "a wise woman from pre-Islamic times, sometimes (probably erroneously) equated with the magician" Zarqa' al-Yamama" (287–288). Further complications arise since there are many namesakes among the kings as well. The first Nuåman al-Mu<u>th</u>hir reigns circa 400–418, he is then succeeded by a great grand son, al-Nuåman the Second (499–503), who is himself succeeded by Nuåman al-Mu<u>th</u>hir the Third (his great grandson) whose reign spans from 580–602 A.D. According to al-<u>T</u>abari, it was the son of Nuåman al-Mu<u>th</u>hir II, al-Mu<u>th</u>hir III, who married Hind. He reigned from 504–554 A.D. See *Tarikh al-<u>T</u>abari*, xxviii . Hind has also been said to be the mother of al-Mu<u>th</u>hir I (418–462) (*Tarikh al-Tabari*, 125). Therefore it is not clear which Queen Yemeni intended, who ruled during the Lakhimid Dynastic rule over Persia and the lands known as Hirrah. At any rate, one thing is certain; this story refers to a pre-Islamic period. Please see author surnames in the Bibliography for full publication details.
21. Bernadette Brooten "Lesbian Historiography Before the Name: A Response," GLQ 4, no 4 (1998): 624.
22. Martin Duberman, Martha Vicinus, and George Chauncey, Jr., eds. & intro. *Hidden from History: Reclaiming the Gay and Lesbian Past* (New York: Penguin, 1990), 6. Hereafter cited in text as "Duberman et al."
23. Lillian Faderman, *Surpassing the Love of Men: Romantic Friendship and Love Between Women from the Renaissance to the Present* (New York: Morrow, 1981).
24. This definition of homosexuality is, ironically, not dissimilar for David Halperin's remark that "Homosexuality refers to all same-sex sexual desire and behaviour, whether hierarchical or mutual, gender-polarized or ungendered, latent or actual, mental or physical." See David Halperin, *How To Do the History of Homosexuality* (Chicago: University of Chicago Press, 2002), 132.
25. Valerie Traub, *The Renaissance of Lesbianism in Early Modern England* (Cambridge: Cambridge University Press, 2002), 360. Hereafter cited in text as "*Traub*."
26. "Zoo Tempts Gay Penguins to Go Straight" *Annanova*. http://www.annanova.com/news/story/sm_1275591.html 01/23/2006.
27. *ABC News Online* "German Zoo Says Penguins Can Stay Gay" (February 15, 2005), http://www.abc.net.au/news/newsitems/200502/s1303702.htm 01/23/2006,

28. Alas, later in 2005 Central Park Zoo's gay penguin couple Roy and Silo separated. An internet news report revels in the latest development and notes that the gay couple separated when "Roy [ran off] with another penguin, Scrappy [female], who moved into the neighborhood and caught his attention. Scientists have no idea what caused the gay couplings, nor the flip-flop in Roy's sexual identity." Roy cannot be a bisexual penguin, nor can the homosexuality of other penguins be seen as anything potentially more complicated than being part of a "flip-flop" or having that ever elusive "cause." http://www.aversion.com/news/news_article.cfm?news_id=5104 09/27/2005.
29. Joan Roughgarden, *Evolution's Rainbow: Diversity, Gender, and Sexuality in Nature and People* (Berkeley: University of California Press, 2004). Hereafter cited in text as "Roughgarden."
30. We might strain to overlook Roughgarden's suggestion that one female "copies" the male role — as though the male role is a kind of original while the "mounting female" acts as a simulacrum, but we must remember that she is a scientist writing within an institution which is greatly conservative, a conservatism she ironically criticizes at length, even though she misses how this conservatism has affected her own modes of expression at times. Roughgarden writes: "scientists cover up homosexuality in animals .... [because] they are homophobic, refusing even to consider homosexuality, while others are embarrassed or fear they might be suspected of being gay themselves if they talk positively about homosexuality. Some may think that homosexuality is evolutionarily impossible and doubt their own eyes when they see homosexual behaviour. A final reason is an absence of consensus that homosexuality is theoretically important" (Roughgarden, 128).
31. Bruce Bagemihl, *Biological Exuberance: Animal Homosexuality and Natural Diversity* (New York: St Martin's Press, 1999), 123. Hereafter cited in text as "Bagemihl."
32. The illustrations include one Antelope's stimulation of another's genitals with its fore-legs, while the "active" partner is positioned behind the other. In the other instance, the female antelope mounts her sexual partner from the rear, providing her thigh for the purposes (presumably) of grinding or rubbing. The third illustration involves one antelope performing the equivalent of cunnilingus on its female partner (also approaching from the rear, this is called "inguinal nuzzling") and finally the fourth illustration in what is termed "pincers movement," this involves the genital stimulation with one partner's use of its fore-hoof as it stands at a perpendicular intersection with the body of its partner.
33. Eve K. Sedgwick "How to Bring your Kids up Gay," *The Children's Culture Reader* ed. Henry Jenkins (New York: New York University Press, 1998), 232–233.
34. Matthew DeCamp and Jeremy Sugarman, "Ethics in Behavioral Genetics Research," *Accountability in Research* 11 (2004): 28.
35. William Byne and Bruce Parsons, "Human Sexual Orientation. The Biologic Theories Reappraised," *Archives of General Psychiatry 50, no. 3 (1993): n.p.* Hereafter cited in text as "Byne & Parsons."
36. LeVay, *Sexual Brain*, xii, my emphasis. Hereafter cited in text as "Le Vay."
37. Laura Allen and Roger Gorski, "Sexual Orientation and the Size of the Anterior Commissure in the Human Brain," *Proceedings of the National Academy of Sciences of the United States of America 89, no 15, (1992):* 7199. Hereafter cited in text as "Allen & Gorski."

38. Windy M. Brown et al., "Differences in Finger Length Ratios Between Self-Identified 'Butch' and 'Femme' Lesbians," *Archives of Sexual Behaviour* 31, no. 1 (2002): 123. Here after cited in text as "Brown et al."
39. For more on this see M.L. Collaer and M. Hines "Human Behavioral Sex Differences: A Role for Gonadal Hormones During Early Development?" *Psychological Bulletin* 118 (1995): 55–107; also see Terrance Williams et al. "Finger-length ratios and sexual orientation," *Nature* 404, no. 6777 (2000): 455–456; Windy M. Brown et al. "Masculinized Finger Length Patterns in Human Males and Females with Congenital Adrenal Hyperplasia" *Hormones and Behaviour* 42, (2002): 380–386; Lynn S. Hall and Craig T. Love "Finger-Length Ratios in Female Monozygotic Twins Discordant for Sexual Orientation," *Archives of Sexual Behaviour* 31, no. 1 (2003): 63–71. For specifically lesbian-oriented studies which deal with the effects of prenatal and perinatal exposure to steroid hormones on female (homo)sexual orientations see Windy M. Brown et al. "Differences in Finger Length Ratios Between Self-Identified "Butch" and "Femme" Lesbians," *Archives of Sexual Behaviour* 31, no 1 (2002): 123–127; and Devendra Singh et al. "Lesbian Erotic Role Identification: Behavioral, Morphological, and Hormonal Correlates," *Journal of Personality and Social Psychology* 76, no. 6 (1999): 1035–1049.
40. Typically, men have a higher waist to hip ratio than women. This study confirmed that "butch" lesbians had a higher WHR ratio than "femme" lesbians, who did not differ in WHR from heterosexual women. The distribution or deposit of body fat is believed to be regulated by the amount of perinatal androgen exposure experienced by the fetus. Typically, male fetuses experience longer exposure to androgen, leading the deposit of fat to be more focused around the waist region.
41. Devendra Singh et al. "Lesbian Erotic Role Identification: Behavioral, Morphological, and Hormonal Correlates," *Journal of Personality and Social Psychology* 76, no. 6 (1999): n.p. Hereafter cited in text as "Singh et al."
42. Edward M. Miller, "Homosexuality, birth order, and evolution: Toward an equilibrium reproductive economics of homosexuality," *Archives of Sexual Behavior* 29, no. 1 (2000): n.p. Hereafter cited in text as "Miller."
43. For a scientific critique of this ideological assumption in science see S. Marc Breedlove et al. "The Orthodox View of Brain Sexual Differentiation," in *Brain, Behavior and Evolution* 54, no. 1 (1999): 8–14. For examples of these "perfect female" and "perfect male" templates see Jared Diamond's *Why is Sex Fun: The Evolution of Human Sexuality* (London: Weidenfeld & Nicolson, 1997); and *Battle of the Sexes*. Channel Four Studios, 1997. Both of these examples were written for the layman and both indicate, in their own way, the biological elements involved in originating patriarchal thought.
44. Irina Pollard, "Preconceptual Programming and Sexual Orientation: a Hypothesis," *Journal of Theoretical Biology* 179, (1996): 271.
45. n the same study, Miller compellingly argues that the family unit would benefit from genetically diversified siblings, firstly in that together they can be in possession of a variety of skills and intellects and secondly their interests (including pursuit of sexual partners) would not conflict. He notes that, for example, having several brothers in one family may mean that if all the brothers were heterosexual that they might end up in competition against each other for the affections and interest of the same target of women. Should one or two of these brothers become interested in other males who are also not interested in women, this will significantly reduce the competitiveness within a family. "If two brothers both bid for leadership, they may neutralize each other's efforts and neither achieve leadership. Having one brother with a personality suited to a bid for leadership and the other with a cooperative per-

sonality, inclined to support the first brother in his bid, is desirable. It would be in the parent's genetic interest to have a mechanism such that offspring differ in personality and follow different strategies" (n.p). Miller's study is one of several which focus on the relationship between sibling birth order and homosexuality in males. Other studies to this effect include James M. Cantor et al. "How Many Gay Men Owe Their Sexual Orientation to Fraternal Birth Order?" *Archives of Sexual Behaviour* 31, no. 1 (2002): 63–71; and Ray Blanchard's "Birth Order and Sibling Sex Ratio in Homosexual Versus Heterosexual Males and Females," *Annual Review of Sex Research* 8 (1997): 27–67.

3 AN OVERVIEW OF MEDIEVAL LITERATURE CONCERNING FEMALE HOMOSEXUALITY

1. Muṭhana Bin Zuhair cited in Samir Saåeedi, *Asil al-Åeela al-Årabiya Wa Anwå al Jawaz al-Qadeema åind al-Årab* (Beirut: Dar al Multaqa, 2000), 157–158.
2. al-Raghib al-Asfahani's birth and death dates are uncertain and very little biographical information about him has been collected. A brief but complex entry in the *Encyclopaedia of Islam* states that al-Zuhri is a reliable source for dating al-Asfahani's death to the early eleventh century. See E.K. Rowson, "al-Raghib al-Isfahani" in *Encyclopaedia of Islam*, Vol. 8, eds. C.E. Bosworth et al. (Leiden: E.J. Brill, 1983), 389. Asfahani's Muĥadarat *al-Udaba* is an encyclopedic work containing adab and mujun literature. *Muĥadarat* is a primarily literary work, however its veracity can be found in the scholar's attention to actual sayings, poems and stories in oral circulation that he combined and recorded under various chapter headings. The scholarly intent to correctly relate culturally accurate information lurks behind the playful and "trivial" spirit of the material related. Extrapolating from this fact Rowson notes "that mujun had by the fifth/eleventh century acquired a respectable niche in both poetry and prose literature is clear from its inclusion in literary encyclopedias by such authors as" al-Asfahani. E.K. Rowson "Mujun," in *Encyclopedia of Arabic Literature*, Vol. 2, eds. Julie Scott Meisami and Paul Starkey (London and New York: Routledge, 1998), 547. Most Arabic studies of Asfahani engage with his *Islamiyat* (those books he devoted to the study of the Quran and the Ĥadiṭh), for example, see entries for Ĥilmi and al-Åjmee in the bibliography. I first cited Jurjani's and Asfahani's texts in Rowson's "The Categorization of Gender and Sexual Irregularity in Medieval Arabic Vice Lists" in *Body Guards: The Cultural Politics of Gender Ambiguity*, eds. Julia Epstein and Kristina Straub New York: Routlegde, 1991. 50–79. (This work is hereafter cited as "Medieval Vice Lists"). I am also indebted to Rowson's scholarship on the Mukhanaṭh in his "Effeminates of Early Medina," *Journal of the American Oriental Society* 111, (1991): 671–693.
3. This is al-Qadi Abi Åbbas Aĥmad bin Moĥamad bin Aĥmad al-Jurjani al-Ṭhaqafi (d.1089) and *not* al-Qadi Åli ibn Åbd al-Åziz al-Jurjani (d. 1002) or Åbd al-Qahir al-Jurjani (d.1081). Although the latter two have received scholarly attention in English language studies, al-Ṭhaqafi remains a largely obscure figure. Ĥaq Shamsi and Moĥamad Shamsul eds. provides the only source known to me about al-Jurjani al-Ṭhaqafi, in their modern edition of *Min Kinayat al-Udaba' wa Isharat al-Bulagha* (Osmania: Da'iratu al-Måarif al-Åosmaniya, 1983).

4. al-Imam al-Adeeb al-Raghib al-Asfahani, *Muĥadarat al-Udaba Wa Muĥawarat al-Shuåra wa al-Bulagha* ed. & intro. Omar Tabaå, 2 vols., (Beirut: Dar al-Arqam Bin Abi Arqam, 1999). Hereafter cited in text as *Muĥadarat*.
5. About "mujun" Rowson writes that "behaviorally [mujun means] open and unabashed indulgence in prohibited pleasures, particularly the drinking of wine and, above all, sexual profligacy. Mujun literature describes and celebrates this hedonistic way of life, frequently employing explicit sexual vocabulary, and almost invariably with primarily humorous intent" (Rowson, "Mujun," 546). Also see Rowson's "Medieval Vice Lists."
6. E.K. Rowson "al-Raghib al-Isfahani," 390.
7. Stephen O. Murray demonstrates that "role versatility was recognized long ago" by using quotations from Tifashi's *Nuzhat al-Albab* (I do not share Murray's reluctance to see this text as authentically thirteenth century) and by upplementing this information with an image whose caption reads: "Male youth penetrating adult male, nineteenth century Turkey. Museum of Turkish and Islamic art, Istanbul." See Murray, "The Will not to Know," *Islamic Homosexualities*, eds. Stephen O. Murray and Will Roscoe (New York and London: New York University Press, 1997), 33. In addition, Everett K. Rowson's attention to the concept of reciprocity (*mubadala*) is more convincing in establishing that such trends in behaviour were known. See "Medieval Vice Lists," 66–67.
8. Craig A. Williams, *Roman Homosexuality: Ideologies of Masculinity in Classical Antiquity* (Oxford: Oxford University Press, 1999), 210–211.
9. This form of criticism is held throughout the exceptionally substantiated book *Islamic Homosexualities*; its editors write: the "thrust of [*Islamic Homosexualities*] is to challenge the dominant, Eurocentric model of gay/lesbian history and the implicit, occasionally explicit, assertion in many social constructionist accounts that contemporary homosexuality is somehow incomparable to any other pattern (or that there are no other patterns). The implication is that nothing at all preceded modern homosexuality or that whatever homosexual behavior occurred earlier was too disorganized, spontaneous and insignificant to compare with modern homosexuality" (5).
10. Bukhari, "al-Nikaĥ," 4834, *Ĥadiṭh Encyclopedia* Ver. 2.1, Ĥarf, Cairo and Riyadh.
11. Bukhari, "al-Maghazzi," 3980, *Ĥadiṭh Encyclopedia* Ver. 2.1, Ĥarf, Cairo and Riyadh.
12. For example we note in another ĥadiṭh in *Sahiĥ al-Bukhari* that one must "not stand behind a Mukhanaṭh [in prayer] unless absolutely necessary" "al-Athan," ĥadiṭh no. 654, *Ĥadiṭh Encyclopedia* Ver. 2.1, Ĥarf, Cairo and Riyadh.
13. Similarly to what Karma Lochrie has argued in regards to Medieval European discourses, where she suggests that there was no such thing as the "heteronormative" or the "heterosexual". See Karma Lochrie's Introduction to *Heterosyncracies: Female Sexuality When Normal Wasn't* (Minneapolis: University of Minnesota Press, 2005).
14. al-Qadi Abu al-Åbbas Aĥmad bin Moĥamad al-Jurjani al-Ṭhaqafi, *al-Muntakhab Min Kinayat al-Udaba wa Isharat al-Bulagha*, eds. Ĥaq Shamsi and Moĥamad Shamsul (Osmania: Da'iratu al-Måarif al-Åosmaniya, 1983. Hereafter cited in text as *al-Muntakhab*.
15. About Yaĥya Bin Akṭham C.E. Bosworth writes: "Yaĥya Bin Akṭham was appointed the Grand Judge [*Qadi al-Muslimeen*] of Baghdad after having been appointed judge in Basra by al-Hassan b. Sahl in 202/717–818. He soon became a member of al-Ma'mun's court circle as an advisor and

boon-companion, thus exemplifying a trend under this caliph to take legal scholars rather than administrators as political counselors. He accompanied al-Ma'mun to Syria and Egypt and on the campaign against Byzantium of 216/831. There were persistent accusations against him of pederasty, and on al-Ma'mun's death he fell from power. Re-appointed Grand Judge under al-Mutawakkil during the years 237–240/851–855, he again fell into disgrace, departed for Pilgrimage but died at al-Rabadha near Medina at an advanced age .... He is said to have been the author of various works of fiqh, none of which has survived." See C.E. Bosworth "Yahya Bin Aktham" in *Encyclopaedia of Islam*, Vol. 11, eds. C.E. Bosworth et al. (Leiden: E.J. Brill, 1983), 246. Bin Akṭham is rarely mentioned as a historical figure in his own right, however, scanty references to him exist wherever there is discussion of al-Ma'mun and al-Mutawakkil under whose caliphates he served.

16. The word in the original is *Qamar*, which is the word used to denote a person, usually a woman, of exceptional beauty. A woman can be a Qamar or like the Qamar (the moon), both of which mean she is in possession of exceptional beauty.
17. Very little biographical information on Abu Nasr al-Samaw'uli exists. There are no modern editions of Nuzhat al-Asĥab, however the dissertation work of Taher Ĥaddad and Fadi Mansour have, together, made the bulk of the manuscript available to committed researchers. Fadi Mansour dates al-Samaw'uli's birth back to 1125 A.D. in Baghdad, where he lived with his Maghribi Jewish parents for the first part of his life. Later he would travel and settle in Azerbaijan and live there until his death in 1180 A.D. It was not until 1163 that Samaw'uli converted to Islam. See al-Samaw'uli, *Kitab Nuzhat al-Asĥab fi Muåsharat al-Aĥbab*, chapters 1–5, ed. Fadi Mansour (PhD. Diss., Fredrich Aleksander University, n.d.), ix. I am indebted to Dr. Rebecca Beirne for volunteering to translate this and other crucial German texts.
18. al-Samaw'uli, Abu Nasr bin Yaĥya bin Åbbas al-Maghribi al-Isra'ili. *Kitab Nuzhat al-Asĥab fi Muåsharat al-Aĥbab*, chapters 6–8. ed. Taher Ĥaddad (PhD. Diss., Fredrich Aleksander University, n.d.) 3–29. Ĥaddad relied on Goth manuscript # 2045 and Berlin manuscript # 6381. This text is hereafter cited in text as *al-Asĥab*.
19. *Fatat* — an adolescent, not a child and not quite a woman.
20. Unlike some of the other medieval Arab scholars who appear in this study, Ibn Ĥazm (d. 1064) is no stranger to studies conducted about him in the English language. Born in Cordoba in 994, Ibn Ĥazm went on to become one of the most influential and versatile scholars of his time, writing as a jurist, a fiqh scholar, a historian and a belletrist. R. Arnaldez asserts that "As far as the [Quran] is concerned, Ibn Ĥazm's interpretation is always a literal one and a wide one .... [to Ĥadiṭh] he applies very severe standards and, in his juridical controversies, he rejects the majority of those on which his adversaries rely." See R Arnaldez, "Ibn Hazm," *Encyclopaedia of Islam*, vol. 3, eds. C.E. Bosworth et al (Leiden: E.J. Brill, 1983), 795. Ibn Ĥazm's *Zahirriya* (what Arnaldez refers to as "literalism") is apparent throughout his religious works and it informs his opinions regarding female homosexuality in his theological work *al-Muĥalla*, as we see below. Most basically, Ibn Ĥazm rejects *opinions* built around the interpretation of the Quran and asserts that extrapolation is not appropriate when it comes to creating the law. As such Ibn Ĥazm rejects laws, traditions and customs which cannot be corroborated clearly and distinctly by verses in the Quran. There are many modern editions of most of Ibn Ĥazm's works while English critical studies of Ibn *Ĥazm* include Anwar G. Chejne's *Ibn Ĥazm* (Chicago: Kazi Publications, 1982); Ghulam Hadar

Aasi's *Muslim Understanding of other Religions* (Islamabad: International Institute of Islamic thought and Research, 1999); and Muhammad Abu Leyla's *In Pursuit of Virtue* (London: Taha, 1990). Exemplary journal articles on Ibn Ĥazm include Israel Friedlaender's "The Heterodoxies of the Shiites in the Presentation of Ibn Ĥazm," *Journal of the American Oriental Society* 29 (1908): 1–183 and Josep Puig Montada's "Reason and Reasoning in Ibn Ĥazm of Cordova (d. 1064)" *Studia Islamica* 92 (2001): 165–185.

21. Ibn Ĥazm. *al-Muĥalla.* MT, 08/24/2006. Hereafter cited in text as *al-Muĥalla.*
22. Ĥassan al-Basri (d.728) was the imam of Basra, Baghdad. He collected and transmitted many aĥadiṭh and is considered to be a highly reliable source due to his temporal proximity to the time of the prophet (he was in the generation following — a tabiåee). al-Basri is often thought to be a progenitor of early Sufist thought and mysticism although this remains disputed. Ample studies on al-Basri, his life and works have been conducted in English, Arabic and German. Suleiman Ali Murad's *Early Islam between Myth and History* (Leiden and Boston: Brill, 2006) is the most recent book-length study on al-Basri's contributions to and impact on ĥadiṭh scholarship. The book also provides a biographical sketch of Basri's life and times.
23. In another example of "licensed" homosexuality, Jurjani relates that homosexual sodomy (i.e. liwa̱t) among some monks who followed the order of Mani was sanctioned (*al-Muntakhab*, 89). Mani dwelled in the third century A.D. and devised a religion based on the teachings of Christ, but he was not Christian. Several recent studies have been conducted on the person and history of Mani and his religious order but none of them discuss the point brought up passingly by Jurjani. See L.J.R. Ort's *Mani: A Religio-Historical Description of his Personality*; Patrick Leigh Fermor *Mani* and Geor Widengren's Mani *and Manichaeism.* See Bibliography for full publication details.
24. Abu Faraj al-Asfahani (d.972) was a renowned poet, anthologist and scholar who thrived under the Abbasid caliphate in Baghdad of the tenth century. His most famous work, *Kitab al-Aghani* is often used not only as a repository of Arab oral literature, lyrics and music but also as a historical resource for uncovering biographical information and sketching cultural histories. Very little scholarship on Asfahani has been conducted in English, though Arabic studies naturally abound. I have included a selection of Arabic studies on Asfahani in the bibliography; please see the following entries: al-Åmeer, Khalf-Allah and Maktabi.
25. al-Asfahani, Abu Faraj. *Kitab al-Aghani.* MT. 08/24/2006. Hereafter cited in text as *Aghani.*
26. Caliph al-Ma'mun was the seventh Abbasid caliph, who ruled contentiously from 813 to 833. He is particularly remembered for his patronage of the arts and for seeking the advisement and counsel of scholars (such as Yaĥya Bin Akṭham) and philosophers for his political affairs. al-Ma'mun also instigated a Miĥna — an inquisition of religious leaders and teachers to pressure them into accepting and hence disseminating the belief that the Quran was created — this would make the Quran an artifact and not necessarily an infallible one (for more on Miĥna see John A. Nawas "A Reexamination of Three Current Explanations for al-Ma'mun's Introduction of the Mihna," *International Journal of Middle East Studies* 26, no. 4 (1994): 615–629. al-Ma'mun deposed his brother al-Mu'taman and ignited a civil war which culminated in the capture and murder of his younger brother al-Amin (see J.S. Meisami, "Abbasids," *Encyclopedia of Arabic Literature,* Vol. 1, eds. Julie Scott Meisami and Paul Starkey (London: Routledge, 1998), 5. And although his politi-

cal behaviour leaves a lot to be desired, al-Ma'mun has been referred to as the face of humanism, no doubt due to his generous patronage of the arts, sciences and culture. On this subject Meisami asserts that al-Ma'mun's "patronage of scholarship was extensive, and he founded the Bayt al-Hikma ('House of Wisdom') in Baghdad as a centre for the translation of Greek works into Arabic" (Meisami, "Åbbasids," 6). Charles Michael Stanton asserts that the motivation behind the founding of Bayt al-Ĥikma and similar patronage endeavors was to promote and further knowledge of the notion of a created Quran (hence supporting his Miĥna). This concept being the product of a religio-philological school of thought later named the Muåtazili school. "He hoped to strengthen their [the Muåtazilis] ideas by increasing the availability of Arabic translations of Greek and Syrian manuscripts — particularly those that dealt with philosophy." Charles Michael Stanton, *Higher Learning in Islam* (Maryland: Rowan & Littlefield, 1990), 65. There is a large corpus of critical studies on al-Ma'mun in Arabic, for some examples please refer to the following entries in the Bibliography: Åbedeen; al-Åmraji; Radi and Amin. For more information in English see Michael Cooperson's *al-Ma'mun* (Oxford: OneWorld, 2005).

27. *Khuld* is both a dwelling and the word for "eternity," i.e. *khulud*.
28. Ibn Abi Ĥajala (d.1375) was a poet and anthologist who first studied in Damascus and later settled in Cairo where he became "the director of a Sufi community outside the walls of Cairo," L.A. Giffen, *Theory of Profane Love Among the Arabs* (New York: New York University Press, 1971), 39. Giffin also asserts that *Diwan al-Sababa* or "The Anthology of Ardent Love, is [Ibn Abi Hajala's] most famous work. The theme is chaste, profane love, and the aim is to please while edifying and informing" (Giffen, *Profane Love*, 39).
29. Ibn Abi Ĥajala, *Diwan al-Sababa*. MT, 08/25/2006. 87.
30. About al-Nuwayri H. Kilpatrick writes "Shihab Adeen Ahmad ibn 'Abd al-Wahhab al-Nuwayri was an encyclopedist. The son of a civil servant, al-Nuwayri was born in Upper Egypt but studied in Cairo, where he distinguished himself in jurisprudence and calligraphy." See H. Kilpatrick's "al-Nuwayri," *Encyclopedia of Arabic Literature*, Vol. 2, eds. Julie Scott Meisami and Paul Starkey (London: Routledge, 1998), 590.
31. The Quran makes two passing mentions of the people of Rus in Qaf: 12 and al-Furqan: 38. The people of Rus are used in conjunction with the example of the people of Ţhamood and the people of Lot, all of whom, tradition informs us, disobeyed the prophets sent to them by Allah and continued in their "immoral" and idol worshipping ways. It is not difficult to perceive in this light why for al-Nuwayri it seemed appropriate to associate such a group with the moral wrong-doings of various sexual perversions. The people of Rus are named after their first king and the river around which they lived; this area is now part of modern Saudi Arabia. A thriving and modern county by the same ancient name continues to exist today. A number of scholarly works have been dedicated to the history of Rus, this includes articles by al-Jaser; al-Åboudee; al-Qublan; and Åmer. Please see bibliography for full details.
32. al-Nuwayri. *Nihayat al-Arb Fi Funoon al-Adab*. MT. 1323.
33. I am again reminded of the possibility posited by Boswell which was heavily dismissed by his critics, where he sought to demonstrate that religious faith was not in conflict with "sexual variances" (to borrow Vern L. Bullough's term), perhaps intending to show that faith did not produce something akin to homophobia but rather that the prejudice was pre-existent (for more on this see Byrne Fone's *Homophobia: A History*). Percy and Johansen were quick to criticize this: "We cannot find a single Christian father,

Penitentialist, scholastic or canonist [etc.] ...who ever wrote even a neutral, much less a kind, word about sodomites" (158). At least as far as the early Islamic scholars were concerned something similar to tolerance, perhaps even a schizophrenia appears, where a pious theologian can find himself writing unabashedly and without the violent rhetoric we observe in other treatises on sexual deviations.

34. Although al-Mutqi al-Hindi is a well-known ĥadiṭh and fiqh scholar I was not able to find any significant biographical information on this author. Modern editions of *Kanz al-Åumal* are in circulation and the book is often cited by modern Muslim scholars.
35. al-Hindi. *Kanz al-Åumal.* MT, 08/24/2006. 675. Hereafter cited in text as *Åumal.*
36. Zahir Th̲at̲h̲a, a researcher and editor for alwaraq.com web site, which hosts the only available copy of Mashtoolee's *Salwat al-Aĥzan*, rightly distinguishes this book from Abu Bakr al-Khafaf's (d.1148) book by the same title, of which a modern edition survives and is edited by T̲ariq al-T̲ant̲awi (see Bibliography and pages 95–97 for discussion of *liwat̲*).
37. al-Mashtooly, Salwat al-Aĥzan Lil-Ijtinab ån Mujalasat al-Aĥdaṭh Wa al-Niswan. MT, 08/25/2006. 49. Hereafter cited in text as *Salwat.*
38. These aĥadiṭh appear in *Sunan Abu Dawud*, "al-Libas," 3574; and in *Sunan al-Tarmithee*, "al-Adab," 2708, both accessible through the *Ĥadiṭh Encyclopedia* Ver. 2.1, Ĥarf, Cairo and Riyadh.
39. al-Zuhri's claims are supported by his reputation for being a thorough scholar. As Duri writes: "Zuhri's method of verification is based on the *isnad* — or chain of transmission. His attitude is that of a sound traditionist of his period, where a report of a tabi' — the generation following the companions of the Prophet — is sometimes sufficient," see A.A. Duri's "al-Zuhri: A Study on the Beginnings of History Writing in Islam," *Bulletin of the School of Oriental and African Studies* 19, no. 1 (1957): 8; also see A. Rippin's "al-Zuhri, "Naskh al-Qur'an" and the problem of early "tafsir" texts," *Bulletin of the School of Oriental and African Studies* 47, no. 1 (1984): 22–43.
40. There are innumerable texts written as means of introducing the history and methodology of ĥadiṭh documentation and the means of measuring reliability and authenticity in English and Arabic. I recommend the recent translation of Ibn al-Salaĥ al-Shahrazuri's (d.1245) *Kitab Mårifat Anwå åilm al-Ĥadiṭh/An Introduction to the Science of Hadith*, trans. Eerick Dickinson (n.p: Ithaca, 2006); or, for a more recent outlook, which is also based on al-Shahrazuri's work, see Suhaib Hasan's *An Introduction to the Science of the Ĥadiṭh* ([Saudi Arabia]: Dar al-Salam, 1995).
41. Abu Dawud, "al-Ĥudood," 3869, *Sunan Abu Dawud*, *Ĥadiṭh Encyclopedia* Ver. 2.1, Ĥarf, Cairo and Riyadh.
42. al-Thahabi (d.1347) was a fiqh scholar who is better known for his voluminous work *Tarikh al-Islam* which is available in several annotated modern editions. His *al-Kaba'er* is also available in several edited modern editions including the most recent one edited by Åmar Aĥmad Åbd Allah and published by al-Fayĥaa' in 1999.
43. Abu Hureira (d. 677) is one of the most renowned early ĥadiṭh transmitters; he was a direct companion of the prophet, therefore his authority is not questioned. There are copious studies on Hureira's work and contributions to ĥadiṭh transmission written in Arabic. Although Abu Hureira may have transmitted the ĥadiṭh that Thahabi cites above, Saĥiĥ al-Bukhari authenticates only a milder version of this ĥadiṭh under a sub-section named "clothing" where the prophet damns effeminacy in men as well as masculinity in

women. Although this may very well be an indirect prohibition of (at least some) homosexual acts/identities/behaviours, it remains an inexplicit one, and it is interesting that only the mild ĥadiţh on the subject can be authenticated.

44. al-Thahabi. *al-Kaba'er.* MT, 08/25/2006.18–19.

4 A CLOSE READING OF AĤMAD IBN YUSUF TIFASHI'S NUZHAT AL-ALBAB: TOWARD RE-ENVISIONING THE ISLAMIC MIDDLE EAST

1. Michel Foucault, *The History of Sexuality*, vol. 1, trans. Robert Hurley (Harmondsworth: Penguin, 1984).
2. Some critics who have implied this theoretical assumption in their readings of homosexuality are Bruce Dunne, Mervat Hatem, E.J. Haeberle, Robert L.A. Clark, Karma Lochrie, James T. Monroe, Everett K. Rowson, J.W. Wright, David Halperin, Henry Abelove, Craig C. Williams, Joseph Massad, and David Greenberg.
3. Take for example the title of an anthology of essays on the subject of medieval female homosexuality: *Same Sex Love and Desire Among Women in the Middle Ages*, which obviates, quite meanderingly but meaningfully, the use of words such as 'homosexual', 'homoerotic' or 'lesbian'.
4. Stephen O. Murray and Will Roscoe, eds. *Islamic Homosexualities: Culture, History and Literature.* (New York: New York University Press, 1997). Murray and Roscoe's anthology of critical essays focuses almost entirely on male Islamic homosexualities, an imbalance that this book and subsequent research, hope to redress. Another anthology on the subject of Arabian homosexuality is J.W. Wright Jr. and Everett K. Rowson, eds. *Homoeroticism in Classical Arabic Literature* (New York: Columbia University Press, 1997). This collection deals exclusively with male homosexuality. The most recent and remarkable work on male homosexuality in the Middle East was conducted by Khaled El-Rouayheb in *Before Homosexuality in the Arab-Islamic World, 1500–1800* (Chicago: University of Chicago Press, 2005). From its title it is clear that El-Rouayheb favors constructionist views of sexuality such as those devised by Halperin and Abelove and argued by Joseph Massad. Although El-Rouayheb's work is thorough and intriguing, I do not support his argument that "homosexuality" is a modern term for which there was no Arabic equivalent, but I do not deal either with the time period he interrogates in his study nor with the subjects (i.e. male sexual deviations) he treats.
5. As'ad Abu Khalil, "A Note on the Study of Homosexuality in the Arab/Islamic Civilization," *Arab Studies Journal* 1/2 (1993): 33. Hereafter cited in text as "AbuKhalil."
6. Hassan Rifat discusses a similar point in regards to the importance of sexuality in Islam. He supports the argument against celibacy with the following Quranic verse: "and among his signs/is this, that he created/for you mates from among/Yourselves, that ye may/Dwell in tranquility with them, / And he has put love/And mercy between your (hearts)/Verily in that are signs/For those who reflect. (30:21)." See Hassan Rifat, "An Islamic Perspective," *Women, Religion and Sexuality: Studies on the Impact of Religious Teachings on Women*, ed. by Jeanne Becher, (Philadelphia: Trinity Press, 1991), 99.

7. Abdelwahab Bouhdiba, *Sexuality in Islam*, trans. Alan Sheridan (London: Routledge & Kegan Paul, 1985), 79–82. On page 82 Bouhdiba writes: "From the Christian point of view for example, it is unthinkable that the working of the flesh, a source of original sin, could find its place in the hereafter. The redemption of man was obtained at the price of renunciation of sensuality, whose mission is at most earthly. For Islam, on the other hand, there is something essential in Eros."
8. Peter Brown, *The Body and Society: Men, Women and Sexual Renunciation in Early Christianity* (New York: Columbia University Press, 1988).
9. Boswell writes: "Among medieval Christian Europeans divorce remained common, "lover relationships" were common, and concubinage quite common, even in widely Catholic societies like twelfth century Europe during the most thorough development of canon law regarding matrimony. Divorce and remarriage after the death of the spouse ... were officially prohibited by early theologians [but] both were still familiar in Christian Europe." See John Boswell's "The Development of Nuptial Offices," in *The Marriage of Likeness: Same-Sex Unions in Pre-Modern Europe* (London: Fontana Press, 1995), 172.
10. See Margaret McGlynn and Richard J. Moll's "Chaste Marriage in the Middle Ages: 'It Were to Hire a Great Merite,'" *Handbook of Medieval Sexuality*, eds. Vern L. Bullough and James A. Brundage (New York: Garland, 1996), 103–122.
11. A thorough presentation of this point of view is to be found in Fatna A. Sabbah's work *Woman in the Muslim Unconscious* (New York: Pergamon Press, 1984). Also see As'ad AbuKhalil, "Gender Boundaries and Sexual Categories in the Arab World," *Feminist Issues* 15, no. 1-2 (1997): 91–104.
12. Evidence of this is to be found in Murray and Roscoe's collection as well as Abu Khalil's brief but polemic essay on the subject.
13. See Alain Blottière's *L'Oasis Siwa* (Paris: Quai Volaire, 1992). Reference to this is also cited in the ficto-documentary *Tariq il- Ĥob*, dir. Remi Lange, 2001, DVD.
14. Haeberle is citing Abu Nasr al-Samaw'uli's *Nuzhat al-Asĥab*.
15. The recent advances in electronic research have made the task of research less time consuming and more productive, in the sense that electronic databases and search engines have given the researcher a form of panoptic surveillance of various literatures and texts. Therefore I cannot but commend the earlier generation of researchers for their efforts in a research environment yet unsupported by electronic research tools.
16. See Remke Kruk, "The Bold and the Beautiful: Women and 'Fitna' in the 'Sirat Dhat al-Himma': The Story of Nura." In *Women in the Medieval Islamic World.* Edited by Gavin R.G. Hambly. New York: Saint Martin Press, 1998, 99–116. Hereafter cited in text as "Kruk, 1998." Also see Kruk's other works: "Warrior Women in Arabic Popular Romance: Qannâsa bint Muzâhim and Other Valiant Ladies: Part One," *Journal of Arabic Literature* 24, no. 3 (1993): 213–230. Hereafter cited in text as "Kruk, 1993"; "Warrior Women, Part Two," *Journal of Arabic Literature* 25, no. 1 (1994): 16–33; and "Clipped Wings: Medieval Arabic adaptations of the Amazon myth," *Harvard Middle Eastern and Islamic Review* 1, no. 2 (1995): 132–154.
17. *Quta Åla Nar/Cat on Fire*, dir. Samir Seif, 1977, video cassette.
18. *al Mutåt wal Åzab*, dir. Niasi Mus̱tafa, c.1971 DVD.
19. *Queen Christina*, dir. Rouben Mamoulian, 1933, video cassette.
20. *Calamity Jane.* Directed by David Butler. 1953. The discussion of closeting and representation in American film is expounded upon in the book and subsequent

documentary based on the book, *The Celluloid Closet* (see Bibliography for full details). I also deal with cinematic closeting in chapter six of this work.

21. Jamal Jomåt, Introduction to *Nuzhat al-Albab Fima La Youjad Fi Kitab*, by al-Tifashi (London: Riad El Rayyes, 1992), 38–39.
22. Shehab Adeen Aĥmad Ibn Yusuf al-Tifashi , *Nuzhat al-Albab Fima La Yujad Fi Kitab*, ed. *Jamal Jomåt* (London, Riad El Rayyes, 1992). Subsequent references are indicated in text as *Nuzhat*.
23. Aĥmad Yusuf Ĥasan and Maĥmood Bayounie Khafajee, eds., *Nuzhat Azhar al-Afkar Fi Jawahir al-Aĥjar* (Cairo: al-Hay'a al-Masriyah al-Åma Lil Kitab: 1977). Hereafter cited in text as "Ĥasan & Khafajee."
24. Gavin R. G. Hambly, Introduction to In *Women in the Medieval Islamic World*, ed. R.G. Hambly (London: Macmillan Press, 1998), 12.
25. Peter Jackson, "Sultan Radiyya Bint Iltutmish," in *Women in the Medieval Islamic World*, ed. Gavin R.G. Hambly (New York: Saint Martin Press, 1998), 181–198.
26. Farhad Daftary, "Sayyida Hurra: The Isma'ili Sulayhid Queen of Yemen," in *Women in the Medieval Islamic World*, ed. Gavin R.G. Hambly (New York: St Martin Press, 1998), 118.
27. For patronage of Hajj and architecture see William C. Young's "Ka'ba, Gender, and the Rites of Pilgrimage," *Journal of Middle East Studies* 25 (1993): 285–300; and Marina Tolmacheva's "Female Piety and Patronage in the Medieval Hajj," in *Women in Medieval Islam*, ed. R.G. Hambly (London: Macmillan Press, 1998), 161–180.
28. See Johnathan Berkey, *The Transmission of Knowledge in Medieval Cairo*, (Princeton: Princeton University, 1992), 162–167; Michael Chamberlain, *Knowledge and Social Practice in Medieval Damascus, 1190–1350* (Cambridge: Cambridge University Press, 1994), 52–53 & 82.
29. The chapter "Fi Adab al Saĥq Wal Musaĥiqat" is divided into subsections. The first is a general introduction to the matter, relating news and anecdotes. The second section is entitled "In praise of grinding" and the final section entitled "The denunciation [or censure] of grinding."
30. The "illicit" here is more figurative rather than literal, but it demonstrates this lesbian community's positionality within the wider culture, which, politically speaking, is not very different from their medieval counterparts.
31. Jieming. "Guestbook for Grinding Tofu" *Grinding Tofu* 05/12/2000, http://www.geocities.com/Tokyo/Towers/4289/geobook.html 08/27/2006.
32. In *Kitab-al-Aghani*, Abu-Faraj al-Asfahani describes Bathal, the courtly entertainer discussed in chapter 3, who is evidently a woman-inclined-woman, in the following manner: "she had a pretty face and was *tharifa*" (*Aghani*, 1904).
33. Abu Nasr al-Samaw'uli writes (more than half a century before Tifashi) that "some [grinders] exceed others in intelligence and deception and in their nature there is much that resembles men ... The greatest number of [grinders] who possess [masculine] traits are among the witty women, and the writers and the Quranic readers and the scholars" (*al-Asĥab*, 16).
34. One of the main and most frequent reasons that (Arab) scholars provide for women turning to same gender sex is the fear of pregnancy or the heaviness of restriction against the mingling of the sexes in private quarters.
35. In his *al-Ĥayat al-Jinsiya åind al-Årab*, al-Munajjid attributes this idea to al-Kindi, page number unknown.
36. Fedwa Malti-Douglas, "Tribadism/Lesbianism and the Sexualized Body in Medieval Arabo-Islamic Narrative," in *Same Sex Love and Desire Among Women in the Middle Ages*, eds. Francesca Canadé Sautman and Pamela Sheingorn (New York: Palgrave, 2001), 133.

37. The title of the book roughly translates into "The promenade of hearts into what won't be found in any book."
38. Fatna A Sabbah, *Woman in the Muslim Unconscious* (New York: Pergamon Press, 1984), 39.
39. See Maĥmood, *al-Mutåt al-Maĥthoora* (Beirut: Riad El-Rayyes, 2000) 299–304 & 318–319.
40. In fact, citation of homosexual subjects is significantly reduced among Arab scholars as homosexuality became more explicitly outlawed in the Islamic tradition.
41. Examples of the observation of this distinction can be found in al-Yemeni's (d.845 A.D.) *Rashd al-Labeeb*, 124–125; al-Samaw'uli's *Nuzhat al-Ashab*, 16; and a citation from al-Jaĥeth (d.875) in Saåeedi's *Asl al'Åeela al-Årabiya*, 158.
42. The metaphor of the saffron stigmas is significant in that these are the female reproductive organs of the plant, which are grinded to produce saffron.
43. Aĥmad al-Yemeni attributes this verse (with slight but significant variations) to the poet Abu Nuwas, who was well known for his love of men, and occasionally, women. Abu Nuwas was hardly a religious figure and rather than moral or religious concern, his lack of comprehension and condemnation might stem from his own preference for the phallic. See *Rashd*, 132
44. Richard Burton, trans. "Tale of Kamar al-Zaman" in *The Arabian Nights*, vol. 3, ([Iran]: Printed by Burton Club, [c.1888]), 303.
45. This poem has been attributed to a man named Abu al-Åtiha, who was unrequitedly in love with a woman whom he later accused of grinding. See Asfahani's *al-Aghani*, 352 &1717.
46. Ibn Abi Ĥajala *Diwan al-Sababa*, MT, 87.
47. This is reminiscent of Derrida's concept of "double writing" which "must inevitably partition itself along two sides of a limit and continue (up to a certain point) to respect the rules of that which it deconstructs, of which it exposes the deconstructibility. Hence, it always makes the dual gesture, apparently contradictory, which consists in accepting, within certain limits — that is to say, in never entirely accepting — the givenness of a context, its closetedness and its stubbornness." See Jacque Derrida's Afterword to *Limited Inc* (Evanston, IL: Northwestern University Press), 152.
48. Ironically the same orthodox ideology which negates women's ability to master their sexuality also commissions them with *fitna* — that element of distinctly female licentiousness of which Eve is mortally (and famously) guilty.
49. The Arabic expression "to fly" means to be delighted by something.

5 CONTEMPORARY REPRESENTATIONS OF FEMALE HOMOSEXUALITY IN ARABIC LITERATURE AND CRITICISM

1. A shorter version of this chapter appears in *Entertext* 5, no. 3 (2006): 201–235.
2. Elham Mansour, *Ana Hiya Anti*, (Beirut: Riad El-Rayyes, 2000), 93–94. All translations are mine and are taken from a complete and yet unpublished manuscript of the novel, entitled *I Am You*. Present and subsequent in text page numbers refer to the Arabic edition cited above.
3. I refer to *I Am You* as the first "lesbian-centred" novel because the entire novel is dedicated particularly to the subject of female homosexuality. Other

Arab writers of fiction have depicted homoerotic relations among women but have treated sexual relationships between women as a side-effect of poor relations between men and women in patriarchal societies. Nawal Sadawi's novel *Janat Wa Iblis* (Beirut: Dar al-Adab, 1992) deals briefly and obscurely with the subject, particularly in the chapter entitled "al Ĥub al Aţhim" ("Sinful Love") 117–137; Ĥannan al Sheik's *Misk al Ghasal* (Beirut: Dar al-Adab, 1988) depicts a sexual relationship between two married women living with their husbands in an unnamed Arab Gulf country. The relationship between Suha and Nour spans the first two volumes of the novel and is intended to depict a critique of Arab societies' alienation of women from men. Two other novelists, Ghada al-Saman and Samia Kaĥluni have written about female homosexuality in their stories *al-Muwa'* and *Layinat al-Malamiss* (respectively). Unfortunately I have not yet been able to procure these texts and although I know of their existence I eagerly await the opportunity to locate these texts and to critique them. An impediment to the discovery of these texts has been their fade into obscurity. Although both Kaĥluni and Saman are prominent feminist Arab writers, significant reference to these stories and any bibliographical information has been impossible to find. I am indebted to Moody Biṯar for referring to these works in "Kira'a Fi Riwayat Elham Mansour 'Ana Hiya Anti,'" *Alhayat*, 14 Oct., 2000, 15.

4. With thanks to the Lesbian Herstory Archives' 1950s lesbian pulp fiction collection viewed in Brooklyn, New York, in November 2004. I am also indebted to M. McClarnon and Sally Bingham's Internet collection of *Lesbian Pulp Fiction*, http://scriptorium.lib.duke.edu/women/pulp.html 12/01/2005.
5. A list of Bannon's lesbian-positive novels can be viewed at http://www.annbannon.com/books.html (06.06.2005). Also see Diane Hamer's "'I Am a Woman:' Ann Bannon and the writing of Lesbian Identity in the 1950s," in *Lesbian and Gay Writing: An Anthology of Critical Essays*, ed. M. Lilly (Philadelphia: Temple University Press, 1990), 47–75.
6. Through oral communication with Dr Elham Mansour, August 2003.
7. Jihad, "Ĥiwar Må al-Doctora Elham Mansour Ĥawl Riwayatuha al-Jadida *Ana Hiya Anti*," *al-Ĥawadeth*, 8 September, 2000, 58. All translations from this text are mine. Hereafter cited in text as "Jihad."
8. The reception of *I Am You* reminds us of the critical appraisal of Radclyffe Hall's *Well of Loneliness* upon its publication in England in 1928. On this subject Lisa Walker writes that "[n]ot without cause, Hall's writing has been called dull, over-wrought, melodramatic, maudlin, old-fashioned and stilted, and *The Well* is often regarded as pioneering for its open representation of lesbianism rather than for its literary achievements." See Walker's *Looking Like What You Are: Sexual Style, Race, and Lesbian Identity* (New York and London: New York University Press, 2001), 22.
9. Pierre, Shalhoob, "Åtash Ila al-Mustaĥeel!" *A-Naqid*, 7–17 August, 2000, 33. All translations from this text are mine. Hereafter cited in text as "Shalhoob."
10. Qasim Nouri Åbood, "Ightiyal al-Riwaya," *A-Naqid*, 25 October, 2000, 32. All translations from this text are mine.
11. Yassin Rafåaya, "Khiyanat al-Fan," *A-Naqid*, 11-22 September, 2000, 31. All translations from this text are mine. Hereafter cited in text as "Rafåaya."
12. Ghusun, Amina "Elham Mansour Fi *Ana Hiya Anti*: Ma Jadwa Riwaya Talhath al Iftiål Wal-Fadiĥa?" *Alĥayat*, 18 August, 2000, 13. All translations from this text are mine.
13. Bitar, "Kira'a Fi Tiwayat Elham Mansour 'Ana Hiya Anti,'" *Alhayat*, 14 Oct., 2000, 15. Translations from this text are mine.

14. Maree Qasifi, "*Ana Hiya Anti* Li Elham Mansour," *An-Nahar*, 2 August, 2000, n.p. All translations from this text are mine.
15. Independent American Film *But I'm A Cheerleader*, dir. J. Babbit, Lions Gate Entertainment, 1999, comically presents this as the concept of the "root." In a camp for teenagers that converts homosexuals into ex-homosexuals by teaching them "true" gender distinctions and roles, the "patients" are invited to discover the event which *caused* their homosexuality. The film is satirical in its take as one young lady comments that she is gay because she was born in France, another that it was because her mother "got married in pants," while a young man claims that it was "varsity wrestling" that did it — all examples leading to the absurdity of the question rather than simply to the absurdity of the answers themselves.
16. Zeena Bizzie, [Interview with Elham Mansour] in *al-Kifah al-Årabi*, 18 Oct. 2000, 14. Translation mine. Hereafter cited in text as "Bizzie."
17. Mansour's experimentalism with language was noted and closely explored in Michelle Hartman's "Ilham Mansur's 'Ila Hiba: sira ula and Hiba fi rihlat al-jasad: sira thaniyya'" *Arabic and Middle Eastern Literatures* 2, no. 2 (1999): 141–158. Hartman notes Mansour's use of English and French words within her conversational Arabic narrative style and ponders the significance of this. In *Ana Hiya Anti* Mansour continues this technique of supplementing Arabic words with English or French terms. For example she uses the term "homosexualité" (*I Am You*, 93); the term "gay" appears several times (see *I Am You*, 170–173); "garçon manqué" (*I Am You*, 11); "la bisexualité" appears on page 173 and the peculiar use of the word "fuck" on page 166. Hartman asserts that Mansour uses European language terms in her writing because they do not have their equivalent in Arabic. In the case of *Ana Hiya Anti* however, with the exception of the term "gay" which is particularly western, the above terms all have their equivalent (homosexuality: Mithliya; garçon manqué: Ĥassan Sabi; bisexuality: Izdiwaj al-Jinsiya and fuck: Neek or Nayk). In this instance Mansour may be reflecting the reality of integrated Lebanese-Arabic speech, which cannot be divorced from the imperialist (through globalization) and colonial nations which have influenced and shaped this culture, particularly among the educated.
18. Mansour is referring to the notion of love as discussed by Aristophanes and penned by Plato in *The Symposium,* trans. W. Hamilton (Middlesex: Penguin, 1976), where, as the tale goes, humans were originally eight-limbed creatures who were bisected by Zeus (for their insubordination). Love, Aristophanes explains, is the urge of the one half to be re-united with its other half. Initially, Aristophanes explains, there were three sexes, not two: male, female and the hermaphrodite and thus those "men who are halves of a being of the common sex, which was called...hermaphrodite, are lovers of women, and most adulterers come from this class, as also do women who are mad about men...Women who are halves of a female whole direct their affections towards women and pay little attention to men; Lesbians [sic] belong to this category" (62). For Mansour, it is not the myth of the eight-limbed creatures which is of interest, but the notion that humans, in love, search for one who is *like* and *of* them, even though it appears as though humans are attracted by each other's differences.
19. This is not to say in the least that love itself manifests itself singularly, but here, the notion of love that is conjured up is particularly platonic and love comes to mean that particular emotion which is entirely divine, affirmative and beautiful, therefore good. See *The Symposium*, 45–46.

20. Ĥaneen Ghadar, "al-Jins Fi Riwayat Årabiya: al-Mar'a Miţhlama Yarghabuha al-Rajul," *al-Mulhaq*, 10 February, 2001, 7. All translations form this text are mine. Hereafter cited in text as "Ghadar."
21. George Ṯrad, Title unknown, *A-Naqid*, 19-21 August, 2000, 31. Translation mine.
22. Ĥassan Åbd Allah, "Ila Elham Mansour," *A-Naqid*, 11 December, 2000, 35. Translation mine.
23. Eve K. Sedgwick, *Epistemology of the Closet* (Berkeley: University of California, 1990), 77.
24. Nuray Sakalli and Ozanser Uğurlu, "The Effects of Social Contact with a Lesbian Person on the Attitude Change Toward Homosexuality in Turkey" *Journal of Homosexuality* 44, no. 1 (2002): 111.Hereafter cited in text as "Sakalli & Uğurlu."
25. Michelle A. Mazur and Tara M. Emmers-Sommer, "The Effect of Movie Portrayals on Audience Attitudes about Nontraditional Families and Sexual Orientation," *Journal of Homosexuality* 44, no. 1 (2002): 157. Hereafter cited in text as "Mazur & Emmers-Sommer."
26. See "Lebanon" *CIA World Fact Book*, http://www.cia.gov/cia/publications/factbook/geos/le.html 02/06/2005.
27. Who, incidentally, *requested the presence of* the Syrian army as assistance to quash the allied Lebanese and Palestinian militias. Eventually, the Syrian army was of no use but also failed to leave; Syrian presence in Lebanon continued well beyond the end of the civil war in 1990. The assassination of former Lebanese Prime Minister Rafiq Ĥariri in February 2005 gained the sympathies of the international community, and the United States was able to apply pressure on Syria to withdraw its troops in the following month of the same year.
28. Miriam Cooke, "Beirut Reborn: The Political Aesthetics of auto-destruction," *Yale Journal of Criticism* 15, no. 2 (2002): 403–404.
29. Evelyn Accad, *Sexuality and War* (New York: New York University Press, 1990), 19.
30. See Elham Mansour *Ĥina Kuntu Rajulan* (Beirut: Riad El Rayyes, 2002), 187, where the protagonist Hiba remarks: "In all the women's meetings I used to insist in particular that the woman needed to possess her body and all the things related to that possession. This possession would act as a first step on the road to her liberation. Of what I said they understood moral depravity. Maybe I meant that precisely. For this reason I used to always object and my opinion was rejected in regards to this matter. It was always perceived to be out of its time: 'It's time now for fighting and to run things that are related to the war and the nations and their liberation and ... all the big important banners, it's not time for pleasure and wasting time in discussing trivial and small things.' And this was the way I was always responded to whenever I proposed the matter."
31. Mansour's notion of the "feminine discourse" is a hybrid of feminist discourse and feminine ideals. She perceives that old-school feminist ideals (particularly in the Middle East) strive to emulate male-centred and patriarchal discourse. In her interview with Bizzie, Mansour asserts that "there is a lot of women's writing but most of it is written within a male-centred framework, even if it may appear revolutionary. Woman's discourse [i.e. feminist discourse] is not self-aware and it adopts the same values, senses and sensations that are adopted by the man. The woman has not established a sensory, intuitive or reactionary basis for her own personal speech, because she is suffering from some sort of denial of her herself .... All the feminist movements

in the world are attempting to turn women into men and to adopt the values held by men, thus jettisoning femininity altogether" (14). I suspect that by "world" Mansour is referring to the Arab world (and is deliberately overlooking the French Feminist School with which she is familiar). In her interview with Michel Mackey, Mansour reasserts this notion, that a feminist (and *feminine*) discourse, distinct from male (and masculine) discourse, is desperately in need of establishing. She remarks that "what I am striving towards is equality based on difference. Man and woman are different, but this does not eliminate the fact that they are entitled to equal rights .... Feminist movements have failed because they attempted to transform women into men." see Michel Mackey, "Elham Mansour Ån Riwayatooha al-Jadida 'Ana Hiya Anti,'" *al-Ĥiwar*, 28 October, 2000, n.p.

32. For more on this see Evelyn Accad's "Sexuality and Sexual Politics: Conflicts and Contradictions for Contemporary Women," in *Sexuality and War: Literary Masks of the Middle East*, 11–38.
33. This patriarchal taxonomy is discussed by Layal and Siham in the novel. Siham claims that when a man "possesses a woman's body...[he] strips her of her love for herself and takes her, consenting or forced, so that he could empty what is inside her of energy" (*I Am You*, 167). Even Meemee seems to register this inequality in this kind of heterosexual act (apologies for the generalization) when she states that men use "us as receptacles for receiving their filth" (*I Am You*, 143). Nawal Sadawi has discussed this concept in "al-Rajul Wal Sadeeya" ("Man and Sadism") in *al-Rajul Wal Jins* (Alexandria: al-Mustaqbal, 1990), 127–160.
34. The possibility of a butch-femme dyad forming a powerful feminist subject position has been discussed in texts such as Sue-Ellen Case's "Towards a Butch Femme Aesthetic," (1989) while writers such as Cherrie Moraga and Amber Hollibaugh in "What We're Rollin' around in Bed With: Sexual Silences in Feminism" (1984) and Joan Nestle's "The Fem Question" (1984) resignify lesbian femininity from passivity into an active subject position. See bibliography for full publication details.
35. Atel Adnan, "Growing up to be a Woman Writer in Lebanon," (1986) in *Opening the Gates: A Century of Arab Feminist Writing*, eds. M. Badran and Miriam Cooke (Bloomington: Indiana University Press, 1990), 7.
36. Conflation of transgenderism and homosexuality is highly common in societies where homosexuality is forbidden. This follows from the basic premise about sexuality and gender, that men are necessarily masculine and desire women, whilst women are feminine and necessarily desire men. Women who desire other women are therefore either seen as men or aspiring to be men.
37. See http://beirut.helem.net/index.htm (06/20/2005).
38. See http://www.helem.net/barra.zn (08/28/2006).
39. Ţhani al-Suwaydee, *Diesel* (Beirut: Dar al-Jadid, 1994). All subsequent references are marked in text as *Diesel*.
40. This may be an abstract reference to Nawal Sadawi's book *al-Untha Hiya al-Asl* (*Woman is the Origin*) in which Sadawi writes that: "recent studies in Embryology have disproved the theories that the fetus is initially born as a hermaphrodite and that the fetus, in all mammals, initially forms female genetalia." See Nawal Sadawi's *al-Unțha Hiya al-Asl* (Alexandria: al-Mustaqbal, 1990), 64. Translation mine. Sadawi's discussion of male homosexuality however, leaves a lot to be desired, given that she reads male homosexual desire as originating from a hatred for and rejection of women. See her argument in "al-Rajul Wal Shuthooth al-Jinsi" ("Man and Sexual Deviation [i.e.

homosexuality]" in *al-Rajul Wal Jins* (Alexandria: al-Mustaqbal, 1990), 198–209.

41. From an interview with Ṭhani al-Suwaydee on al-Jazeera's literary program *Awraq Ṭhaqafeeya* which aired on 05/04/2004. Reporter: Juwad al-Omree; tanslation mine. Transcripts available at http://www.aljazeera.net/NR/exeres/3DBF6CA7-557F-406C-BF1A-931970320540.htm 02/02/2005.
42. Tawfiq Taha, presenter of *Awraq Ṭhaqafeeya* referred to the novel as "Riwayat al-Saddem," which translates into "shock value novel."
43. Saad Elkhadem, Preface to *A Leader of Men* by Yusuf Idris (Fredericton [Canada]: York Press, 1988), 1.
44. Saad Elkhadem notes that "originally Yusuf Idris wanted to call this story "al-Kumun" (= latency), but for fear that it may be read "al-kammun" (=cumin), since, in Arabic, both words have the same spelling..." he settled for "Abu A-Rijal" See his Preface to *A Leader of Men*, 1. Idris's narrative, in my opinion, tends to portray a process of transformation, physical and mental (i.e. the aging and the shedding of the hair as symbol of loss of "true" masculinity) which culminates in "effeminate" homosexuality, which is read to be always anally receptive. It does not appear to be simply a process of realization, or "coming to terms," as Elkhadem notes, but a process of transformation brought on by the loss of physical power and strength (through the metaphor of aging).
45. Saad Elkhadem "Yusuf Idris and his Gay 'Leader of Men,'" *International Fiction Review* 17, no. 1 (1990): 27.
46. Ramzi Salti, "A Different Leader of Men," *World Literature Today* 75, no. 2 (2001): 246.
47. Yusuf Idris, *A Leader of Men*, trans. Saad Elkhadem (bilingual edition) (Fredericton [Canada]: York Press, 1988), 12.

6 SOME LIKE IT LUKE-WARM: A BRIEF HISTORY OF THE REPRESENTATION OF (HOMO)SEXUALITY IN EGYPTIAN FILM

1. Viola Shafik, *Arab Cinema: History and Cultural Identity* (Cairo: American University in Cairo Press, 1998), 34. Hereafter cited in text as "Shafik."
2. Vito Russo, *The Celluloid Closet: Homosexuality in the Movies* (New York: Harper & Row, 1987); and *The Celluloid Closet*, dir. Rob Epstein and Jeffrey Friedman, Columbia Tristar, 1996. Hereafter cited in text as "Russo."
3. For more on this see Harry M. Benshoff's Introduction to *Monsters in the Closet: Homosexuality and the Horror Film* (Manchester: Manchester University Press, 1997), 1–30.
4. I am indebted to the Internet Movie Database for filmographies of these directors and to an anonymously written note "issued by Channel Four television to accompany a season of Arab films shown on British TV in the late 1980s, see http:www.al-bab.com/media/cinema/film1.htm last accessed 06/07/2005, now discontinued.
5. Ibrahim al-Åris asserts that it was Musṯafa who inspired and launched Abu Seif's career, he also notes that the two collaborated in the 1990s on the film *al-Åzima*, while Ibrahim al-Fawal claims that it was Musṯafa who helped Chahine get his film *Nile Boy* screened at the Venice Film festival in 1951. Fawal also notes Saheen and Abu Seif's lifelong friendship which was consolidated in 1975 when Abu Seif directed the film *Death of the Water Bearer*

at the commission of Chahine's newly formed production company. See Ibrahim Fawal, *Youssef Chahine* (London: British Film Institute, 2001), 40 & 47.

6. *Some Like it Hot*, dir. Billy Wilder, MGM, 1959.
7. *Firqat Banat Wa Bass*, dir. Sherif Shåban, c2003.
8. This is forbidden in Islam, but this is a rule which is usually only observed by orthodox followers.
9. *The Adventures of Priscilla Queen of the Desert*, dir. & screenplay by Stephan Eliott, MGM, 1997.
10. *Sukkar Hanim*, dir. al-Sayed Bedeir, 1960.
11. Garay Menicucci, "Unlocking the Arab Celluloid Closet: Homosexuality in Egyptian Film," *Middle East Report* 206 (1998): n.p. http://www.merip.org/mer/mer206/egyfilm.htm 03/30/2003. Hereafter cited in text as "Menicucci."
12. *Muthakarat Muraheeqa*, dir. Inas Degheidi, 2001.
13. Degheidi's unconventional and audacious depiction of sexuality manages to offend critics time and time again. In 2002 Degheidi was taken to court by an "Alexandria lawyer who called for expelling the filmmaker from the [Cinematic Profession's] Syndicate." See "El-Degheidi Retained." *al-Ahram Weekly*. 607, 10–16 October, 2002. http://weekly.ahram.eg/2002/607/cu5.htm 06/07/2005. The court case was dismissed and Degheidi was never expelled from the Syndicate. In addition, it is alleged that Degheidi was on the assassination hit list of a group of independently operating Islamist militants. See Khaled Dawoud's "Trying Times for Islamists." *al-Ahram Weekly* 568, 10–16 January, 2002. http://weekly.ahram.org.eg/2002/568/eg6.htm 06/07/2005.
14. *Dentelle*, dir. Inas Degheidi, 1993, DVD.
15. See *The Celluloid Closet*, dir. Rob Epstein and Jeffrey Friedman, Columbia Tristar, 1996.
16. The Ministry of Information is responsible for the censorship of all forms of information and media, particularly focusing on news media. However, as the editors of the Egyptian English language publication *Middle East Times* point out "the censor is very arbitrary — sometimes these things go through, sometimes they don't." See http://www.metimes.com/censored 06/09/2005.
17. Emma Donoghue, *Passions Between Women: British Lesbian Culture 1668–1801* (London: Scarlet Press, 1993).
18. See Faderman, Lillian. *Surpassing the Love of Men* (New York: Morrow, 1981); also see Bibliography for entries under McGlenen, Mamet, and Rothblum.
19. Adrienne Rich, "Compulsory Heterosexuality and Lesbian Existence," *Signs* 5, no. 4 (1980): 631–660.
20. This issue was discussed by Degheidi when she appeared for an interview on the Lebanese Television station LBC for the celebrity-interview show *Li Man Yajru' Faqat*, hosted by Tony Khalifeh, which aired on 08/05/2005.
21. *Tariq il-Ĥob*, in "DVD extras: interviews," dir. Remi Lange, 2001, DVD.
22. *Ĥamam al Malatily*, dir. Salaĥ Abu Seif, 1973.
23. As Yussuf Idris's short story *A Leader of Men* depicts, bestiality was a form of sexual release resorted to in some rural communities in order to alleviate sexual frustration, which, like most instances of homosexual behaviour, was brought about due to restrictions on heterosexual conduct.
24. For example see al-Yemeni's chapter "Fi Tafdeel al-Ghulman åla al-Jawari al-Ĥussan," ("Preferring Male Slaves Over Female Slaves") in *Rashd*, 133–163; and Tifashi's chapter in *Nuzhat* "Fi Shuroot al-Lata Wal Mu'ajereen" ("Rules for Sodomy and Male Prostitution"), 139–146.

25. *Bint Ismaha Maĥmood*, dir. Niasi Mus̲tafa, 1975.
26. In her now seminal work *Gender Trouble* (New York: Routledge, 1990), Judith Butler argues against essentialist notions of gender, demonstrating that the demarcations of gender involve phenomenal illusions, which can be performed, impersonated, subverted.
27. *Lil Rijal Faqat̲*, dir. Maĥmood Zulfikar, 1965.
28. For a brief analysis of this film see Menicucci, "Arab Celluloid Closet," n.p.
29. al-*Mutåt wal Åzab*, dir. Niasi Mus̲tafa, c.1971
30. This is a rendition of Tennessee Williams's play *Cat on a Hot Tin Roof*, of which a film was made in 1958, starring Elizabeth Taylor and Paul Newman. See Bibliography for details. The Egyptian version of this story suggests that Amin (Brick in the English version) is exclusively homosexual and not at all interested in women, despite the illogical passionate kiss between Amin and his wife which seals the narrative. Throughout the film both portrayal of homosexuality and the protagonist is cast in a sympathetic light. At one point the protagonist's father reproaches him saying "if you knew you were .... then why did you marry? Why do you torture decent girls?" Similarly to *Ĥamam* the word "lut̲i" or its equivalent is never uttered, instead a brief pause or silence becomes the equivalent of Amin's unspeakable sexual orientation which is, ironically, being spoken about. It is interesting to note that in the Hollywood version, the homosexual subtext is diminished significantly.
31. Ostensibly to prevent her from contacting the police about a man who has been blackmailing her and her friends. What Nana does not know at this point is that Ådel is in conspiracy with Nana's blackmailer.
32. I would like to note Gore Vidal's comment regarding the making of films with homoerotic subtext within an environment laden with moral restriction and censorship: "You did learn how to write between the lines, or photograph between the lines, you do it with a look or something...." In *The Celluloid Closet*, dirs. Epstein and Friedman.
33. On this subject Benshoff writes: "while horror films and monster movies are frequently dismissed as children's fare or vacuous, meaningless escapism, the demonization (or "monsterizartion") of homosexuals in American society is a very serious life and death issue." *Monsters in the Closet*, 3.
34. *al-Suåood Ila al-Hawiya*, dir. Kamal Sheik, 1979.
35. *Genoun al-Shabab*, dir. Khalil Shawqi, 1980.
36. *Alexandria Why?* dir. Youssef Chahine, Fox Lorber Studios, 1979. DVD.
37. Examples of extremely minor homosexual subplots are evident in *The Nile and Its People* (1968), *Destiny* (1997), *Adieu Bonaparte* (1985), *Alexandria Why?* (1978), *Alexandria Again and Again* (1990) and *An Egyptian Story* (1982).
38. Ibrahim Fawal, *Youssef Chahine*, 1. I note the peculiar exception on page 126, but which suggests that Fawal was watching *Alexandria Why?* in rewind, or else there is another version of the film out there of which I am not aware. Avoiding the real intimacy between Tommy and Ådel, Fawal writes of their farewell scene: "It is an effective scene. Primarily because of Tommy's wholesomeness." Furthermore, in his discussion of *The Nile and its People* Fawal does not mention the homosexual subplot at all (see *Youssef Chahine*, 45).
39. All of Degheidi's films to date have centred on issues of sexuality, sexual freedom and the social inequality imparted upon the sexes. These include: *Kalam al-Layil* (2003) *Muthakarat Muraheeqa* (2001) *Dentelle* (1993) and *Asrar al Banat* (2001).

40. *Daughter of the Sun*, dir. Maryam Shahriar, Farabi Cinema Foundation, 2000, DVD.
41. *Steam: The Turkish Bath*, dir. Ferzan Ozpetek, Strand Releasing, 1998.
42. *His Secret Life*, dir Ferzan Ozpetek, Strand Releasing, 2002.
43. *Diary of a Male Whore*, dir. and screenplay Twafiq Abu Wael, Trabelsi, 2001.
44. *Shou Bañibak* (a.k.a. *Crazy of You*), dir. and screenplay by Akram Zåtari, Majnounak Distributors, 2001.
45. *I Exist*, dir. Peter Barbosa, Arab Film Distributors, 2003. This is a documentary about Gays and Lesbians of Middle Eastern origin living in the United States.

7 CONCLUSION: HOMOSEXUALS, THE PEOPLE OF LOT AND THE FUTURE OF ARABIC HOMOSEXUALITY

1. Portions of this chapter appear in "Queering the Middle East and the New Anti-Semitism," *Entertext* 3, no. 2 (2003): 52–71.
2. Yusuf Qardawi, "Islamic Stance on Homosexuality," ed. Nadia El-Awady, *Islam Online*: http://www.islamonline.net/english/Contemporary/2003/02/article01-1.shtml 08/25/2006. Hereafter cited in text as "Qardawi."El-Awady, the editor of this site, further reasons on behalf of Qardawi: "the matter of vocalizing one's sexual preference even in the case of normal marital relations is prohibited in Islam, let alone forming groups based on sexual preferences."
3. Need I remind the reader that although Bin Laden explicitly allied himself with the Palestinian cause, Arafat was quick to make his sympathy for the Americans very clear, when he donated blood to the World Trade Center victims? The reader should also be aware that the Palestinian war with the state of Israel has been predominantly one of secular (Christian and Muslim) civilian survival as opposed to the global Islamist militancy with which the *intifadas* are often associated.
4. Women in Black, http://www.womeninblack.net/mission.html 02/17/2006.
5. See Lars Krause's "The Queer Community in Israel: Findings of Research for the HBF April-June 2002," http://www.boell.de/downloads/gd/queer_report_israel.pdf, page 16, 02/17/2006. It is noteworthy that "according to Lior [of the pro-Zionist gay and lesbian organization Agudah] that gays and lesbians and trangenders share political attitudes from the left to the right to almost the same degree found in the general public (there was an inquiry being conducted a couple of years ago, discovering this amazing result)." This is countered by Jerusalem's first Pride Parade (of June 7, 2002) which was dubbed "A march against hatred" in which five thousand Israelis participated. 03/25/2003.
6. Hagai El-Ad, "Gay Israel: No Pride in Occupation," *The Gully* 02/21/2002 http://www.thegully.com/essays/israel/020220_gays_meet_sharon.html 02/17/2006.
7. "Queer "Settlers" Land on Berkeley Starbucks: Analogy to Israeli Colonists" *San Francisco Independent Media Center* 18/8/2002 http://sf.indymedia.org/news/2002/08/141433.php 02/17/2006.
8. Additionally, the Israeli feminist lesbian group, Claf, established a brief contact with Kayan — a Palestinian women's movement group — even though Claf had been traditionally a supporter of state Zionism. For more on this see

Yael Ben-Zvi, "Zionist Lesbianism and Transsexual Transgression: Two Representations of Queer Israel," *Middle East Report* 28, no. 1 (1998): 26–28 & 37. I more recent years there have been developments that may suggest a change of political motivation within Claf. For example, Claf's web site is now available in Arabic as well as Hebrew and English, which suggests that an Arab-Israeli audience as well as a non-Hebrew speaking Palestinian audience is targeted. Furthermore, Jerusalem's centre for LGBT citizens, the Jerusalem Open House, welcomes Palestinian and Arab-Israeli visitors and has recently begun acquiring material written in Arabic. The 2006 Jerusalem Pride Parade will focus on the theme of "Love without borders" (see World-Pride.net). For more information on this subject see Samar Ĥabib's "Queering the Middle East and the new Anti-Semitism" *Entertext* 3, no. 2 (2003): 52–71.

9. As'ad Abu-Khalil cited in *I Exist*, 2003.
10. This expression is borrowed from a section which appeared on www.gayegypt.com in 2003.
11. See "Mission of al-Fatiha," in *About al-Fatiha* http://www.al-fatiha.org/nav_about.htm 08/31/2006.
12. The Internet is a living organism which sheds and generates cells at a rate much more rapid than Internet archiving, therefore some of the web sites may not be in operation in the near future, while others are no longer with us but which were in operation in earlier years. Between the period of March 2003 and March 2006 I was able to observe the existence of the following Arab/Muslim queer sites: GayLebanon.info, www.worldpride.net (previously under a different URL), Helem.net, homanla.org, glas.org, glas.org/lazeeza.html, glas.org/ahbab, bintelnas.org, huriyahmag.com, imaan.org.uk, safraproject.org, gaymiddleeast.com, geocities.com/cafe_trans_arab, http://members.aol.com/marinerdc/connect/muslim.htm, well.com/user/queerjhd , geocities.com/khanaye_doost.
13. See http://gaymuslims.wordpress.com/ 06/28/2006.
14. See Arif Raza, "Muslim Canadian Congress Endorses Gay Marriage,"02/13/2005, Queer Day, http://www.queerday.com/2005/feb/13/muslim_canadian_congress_endorses_gay_marriage.html 08/31/2006.
15. Peter Tatchell, "Time to Talk to Gay People, Sir Iqbal," 05/04/2006, in *Guardian Unlimited*'s "Comment is Free," http://commentisfree.guardian.co.uk/peter_tatchell/2006/05/muslim_council_rejects_gay_dia.html 08/31/2006.
16. "Muslim Festival Bars Gays," *Sydney Star Observer*, January 26, 2006, 5.

Bibliography

BIBLIOGRAPHY OF PRIMARY SOURCES

Abu Dawud, "Sunan Abu Dawud." *Ĥadiṭh Encyclopedia* Ver. 2.1, Ĥarf, Cairo and Riyadh.

al-Asfahani, Abu Faraj. *Kitab al-Aghani*. Hypertext accessed at al-Maktaba al-Turaṭheeya (Classical Literature Library www.alwaraq.com). Reference to this electronic collection is henceforth marked as MT. Last accessed 08/24/2006.

al-Asfahani, al-Imam al-Adeeb al-Raghib. *Muĥadarat al-Udaba Wa Muĥawarat al-Shuåra wa al-Bulagha*. Edited and introduced by Omar Tabaå. 2 vols. Beirut: Dar al-Arqam Bin Abi Arqam, 1999. Vol. 1 pages: 5–12. Vol. 2 pages: 264–304.

al-Åskalani, Ĥajar. *Lisan al-Mizan*. MT, 08/24/2006.

———. *Lisan al-Mizan*. Beirut: Dar al-Basha'ir al-Islamiya, 2002.

Ĥajala, Ibn Abi. *Diwan al-Sababa*. MT, 08/25/2006.

———. *Diwan al-Sababa*. Beirut: Dar wa Maktabat al-Hilal, 1999.

al-Hindi. *Kanz al-Åumal*. MT, 08/24/2006.

al-Hindi. *Kanz al-Åumal fi Sunan al-Aqwal Wal Afåal*. Edited by Mahmood Omar al-Dimyati. Beirut: Dar al-Kutub al-Åilmiya, 1998.

Ibn Ĥazm. *al-Muĥalla*. MT, 08/24/2006.

Ibn Ĥazm. *al-Muĥalla*. Beirut: Dar al-Afaq al-Jadida wa Dar al-Jil, 1996.

Idris, Yusuf. *A Leader of Men*. Translated by Saad Elkhadem (bilingual edition). Fredericton, Canada: York Press, 1988.

al-Jaĥeth. "Mufakarat al-Jawari Wa al-Ghulman." *Rasa'il al-Jaĥeth*. Edited by Åbd al-Salam Moĥamad Harun. Cairo: Maktabat al-Khanji, n.d.

al-Jawzi (c. 1197), al-Ĥafith Åbd A-Ruhman Bin Åli Bin. *Kitab Aĥkam al Nisa'*. Beirut: al-Maktaba al-Åsriya, 2003.

al-Jurjani al-Ṭhaqafi, al-Qadi Abu al-Åbbas Aĥmad bin Moĥamad. *al-Muntakhab Min Kinayat al-Udaba wa Isharat al-Bulagha*. Edited by Ĥaq Shamsi and Moĥamad Shamsul. Osmania: Da'iratu al-Måarif al-Åosmaniya, 1983.

Khalifa, Haji. *Kashif al-Thunoon*. MT, 08/24/2006.

———. *Kashif al-Thonoon Ån Asami al-Kutub Wal Funoon*. Edited by Gustav Flugool. Beirut: Dar al-Sader lil Tibaåt Wal Nashr, 1999.

al-Khafaf, Abu Bakr. *Salwat al-Ahzan Lil-Ijtinab ån Mujalasat al-Aĥdaṭh Wa al-Niswan*. Edited by Tariq Tantawi. Cairo: Maktabat Ibn Sina, 1991.

al-Maqbani, Åli Bin Musa et al. *Sirat al-Amira That al-Himma*. 7 vols. Beirut: al-Maktaba al-Ṭhaqafiya, 1980.

Mansour, Elham. *Ĥina Kuntu Rajulan*. Beirut: Riad El Rayyes, 2002.

———. *Ana Hiya Anti/I Am You*. Beirut, Riad El-Rayyes, 2000.

al-Mashtooly. *Salwat al-Aĥzan Lil-Ijtinab ån Mujalasat al-Aĥdaţh Wa al-Niswan.* MT.
al-Nafzawi, al-Sheik. al-Rawd al-Åttir fi Nuzhat al-Khatir. Edited by Jamal Jomåt. London: Riad El Rayess, 1993.
al-Nuwayri. *Nihayat al-Arb Fi Funoon al-Adab.* MT.
———. *Nihayat al-Arb Fi Funoon al-Adab.* Edited by Mufeed Qamiĥa et al. Cairo: Dar al-Kutub al Åilmia, 2004.
al-Quran al-Kareem. n.p: al-Matbåt al-Masriyah Wa Maktabatuha, n.d.
The Holy Quran. Translated by N.J. Dawood. Middlesex: Penguin, 1970.
al-Samaw'uli, Abu Nasr bin Yaĥya bin Åbbas al-Maghribi al-Israili. *Kitab Nuzhat al-Asĥab fi Muåsharat al-Aĥbab.* Chapters 6–8. Edited and compiled from original manuscripts by Taher Ĥaddad. PhD. Diss., Fredrich Aleksander University, n.d. 3–29.
———. *Kitab Nuzhat al-Asĥab fi Muåsharat al-Aĥbab.* Chapters 1–5. Edited and compiled from original manuscripts by Fadi Mansour. PhD. Diss., Fredrich Aleksander University, n.d. 1–17.
al-Suwaydee, Ţhani. *Diesel.* Beirut: Dar al-Jadid, 1994.
al-Suyuţi. *Sifat Saĥib al-Thawq al-Saleem wa Masloob al-Thawq al-la'eem.* MT.
———. *Kitab Fi Sifat Saĥib al-Thawq al-Saleem wa Masloob al-Thawq al-la'eem.* n.p.: Dar Ibn Ĥazm, 1994.
al-Tajee, Muĥamad Bin Aĥmad. *Tuĥfat al-Åroos Wa Nuzhat al-Nufus.* Beirut: Dar al-Jeel, n.d.
al-Tarmithee, "Sunan al-Tarmithee."*Ĥadiţh Encyclopedia* Ver. 2.1, Ĥarf, Cairo and Riyadh.
al-Thahabi. *al-Kaba'er.* MT.
———. *al-Kaba'er.* Edited by Åmar Aĥmad Åbd Allah. Beirut: Dar al-Fayĥaa', 1999.
al-Tifashi. Shehab Adeen Aĥmad Ibn Yusuf. *Nuzhat al-Albab Fima La Yujad Fi Kitab.* Edited by *Jamal Jomåt.* London, Riad El Rayyes, 1992.
———. *Kitab Azhar al-Afkar Fi Jawaheer al-Aĥjar.* Edited and introduced by Ĥasan, Moĥamad Yusuf and Maĥmood Basyooni Khafaji. Cairo: al Hay'a al-Masriya al-Åma Lil-Kitab, 1977.
———. *Awsaf al-Nisa'.* Edited by Hasam Huseyin Aĥmad. Damascus: Dar al-Kitab al-Årabi, n.d.
al-Yemeni, Aĥmad Bin Moĥamad Bin Åli. *Rashd al-Labeeb Ila Muåsharat al-Ĥabib.* n.c: Thala Lil Tibaåt Wal Nashr, 2002.

BIBLIOGRAPHY OF SECONDARY SOURCES

Aasi, Ghulam Hadar. *Muslim Understanding of other Religions.* Islamabad: International Institute of Islamic Thought and Research, 1999.
Åbd Allah, Ĥassan. "Ila Elham Mansour." *A-Naqid*, 11 December, 2000, 35.
Åbedeen, Sami. *al-Itijahat al-Adabeeya fi Qasr al-Ma'mun.* Beirut: Dar al-Åulum al-Adabiya, 1992.
Åbood, Qasim Nouri. "Ightiyal al-Riwaya." *A-Naqid*, 25 October, 2000, 32.
al-Åboudee, Moĥamad Bin Naser. "Mawadiå Tarikhiya fi Bilad al-Qaseem: al-Rus wa al-Rasees." *al-Årab: Majala Shahriya Jamiåt* 14, no. 1 & 2 (1979): 5–29.
AbuKhalil, As'ad. "A Note on the Study of Homosexuality in the Arab/Islamic Civilization." *Arab Studies Journal* 1/2 (Fall 1993): 32–34.
———. "Gender Boundaries and Sexual Categories in the Arab World." *Feminist Issues* 15/1-2 (1997): 91–104.
Abu Leyla, Muhammad. *In Pursuit of Virtue: The Moral Theology and Psychology of Ibn Hazm al-Andalusi.* London: Taha, 1990.

Abu Nuwas. *The Forbidden Texts*. Edited by Jamal Jomåt. London: Riad El-Rayyes, 1994.
Accad, Evelyn. *Sexuality and War: Literary Masks of the Middle East*. New York: New York University Press, 1990.
———. "Sexuality and Sexual Politics: Conflicts and Contradictions for Contemporary Women in the Middle East." In *Third World Women and the Politics of Feminism*. Edited by Chandra Talpade Mohanty and Lourdes Torres, 237–250. Bloomington: Indiana University Press, 1991.
Adnan, Atel. "Growing up to be a Woman Writer in Lebanon (1986)." In *Opening the Gates: A Century of Arab Feminist Writing*. Edited by M. Badran and Miriam Cooke. Bloomington: Indiana University Press, 1990, 3–20.
Ådnani, Khatib. *al-Zina Wal-Shuthooth Fi A-Tarikh al-Årabi*. Beirut: al-Intishar al-Årabi, 1999.
al-Åjmee, Abu Yazbd. "al-Raghib al-Asfahani wa Kitabahu al-Thareeåt ila Maålim al-Shariåt." *al-Faisal: Majala Thaqafiya Shahriya* 20, no. 238 (1996): 42–47.
Aldrich, Robert. *Colonialism and Homosexuality*. London: Routledge, 2003.
Allen, Laura and Roger Gorski. "Sexual orientation and the size of the anterior commissure in the human brain." *Proceedings of the National Academy of Sciences of the United States of America* 89, no. 15 (1992): 7199–7202
Altman, Dennis. "Rupture or Continuity?" In *Postcolonial, Queer*. Edited by John C. Hawley, 19–41. Albany: State of New York University Press 2001.
Åly, Waleed. "An Evolution, not Revolution in Iran." *Sydney Morning Herald*, 17 August 2004, 11.
Åmer, Souåd. "al-Rus." *al-Majala al-Årabiya: Shahriya, Ţhaqafiya* 29, no 330 (2004): 65.
Amin, Aĥmad. *al-Ma'mun Adabeeyan*. Cairo: Maktabat al-Såada, 1990.
Amnesty International, *Breaking the Silence: Human Rights Violations Based on Sexual Orientation*. London: Amnesty International U.K., 1997.
al-Åmir, Ali. "Må Abu Faraj al-Asfahani" *al-Årab: Majalah Shahriya* 4, no. 1 (1969): 64–76.
al-Åmraji, Ahmad Shawqi Ibrahim. *al-Muåtazalla Fi Baghdad Wa Atharuhum Fi al-Ĥayat al-Fikriya Wal Siyasiya*. Cairo: Maktabat Madbulee, 2000.
Armbrust, Walter. "Transgresssing Patriarchy: Sex and Marriage in Egyptian Film" *Middle East Report* (Spring 1998): 29–31.
Åris, Ibrahim. "The Legacy of Salah Abu Seif, Master of Realism in Egyptian Cinema." *al-Jadid* 3, no. 15 (1997): n.p., http://www.aljadid.com/film/0315aris.html 08/30/2006.
Arnldez, R. "Ibn Hazm." *Encyclopaedia of Islam*. vol. 3. Edited by C.E. Bosworth et al., 790–799. Leiden: E.J. Brill, 1983.
Awraq Ţhaqafeeya. "Interview with Ţhani al-Suwaydee." al-Jazeera, 05/04/2004. Reporter: Juwad al-Omree. Transcripts at http://www.aljazeera.net/NR/exeres/3DBF6CA7-557F-406C-BF1A-931970320540.htm 02/02/2005.
Baålbaki, Roĥi. *al – Mawrid: A Modern Arabic – English Dictionary*. Beirut: Dar al-Åilm Lil Malayeen, 2001.
Badawi, Aĥmad Aĥmad. *Al Qadi al-Jurjani*. Cairo: Dar al-Måarif, 1964.
Badran, Margot and Miriam Cooke, eds. *Opening the Gates: a Century of Arab Feminist Writing*. Bloomington, Indiana University Press, 1990.
al-Baghdadi, Ali. *Les fleurs éclatantes dans les baisers et l'accolement*. Translated by René Khawam. Paris: Phébus, 1989.
Bailey, J. Michael et al. "Heritable Factors Influence Sexual Orientation in Women." *General Psychiatry* 50, no. 3 (March 1993): 217–223.
Bannon, Anne. *Books and Publications*, http://www.annbannon.com/books.html 08/25/2006.

Battle of the Sexes. Channel Four Studios, 1997.

Bennett, Judith M. (1998) "'Lesbian-like' and the Social History of Medieval Lesbianism." Unpublished article cited at the Lesbian Herstory Archives, New York, November 2004.

Benshoff, Harry M. *Monsters in the Closet: Homosexuality and the Horror Film*. Manchester: Manchester University Press, 1997.

Ben-Zvi, Yael "Zionist Lesbianism and Transexual Transgression: Two Representations of Queer Israel." *Middle East Report* 28, no. 1 (1998): 26–28 & 37.

Berkey, Johnathan. *The Transmission of Knowledge in Medieval Cairo: A Social History of Islamic Education*. Princeton, NJ: Princeton University Press, 1992.

Bitar, Moody. "Kira'a Fi Riwayat Elham Mansour 'Ana Hiya Anti.'" *Alhayat*, 14 October 2000, 15.

Bizzie, Zeena. [Interview with Elham Mansour] in *al-Kifah al-Årabi*, 18 Oct. 2000, n.p.

Blanchard, Ray. "Birth Order and Sibling Sex Ratio in Homosexual Versus Heterosexual Males and Females." *Annual Review of Sex Research* 8 (1997): 27–67.

Blottiere, Alain. *L'Oasis Siwa*. Paris: Quai Voltaire, 1992.

Boswell, John. *Christianity, Social Tolerance, and Homosexuality: Gay People in Westerm Europe From the Beginning of the Christian Era to the Fourteenth Century*. Chicago: Chicago University Press, 1980.

———. (1994) *The Marriage of Likeness: Same-Sex Unions in Pre-Modern Europe*. London: Fontana Press, 1995.

———. *Rediscovering Gay History*. London: Gay Christian Movement, 1985.

———. *The Royal Treasure: Muslim Communities Under the Crown of Aragon in the Fourteenth Century*. London: Yale University Press, 1977.

———. "Revolutions, Universals and Sexual Categories." *Hidden from History: Reclaiming the Gay and Lesbian Past*. Edited and introduced by Martin Duberman, Martha Vicinus, and George Chauncey, Jr. New York: Penguin, 1989.

Bosworth, Clifford Edmund. *The Medieval Islamic Underworld*. Leiden: E. J. Brill, 1976.

Bouhdiba, Abdelwahab. *Sexuality in Islam*. Translated by Alan Sheridan. London: Routledge & Kegan Paul, 1985.

Breedlove, S Marc, Bradley M. Cooke and Cythia L. Jordan. "The Orthodox View of Brain Sexual Differentiation." *Brain, Behaviour and Evolution* 54, no. 1 (1999): 8–14.

Brooten, Bernadette J. *Love Between Women: Early Christian Responses to Female Homosexuality*. Chicago: University of Chicago Press, 1996.

———. "Lesbian Historiography Before the Name: A Response." *GLQ* 4, no. 4 (1998): 606–630.

Brown, Peter. *The Body and Society: Men, Women and Sexual Renunciation in Early Christianity*. New York: Columbia University Press, 1988.

Brown, Windy M. et al. "Differences in Finger Length Ratios Between Self-Identified 'Butch' and 'Femme' Lesbians." *Archives of Sexual Behaviour* 31, no. 1 (2002): 123–127.

———. "Masculinized Finger Length Patterns in Human Males and Females with Congenital Adrenal Hyperplasia." *Hormones and Behaviour* 42, (2002): 380–386

Burton, Richard, trans. "Tale of Kamar al-Zaman" in *The Arabian Nights*. Vol. 3, 212–348. Iran: Burton Club, c.1888.

Butler, Judith. *Gender Trouble*. New York and London: Routledge, 1990.

Bynen William and Bruce Parsons. "Human Sexual Orientation: The Biologic Theories Reappraised." *Archives of General Psychiatry* 50, no. 3 (1993): 228–239.

Cantor, James M. et al. "How Many Gay Men Owe Their Sexual Orientation to Fraternal Birth Order?" *Archives of Sexual Behaviour* 31, no. 1 (2002): 63–71.

Case, Sue Ellen. "Towards a Butch Femme Aesthetic" *Journal for Theoretical Studies in Media and Culture* 11, no.1 (1988–1989): 55–73.

Castelli, Elizabeth A. et al. "Lesbian Historiography Before the Name?" *Gay and Lesbian Quarterly* 4, no. 4 (1998): 557–630.

Chamberlain, Michael. *Knowledge and Social Practice in Medieval Damascus, 1190–1350*. Cambridge: Cambridge University Press, 1994.

Chejne, Anwar G. *Ibn Ĥazm*. Chicago: Kazi Publications, 1982.

Collaer, M.L. and M. Hines. "Human Behaviorual Sex Differences: A Role for Gonadal Hormones During Early Development?" *Psychological Bulletin* 118, (1995): 55–107.

Cooke, Miriam. "Beirut Reborn: The Political Aesthetics of Auto-destruction." *Yale Journal of Criticism* 15, no. 2 (2002): 393–424.

Cooperson, Michael. *al-Ma'mun*. Oxford: OneWorld, 2005.

Cruz-Malavé, Arnaldo and Martin F. Manalansan IV, eds. *Queer Globalizations: Citizenship and the Afterlife of Colonialism*. New York: New York University Press, 2002.

Daftary, Farhad. "Sayyida Hurra: The Isma'ili Sulayhid Queen of Yemen." In *Women in the Medieval Islamic World*. Edited by Gavin R.G. Hambly, 117–130. New York: St. Martin Press, 1998.

Dawoud, Khaled. "Trying Times for Islamists." *al-Ahram Weekly* 568, 10–16 January, 2002. http://weekly.ahram.org.eg/2002/568/eg6.htm 06/07/2005.

DeCamp, Matthew and Jeremy Sugarman. "Ethics in Behavioral Genetics Research." *Accountability in Research* 11 (2004): 27–48.

"El-Degheidi Retained." *al-Ahram Weekly* 607, 10–16 October, 2002, http://weekly.ahram.eg/2002/607/cu5.htm 06/07/2005.

Derrida, Jacque Afterword to *Limited Inc*. Evanston, IL: Northwestern University Press, 152.

Diamond, Jared. *Why is Sex Fun? The Evolution of Human Sexuality*. London: Weidenfeld & Nicolson, 1997.

Donoghue, Emma. *Passions Between Women: British Lesbian Culture 1668–1801*. London: Scarlet Press, 1993.

Doward, Jamie. "Muslims Are Accused of Gay U-Turn" *The Observer*, April 23, 2006, http://observer.guardian.co.uk/uk_news/story/0,,1759313,00.html 08/23/2006.

Duberman, Martin, Martha Vicinus, and George Chauncey, Jr., eds. *Hidden from History: Reclaiming the Gay and Lesbian Past*. New York: Penguin, 1990.

Dunne, Bruce. "Power and Sexuality in the Middle East" *Middle East Report* 206 (1998), http://www.merip.org/mer/mer206/bruce.htm last accessed 03/30/2003.

———. "Homosexuality in the Middle East: An Agenda for Historical Research," *Arab Studies Quarterly* 12, no. 3& 4 (1990): 55–82.

Duri, A.A. "al-Zuhri: A Study on the Beginnings of History Writing in Islam." *Bulletin of the School of Oriental and African Studies* 19, no. 1 (1957): 8.

Dynes, Wayne R. "Christianity and the Politics of Sex." *Homosexuality, Intolerance and Christianity: A Critical Examination*." New York: Scholarship Committee, Gay Academic Union, 1981.

El-Ad, Hagai "Gay Israel: No Pride in Occupation" *The Gully* (02/21/2002), http://www.thegully.com/essays/israel/020220_gays_meet_sharon.html last accessed 02/17/2006.

Elkhadem, Saad. Preface to *A Leader of Men*, by Yusuf Idris. Fredericton [Canada]: York Press, 1988.

———. "Yusuf Idris and his Gay *Leader of Men*" *International Fiction Review* 17, no. 1 (1990): 25–28.

El-Rouayheb, Khaled. *Before Homosexuality in the Arab-Islamic World, 1500–1800*. Chicago: University of Chicago Press, 2005.

Encyclopaedia of Islam. 11 vols. Edited by C.E. Bosworth et al. Leiden: E.J. Brill, 1983.

Faderman, Lillian. *Surpassing the Love of Men: Romantic Friendship and Love Between Women from the Renaissance to the Present*. New York: Morrow, 1981.

Fawal, Ibrahim. *Youssef Chahine*. London: British Film Institute, 2001.

Fermor, Patrick Leigh. *Mani*. London: John Murray, 1958.

Fone, Byrne R. S. *Homophobia: A History*. New York: Metropolitan Books, 2000.

Foucault, Michel. *The History of Sexuality: An Introduction*. Vol. 1. Translated by Robert Hurley. Harmondsworth: Penguin, 1984.

Friedlaender, Israel. "The Heterodoxies of the Shiites in the Presentation of Ibn Ĥazm." *Journal of the American Oriental Society* 29 (1908): 1–183.

"Further Reading: Sexuality in Middle East Societies [A bibliography]." *Middle East Report* 206 (1998) n.p., http://www.merip.org/mer/mer206/further.htm 08/18/2006.

Fuss, Diana. *Essentially Speaking: Feminism, Nature and Difference*. New York: Routledge, 1989.

"Gay Pride Jerusalem: Making History in the Holy City," http://www.thegully.com/essays/israel/020613_gay_pride_jerusalem.html 05/10/2003.

Gçek, Fatima Múge and Shiva Balaghi, eds. *Reconstructing Gender in the Middle East*. New York: Columbia University Press, 1994.

Ghadar, Ĥaneen. "al-Jins Fi Riwayat Årabiya: al-Mar'a Miţhlama Yarghabuha al-Rajul." *al-Mulhaq*, 10 February, 2001, 7.

Ghusun, Amina "Elham Mansour Fi *Ana Hiya Anti*: Ma Jadwa Riwaya Talhath al Iftiål Wal-Fadiĥa?" *Alĥayat*, 18 August, 2000, 13.

Giffen, Lois Anita. *Theory of Profane Love Among the Arabs: The Development of the*

Genre. New York: New York University Press, 1971.

Gilbert, Arthur N. "Introduction: History and Sexuality." *Journal of Sex Research* 17, no. 3 (1981): 197–203.

Goldie, Terry. Introduction to "Postcolonial and Queer Theory and Praxis." *Ariel* 30, no. 2 (1999): 9–26.

Gostin, Lawrence O. "AIDS in Africa Among Women and Infants: A Human Rights Framework." *The Hastings Center Report* 32 (2002): n.p.

Greenberg, David. *The Construction of Homosexuality*. Chicago: Chicago University Press, 1988.

Guthrie, Shirley. *Arab Women in the Middle Ages: Private Lives and Public Roles*. London: Saqi Books, 2001.

Habib, Samar. "Queering the Middle East and the New Anti-Semitism." *Entertext* 3, no. 2 (2003): 52–71.

———. "The Historical Context and Reception of the First Arabic-Lesbian Novel, *I Am You*, by Elham Mansour." *Entertext* 5, no. 3 (2006): 201–235.

Ĥadiţh Encyclopedia Ver. 2.1, Ĥarf, Cairo and Riyadh.

Haeberle, E. J. "The Manufacture of Gladness: Some Observations on Sex Therapy." In *Challenges in Sexual Science: Current Theoretical Issues and Research Advances*. Edited by C. M. Davis, 8–15. Lake Mills, IA: The Society for the Scientific Study of Sex, 1983.

Haeri, Shahla. "Temporary Marriage and the State in Iran: An Islamic Discourse on Female Sexuality." *Social Research* 59, no. 1 (1992): 201–223.

Ĥafeṯẖ, Åbd al-Ĥalim. *Qusat Ĥayati*. Beirut: Dar al-Åawda, n.d.
———. *Muthakarat Åbd al-Ĥalim Ĥafeṯẖ Kama Sajaluha Bisawtoohu*. Beirut: Dar al- Åawda, n.d.
Hall, Lynn S. and Craig T. Love "Finger-Length Ratios in Female Monozygotic Twins Discordant for Sexual Orientation" *Archives of Sexual Behaviour* 32, no. 1 (2003): 23–28.
Halperin, David. *How to Do the History of Homosexuality*. Chicago: Chicago University Press, 2002.
———. "Lesbian Historiography Before the Name." *GLQ* 4, no. 4 (1998): 559–578.
———. *Saint Foucault: Towards a Gay Hagiography*. Oxford: Oxford University Press, 1995.
———. *One Hundred Years of Homosexuality*. New York: Routledge, 1989.
Ĥamawee, Subĥee et al. *al-Munjid Fi al-Lugha al-Årabiya al-Muåsirah*. Beirut: Dar al-Mashriq, 2001.
Hambly, Gavin R. G. Introduction to *Women in the Medieval Islamic World*. Edited by R.G. Hambly. London: Macmillan Press, 1998.
Hamer, Diane. "'I Am a Woman:' Ann Bannon and the writing of Lesbian Identity in the 1950s." In *Lesbian and Gay Writing: An Anthology of Critical Essays*. Edited by M. Lilly. 47–75. Philadelphia: Temple University Press, 1990.
Ĥamzeh, Åli Abdel-Ĥalim. *al-Kamoos al-Jinsee åind al-Årab*. Beirut: Riad El-Rayyes, 2002.
Hartman, Michelle. "Ilham Mansur's *Ila Hiba: sira ula and Hiba fi rihlat al-jasad: sira thaniyya*" *Arabic and Middle Eastern Literatures* 2, no. 2 (1999): 141–158.
Hasinein, Ådel. *Aghani Wa Ashåar Åbd al-Ĥalim Ĥafeṯẖ*. Beirut: al-Dar al-Masriyah al-Lubnaniyah, 1999.
Hassan, Rifat. "An Islamic Perspective." In *Women, Religion and Sexuality: Studies on the Impact of Religious Teachings on Women*. Edited by Jeanne Becher, (93–128). Philadelphia: Trinity Press, 1991.
Hatem, Mervat. "The Politics of Sexuality and Gender in Segregated Patriarchal Systems: The Case of 18th- and 19th-Century Egypt." *Feminist Studies* 12, (1986): 251–274.
Hawley, John, ed. *Postcolonial, Queer: Theoretical Intersections*. Albany: State of New York University Press 2001.
———. *Postcolonial and Queer Theories: Intersections and Essays*. Westport, CT and London: Greenwood Press, 2001.
Hershberger, Scott L. "A Twin Registry Study of Male and Female Sexual Orientation." *The Journal of Sex Research* 34, no. 2 (1997): 212–223.
Ĥilmi, Musṭafa. "al-Thareeåa Ila Makarim al-Shariåa Kama Yuwadiĥuha al-Raghib al-Asfahani" *al-Darra: Quarterly Review* 3, no. 2 (1977): 206--229.
Hoffman, Richard J. "Vices, Gods, and Virtues: Cosmology as a Mediating Factor in Attitudes toward Male Homosexuality". *Journal of Homosexuality* 9, no. 2/3 (Winter 1983/Spring 1984): 27–44.
Hovannisian, Richrad G. and Georges Sabagh, (1993). *Religion and Culture in Medieval Islam*. Cambridge: Cambridge University Press, 1999.
Ibn al-Salaĥ al-Shahrazuri *Kitab mårifat anwaå åilm al-ĥadiṯẖ*. n.p: Garnett Publishing 2005.
Irwin, R. "al-Suyuti." *Encyclopedia of Arabic Literature*. Vol. 2. Edited by Julie Scott Meisami and Paul Starkey. London: Routledge, 1998. 746.
"Islamic Scholars Ignore Evidence that the Holy Prophet Muhammad (peace be upon him) was 'Gay!'" from GayEgypt.com http://www.gayegypt.com/islam. html 03/17/2003, now discontinued.

Jackson, Peter. "Sultan Radiyya Bint Iltutmish." In *Women in the Medieval Islamic World*. Edited by Gavin R.G. Hambly, 181–198. New York: St. Martin Press, 1998.

James, W.H. "Finger-Length Ratios, Sexual Orientation and Offspring Sex Ratios." *Journal of Theoretical Biology* 212, no. 3 (2001): 273–274.

al-Jaser, Ĥamd Bin Moĥamad. "al-Rus Fi al-Quran al-Kareem wa Aara' al-Baĥiṭheen Ĥawlahu." *al-Årab: Majala Shahriya Jamiåt* 5, no 1 (1970): 1–12.

al-Jawadi, Åbd al Karim Åbd al-Åziz. *Åbd al-Ĥalim Ĥafeth*. Beirut: Dar al-Kitab al Ålamie, 1992.

Jieming. "Guestbook for Grinding Tofu" *Grinding Tofu* 05/12/00, http://www.geocities.com/Tokyo/Towers/4289/geobook.html 08/27/2006.

Jihad. "Ĥiwar Må al-Doctora Elham Mansour Ĥawl Riwayatuha al-Jadida *Ana Hiya Anti*." *al-Ĥawadeth*, 8 September, 2000, 58–59.

Johansson, Warren. "Ex Parte Themis: The Historical Guilt of the Christian Church" *Homosexuality, Intolerance and Christianity: A Critical Examination*. New York: Scholarship Committee, Gay Academic Union, 1981.

Johansson, Warren and William A. Percy. "Homosexuality." In *Handbook of Medieval Sexuality*. Edited by Vern L.Bullough and James A. Brundage (155–189). New York: Garland Press, 1996.

Jomåt, Jamal. Introduction to *Nuzhat al-Albab Fima La Youjad Fi Kitab*, by al-Tifashi. London: Riad El Rayyes, 1992.

Kennedy, Elizabeth L. and Madeline D. Davis. *Boots of Leather, Slippers of Gold*. New York: Penguin, 1993.

Khalf-Allah, Moĥamad. *Sahib al-Aghani Abu Faraj al-Asfahani al-Riwaya*. Cairo: Maktabat Nahdat Misr, 1953.

al-Khoury, George Ibrahim. *Hikayati Må al-Nujoom: Åbd al-Ĥalim Ĥafeth*. n.p.: Juros Press, n.d.

Kilpatrick, H. "al-Nuwayri." *Encyclopedia of Arabic Literature*. Vol. 2. Edited by Julie Scott Meisami and Paul Starkey, 590–591. London: Routledge, 1998.

Krause, Lars. "The Queer Community in Israel: Findings of Research for the HBF April-June 2002," http://www.boell.de/downloads/gd/queer_report_Israel.pdf 03/10/2003.

Kruk, Remke. "The Bold and the Beautiful: Women and 'Fitna' in the 'Sirat Dhat al-Himma': The Story of Nura." In *Women in the Medieval Islamic World*. Edited by Gavin R.G. Hambly, 99–116. New York: St. Martin Press, 1998.

———. "Clipped Wings: Medieval Arabic Adaptations of the Amazon Myth." *Harvard Middle Eastern and Islamic Review* 1, no. 2 (1995): 132–154.

———. "Warrior Women, Part Two," *Journal of Arabic Literature* 25, no 1 (1994): 16–33.

———. "Warrior Women in Arabic Popular Romance: Qannâsa bint Muzâhim and Other Valiant Ladies: Part One," *Journal of Arabic Literature* 24, no. 3 (1993): 213–230.

Lauritsen, John, "Culpa Ecclesiae: Boswell's Dilemma." In *Homosexuality, Intolerance and Christianity: A Critical Examination*. New York: Scholarship Committee, Gay Academic Union, 1981.

LeVay, Simon. *The Sexual Brain*. Cambridge: MIT Press, 1993.

———. *Queer Science*. Cambridge: MIT Press, 1996.

Li Man Yajru' Faqaṯ. "Interview with Inas Degheidi." LBC, 08/05/2005. Hosted by Tony Khalifeh.

Lochrie, Karma. *Heterosyncracies: Female Sexuality When Normal Wasn't*. Minneapolis: University of Minnesota Press, 2005.

Luibhéid, Eithne and Lionel Cantú Jr., eds. *Queer Migrations: Sexuality, U.S. Citizenship, and Border Crossings*. Minneapolis: University of Minnesota Press, 2005.

Lyotard, Jean François. *The Postmodern Condition: a Report on Knowledge*. Translated by Geoff Benington and Brian Massumi. Foreword by Fredric Jameson. Minneapolis: University of Minnesota Press, 1984.

McClarnon, M. and Sally Bingham. Collection of *Lesbian Pulp Fiction*, http://library.duke.edu/specialcollections/bingham/guides/lesbianpulp/ 08/25/2006.

McGlenen, Edward W. *Boston Marriages from 1700-1809*. Baltimore: Genealogical Co., 1977.

McGlynn, Margaret and Richard J. Moll. "Chaste Marriage in the Middle Ages: 'It Were to Hire a Great Merite.'" In *Handbook of Medieval Sexuality*. Edited by Vern L. Bullough and James A. Brundage, 103–122. New York: Garland, 1996.

McGreal, Chris "Woman Faces Death by Stoning 'after Weaning'" *The Guardian*, 20 August, 2002, http://www.guardian.co.uk/international/story/0,3604,777421,00.html last accessed 08/22/2006.

Mackey, Michel. "Elham Mansour Ån Riwayatooha al-Jadida 'Ana Hiya Anti.'" *al-Ĥiwar*, 28 October, 2000, n.p.

Mamet, David. *Boston Marriage*. New York: Vintage Books, 2002.

Maĥmood, Ibrahim. *al-Mutåt al-Maĥthoora/The Forbidden Pleasure: Homosexuality: Sex in Arab History*. Beirut: Riad El-Rayyes, 2000.

Maĥmood, Samra. *al-Qadi al-Jurjani: al-Adib al-Naqid*. Beirut: al-Maktab al-Tijaree Lil Tawzeeå Wal Tibaåt Wal Nashr, 1966.

Maktabi, Natheer Moĥamad. *Jawla Fi Afaq al-Aghany Li abi Faraj al-Asfahani*. Beirut: Dar al-Bashayir al-Islamiya, 1990.

Malti Douglas, Fedwa. "Tribadism/Lesbianism and the Sexualised Body in Medieval Arabo-Islamic Narrative." In *Same Sex Love and Desire Among Women in the Middle Ages*. Edited by Francesca Canadé Sautman and Pamela Sheingorn, 123–141. New York: Palgrave, 2001.

Elham Mansour. *I Am You: An Excerpt*. Translated by Samar Habib. *Entertext* 5, no. 3 (2006): 236–253.

Marsee, Åbd al-Waĥed. *al-Shuthooth al-Jinsy wa Jara'im al Qatl*. n.p: Dar al-Fikr al-Jamiåee, 1998.

Massad, Joseph. "Re-Orienting Desire: The Gay International and the Arab World." *Public Culture* 14, no. 2 (2002): 361–385.

Mazur, Michelle A. and Tara M. Emmers-Sommer. "The Effect of Movie Portrayals on Audience Attitudes about Nontraditional Families and Sexual Orientation." *Journal of Homosexuality* 44, no. 1 (2002): 157.

Meisami, J.S. "Abbasids." *Encyclopedia of Arabic Literature*. Vol. 1. Edited by Julie Scott Meisami and Paul Starkey, 4–11. London: Routledge, 1998.

Menicucci, Garay. "Unlocking the Arab Celluloid Closet: Homosexuality in Egyptian Film." *Middle East Report* 206, (1998), http://www.merip.org/mer/mer206/egyfilm.htm 03/30/2003.

Miller, Edward M. "Homosexuality, Birth Order, and Evolution: Toward an Equilibrium Reproductive Economics of Homosexuality." *Archives of Sexual Behavior* 29, no. 1 (2000): n.p.

Mondimore, Francis Mark."From the Inquisition to the Holocaust." In *A Natural History of Homosexuality*, 107–218. Baltimore and London: Johns Hopkins University Press, 1996.

Monroe, James T. "The Striptease That was Blamed on Abu Bakr's Naughty Son." In *Homoeroticism in Classical Arabic Literature*. Edited by Everett K. Rowson and J.W. Wright Jr., 94–139. New York: Columbia University Press, 1997.

———. (1974) *Hispano-Arabic Poetry: A Student Anthology*. Piscataway, NJ: Gorgias Press, 2004.

Montada, Josep Puig. "Reason and Reasoning in Ibn Ĥazm of Cordova (d. 1064)." *Studia Islamica* 92 (2001): 165–185.

Moraga, Cherie and Amber Hollibaugh. "What We're Rollin' around in Bed With: Sexual Silences in Feminism." In *Desire: The Politics of Sexuality*. Edited by Ann Snitow, Christine Stansell and Sharon Thompson, 404–414. London: Virago Press, 1984.

Mubarak Dahir "Is Beheading Really the Punishment for Homosexuality in Saudi Arabia?" *Sodomy Laws*, December 2002, http://www.sodomylaws.org/world/saudi_arabia/saudinews19.htm 01/23/2006.

———. "Tight T-shirts and a Gay Café in the Saudi Capital" *Sodomy Laws*, 5 November, 2002, http://www.sodomylaws.org/world/saudi_arabia/saudinews027.htm 01/23/2006.

al-Muĥamie, Moĥamad Riffåt. *Muthakart al-Åndaleeb al-Asmar Åbd al-Ĥalim Ĥafeṯẖ*. n.p: Muassasat Åiz Adeen Lil Tibaåt Wal Nashr, 1990.

———. *Åbd al-Ĥalim Ĥafeṯẖ*. n.c.: Dar al-Biĥar, 1998.

al-Munajjid, Talal Adeen, (1958). *al-Ĥayat al-Jinsiya Åind al-Årab*. Beirut: Dar al Kutub, 1975.

al-Munjid Fi al-Lugha Wal-Aålam. Beirut: Dar al-Mashriq, 2003.

Murad, Suleiman Ali. *Early Islam between Myth and History: al-Hassan al-Basri (d. 110H/728CE) and His Legacy*. Leiden and Boston: Brill, 2006.

Murray, Jacqueline. "Twice Marginal and Twice Invisible." In *Handbook of Medieval Sexuality*. Edited by Vern L. Bullough and James A. Brundage, 191–222. New York: Garland Press, 1996.

Murray, Stephen O. *Homosexualities*. Chicago: Chicago University Press, 2000.

———. "Woman-Woman Love in Islamic Societies." In *Islamic Homosexualities: Culture, History and Literature*. Edited by Stephen O. Murray and Will Roscoe, 97–106. New York: New York University Press, 1997.

———. "Gender-Defined Homosexual Roles in Sub-Saharan African Islamic Cultures." In *Islamic Homosexualities: Culture, History and Literature*. Edited by Murray, Stephen O. and Will Roscoe, 222–232. New York: New York University Press, 1997.

———. "The Will not to Know." In *Islamic Homosexualities*. Edited by Stephen O. Murray and Will Roscoe, 14–54. New York and London: New York University Press, 1997.

Murray, Stephen O. and Will Roscoe, eds. *Islamic Homosexualities: Culture, History and Literature*. New York: New York University Press, 1997.

"Muslim Festival Bars Gays." *Sydney Star Observer*, January 26, 2006, 5.

Mustanski, Brian S. et al. "A Critical Review of Recent Biological Research on Human Sexual Orientation." *Annual Review of Sex Research* 13, (2002): 89–131.

Muṯẖhir, Muntasir *al-Mutåt al-Muĥarama: al-Liwaṯ Wal Suĥaq Fi A-Tareekh al-Årabi*. n.p.: al-Dar al-Ålamiya lil Kutub Wal Nashr, 2001.

Nawas, John A. "A Reexamination of Three Current Explanations for al-Ma'mun's Introduction of the Mihna." *International Journal of Middle East Studies* 26, no. 4 (1994): 615–629.

al-Nawdji, Moĥammad. *La Prairie des gazelles: éloge des beaux adolescents*. Translated by René Khawam. Paris: Phébus, 1989.

Nestle, Joan "The Fem Question." In *Pleasure and Danger: Exploring Female Sexuality*. Edited by Carole S. Vance, 232–241. London: Routledge & Kegan Paul Books, 1984.

Ort, L.J.R. *Mani: A Religio-Historical Description of his Personality*. Leiden: E.J. Brill, 1967.

Patton, Cindy and Benigno Sánchez-Eppler, eds. *Queer Diasporas*. Durham and London: Duke University Press, 2000

Petersen, William L.. "On the Study of 'Homosexuality' in Patristic Sources." *Studia Patristica* 20, (1989): 283–288.

Plato. *The Symposium*. Translated by W. Hamilton. Middlesex: Penguin, 1976.

Pollard, Irina. "Preconceptual Programming and Sexual Orientation: a Hypothesis." *Journal of Theoretical Biology* 179, (1996): 269–273.

Qardawi, Yusuf. "Islamic Stance on Homosexuality." *Islam Online*. Edited by Nadia El-Awady, http://www.islamonline.net/english/Contemporary/2003/02/article01-1.shtml 08/25/2006.

Qasifi, Maree. "*Ana Hiya Anti* Li Elham Mansour." *An-Nahar*, 2 August, 2000, n.p.

al-Qublan, Qublan Bin Saleĥ. "Itilå åla Tarikh al-Rus." *al-Duråiya: Fasliya, Muĥakama* 4, no. 16 (2002): 214–242.

"Queer "Settlers" Land on Berkeley Starbucks: Analogy to Israeli Colonists" *San Francisco Independent Media Center* 08/18/2002, http://sf.indymedia.org/news/2002/08/141433.php last accessed 02/17/2006.

Radi, Åli Moĥamad. *al-Ma'mun al-Åbassi: Åsr al-Islam al-Thahabi*. Dar Qawmiyah Lil Tibaåt Wal Nashr, c.1965.

Raditapole, Deborah K. "The Economics of Transmission." In *HIV and AIDS: the Global Inter-Connection*. Edited by Elisabeth Reid. West Hartford, CT: Kumarian Press, 1995.

Rafåaya, Yassin. "Khiyanat al-Fan." *A-Naqid*, 11–22 September, 2000, 31.

Raza, Arif. "Muslim Canadian Congress Endorses Gay Marriage." 02/13/2005, *Queer Day*, http://www.queerday.com/2005/feb/13/muslim_canadian_congress_endorses_gay_marriage.html 08/31/2006.

Reed, Elisabeth. Introduction to *HIV and AIDS: the Global Inter-Connection*. West Hartford, CT: Kumarian Press, 1995.

Reddy, Vasu. "Perverts and Sodomites: Homophobia as Hate Speech in Africa." *Southern African Linguistics and Applied Language Studies* 20, no. 3 (2002): 163–175.

Rich, Adrienne. "Compulsory Heterosexuality and Lesbian Existence." *Signs* 5, no. 4 (1980): 631–660.

———. "Reflections on 'Compulsory Heterosexuality.'" *Journal of Women's History* 16, no. 1 (2004): 9–11.

Rippin, A. "al-Zuhri, "Naskh al-Qur'an" and the problem of early "tafsir" texts." *Bulletin of the School of Oriental and African Studies* 47, no. 1 (1984): 22–43.

Rothblum, Esther D. and Kathleen A. Brehony, eds. *Boston Marriages: Romantic but Asexual Relationships Among Contemporary Lesbians*. Amherst: University of Massachusetts Press, 1993.

Roughgarden, Joan. *Evolution's Rainbow: Diversity, Gender, and Sexuality in Nature and People*. Berkeley: University of California Press, 2004.

Rowson, Everett K. "The Effeminates of Early Medina." *Journal of the American Oriental Society* 111, (1991): 671–693.

———. "The Categorization of Gender and Sexual Irregularity in Medieval Arabic Vice Lists." In *Body Guards: The Cultural Politics of Gender Ambiguity*. Edited by Julia Epstein and Kristina Straub, 50–79. New York: Routlegde, 1991.

———. "al-Raghib al-Isfahani." *Encyclopaedia of Islam*. Vol. 8. Edited by C.E. Bosworth et al., 389–390. Leiden: E.J. Brill, 1983.

———. "Mujun." *Encyclopedia of Arabic Literature*. Vol. 2. Edited by Julie Scott Meisami and Paul Starkey, 546–548. London and New York: Routledge, 1998.

Russo, Vito. *The Celluloid Closet: Homosexuality in the Movies*. New York: Harper & Row, 1987.

Sabbah, Fatna A. *Woman in the Muslim Unconscious*. New York: Pergamon Press, 1984.

Sadawi, Nawal. (1974). *al-Unţha Hiya al-Asl*. Alexandria: al-Mustaqbal, 1990.

———. "al-Rajul Wal Shuthooth al-Jinsee." In *al-Rajul Wal Jins*. Alexandria: al-Mustaqbal, 1990. 198–209.
———. *Janat Wa Iblis*. Beirut: Dar al-Adab, 1992.
Saåeedi, Samir. *Asil al-Åeela al-Årabiya Wa Anwå al Jawaz al-Qadeema åind al-Årab*. Beirut: Dar al Multaqa, 2000.
Sakalli, Nuray and Ozanser Uğurlu. "The Effects of Social Contact with a Lesbian Person on the Attitude Change Toward Homosexuality in Turkey." *Journal of Homosexuality* 44, no. 1 (2002): 111–119.
Salti, Ramzi "A Different Leader of Men." *World Literature Today* 75, no. 2 (2001): 246–256.
Sanders, Paula. "Gendering the Ungendered Body: Hermaphrodites in Medieval Islamic Law." In *Women in Middle Eastern History: Shifting Boundaries in Sex and Gender*. Edited by Nikki R. Keddie and Beth Baron, 75–95. New Haven, CT: Yale University Press, 1991.
Sartain, E.M. Jalal al-din al-Suyuti: Biography and Background, vol. 1. Cambridge: Cambridge University Press, 1975.
Sautman, Françesca Canadé and Pamela Sheingorn, eds. *Same-Sex Love among Women in the Middle Ages*. New York: Palgrave, 2001.
al-Sayyid-Marsot, Afaf Lutfi. *Society and the Sexes in Medieval Islam*. Malibu, CA: Undena Publications, 1979.
Schmitt, Arno and Jehoeda Sofer, eds. *Sexuality and Eroticism among Males in Moslem Societies*. Binghamton, NY: Harrington Park Press, 1992.
Sedgwick, Eve K. *Epistemology of the Closet*. Berkeley: University of California, 1990.
———. "How to Bring your Kids up Gay" In *The Children's Culture Reader*. Edited by Henry Jenkins, 231–240. New York: New York University Press, 1998.
———. Sedgwick, Eve K. *Between Men: English Literature and Male Homosocial Desire*. New York: Columbia University Press, 1985.
Shafik, Viola. *Arab Cinema: History and Cultural Identity*. Cairo: American University in Cairo Press, 1998.
Shalhoob, Pierre. "Åtash Ila al-Mustaĥeel!" *A-Naqid*, 7-17 August, 2000, 33.
al-Sheik, Ĥannan. *Misk al Ghasal*. Beirut: Dar al-Adab, 1988.
Shuåyb, Ålia. *Kalam al-Jasad: Dirasa Ikhlaqiya*. [Kuwait]: Dar Åliya lil-Nashr wa al-Tawzeeå, 2001.
al-Shurbejee, al-Said. *Åbd al-Ĥalim Ĥafeth: Mushwar al-Majid Wal Åthab*. Beirut: Dar al-Kitab al-Ĥadiṭha, n.d.
Singh, Devendra et al. "Lesbian Erotic Role Identification: Behavioral, Morphological, and Hormonal Correlates." *Journal of Personality and Social Psychology* 76, no. 6 (1999): 1035–1049.
Stanton, Charles Michael. *Higher Learning in Islam*. Lanham, MD: Roman & Littlefield, 1990.
Stein, Edward. *The Mismeasure of Desire: The Science, Theory, and Ethics of Sexual Orientation*. New York: Oxford University Press, 1990.
———. Introduction and Conclusion to *Forms of Desire*. Edited by Edward Stein. New York: Routledge, 1992.
Szasz, Thomas Stephen. *The Manufacture of Madness: a Comparative Study of the Inquisition and the Mental Health Movement*. London: Routledge Kegan & Paul, 1971.
al-Ṯabari. *Tarikh al Tabari/The History of al-Ṯabari: The Sasanids, the Byzantines, the Lakhamids, and Yemen*. Translated and annotated by C.E. Bosworth. Albany: State University of New York Press, 1999.
Tabbara, Lina Mikdadi. *Survival in Beirut: a Diary of Civil War*. Translated by Nadia Hijab. London: Onyx Press, 1979.

Tait, Robert. "A Fatwa for Freedom" *The Guardian*, July 27, 2005, http://www.guardian.co.uk/g2/story/0,,1536658,00.html 01/01/2006.

Tatchell, Peter. "Time to Talk to Gay People, Sir Iqbal." 05/04/2006 In *Guardian Unlimited*'s "Comment is Free," http://commentisfree.guardian.co.uk/peter_tatchell/2006/05/muslim_council_rejects_gay_dia.html 08/31/2006.

Taweel, Nour. "'Ana Hiya Anti' Riwayat Elham Mansour." *al-Safir*, 20 December, 2000, n.p.

Thomas, Jon. "Anti-Sex Law Passed in Iran." *Torch*, November 15–December 14, 1982, 15. Rreprinted from *Forward: Newspaper of the Revolutionary Marxist League of Jamaica*, September 27–October 26, 1982, n.p.

Tifashi, Shehab Adeen Aĥmad Ibn Yusuf. *The Delight of Hearts or What you will Not Find in any Book*. Edited by Winston Leylandinston. Translated from French translation by René R. Khawam, by Edward A. Lacey. San Francisco: Gay Sunshine Press, 1988.

Tohidi, Nayereh. "Gender and Islamic Fundamentalism: Feminist Politics in Iran." In *Third World Women and the Politics of Feminism*. Edited by Chandra Talpade Mohanty and Lourdes Torres, 251–267. Bloomington: Indiana University Press, 1991.

Tolmacheva, Marina. "Female Piety and Patronage in the Medieval Hajj." In *Women in the Medieval Islamic World*. Edited by R.G. Hambly. London: Macmillan Press, 1998.

T̲rad, George. Title unknown. *A-Naqid*, 19-21 August, 2000, 31.

T̲rad, Majeed and Khalifah, Rabeeå Moĥamad. *Åbd al-Ĥalim Ĥafet̲h̲: Ĥayatuhu Wa Fanahu*. Beirut: al-Mu'asasa al-Ĥadiṭha Lil Kitab, 1996.

Traub, Valerie. *The Renaissance of Lesbianism in Early Modern England*. Cambridge: Cambridge University Press, 2002.

Ullman, Manfred. *Die Medizin Im Islam.*, 196 & 284. Leiden: Brill, 1970.

Van de Ven, Paul. "Effects on High School Students of a Teaching Module for Reducing Homophobia." *Basic and Applied Social Psychology* 17, no. 1 & 2 (1995): 153–172.

Van De Wijgert , Janneke H.H.M. and Nancy S. Padian. "Heterosexual Transmission of HIV." In *AIDS and the Heterosexual Population*. Edited by Lorraine Sherr, 1–9. Chur, Switzerland: Harwood Academic Publishers, 1993.

Walker, Lisa. *Looking Like What You Are: Sexual Style, Race, and Lesbian Identity*. New York and London: New York University Press, 2001.

Walton, Alan Hull, (1963), ed. & intro. *The Perfumed Garden*, by al-Nafzawi. Translated by Richard Burton. London: Book Club Association, 1982.

Walzer, Lee. "Queer in the Land of Sodom" *The Gully*, 21 February, 2002, http://www.thegully.com/essays/gaymundo/020220_gay_israel_history.html 02/17/2006.

Widengren, Geor. *Mani and Manichaeism*. New York: Holt, Rinehart and Winston, 1965.

Williams, Craig A. *Roman Homosexuality: Ideologies of Masculinity in Classical Antiquity*. Oxford: Oxford University Press, 1999.

Williams, Tennessee. *Cat on a Hot Tin Roof*. New York: New Directions, 2004.

Williams, Terrence et al. "Finger-Length Ratios and Sexual Orientation" *Nature* 404, no 6777 (2000): 455–456.

Wright, David F. "Homosexuals or Prostitutes? The Meaning of *Arsenokoitai* (1 Cor 6:9, 1 Tim 1:10)." *Vigiliae Christianae* 38, (1984): 125–153.

———. "Do You Take this Man — Same Sex Unions in Premodern Europe." *National Review* 46, no. 16 (1994): 59–60.

Wright, J.W. Jr and Everett K. Rowson, eds. *Homoeroticism in Classical Arabic Literature*. New York: Columbia University Press.

Young, William C. "Ka'ba, Gender, and the Rites of Pilgrimage." *Journal of Middle East Studies* 25 (1993): 285–300.

FILMOGRAPHY

The Adventures of Priscilla, Queen of the Desert. Directed and written by Stephan Eliott. MGM. 1997.
Alexandria Why? Directed by Youssef Chahine. Fox Lorber Studios. 1979.
Bint Ismaha Maĥmood. Directed by Niasi Mustafa.1975.
But I'm A Cheerleader. Directed by J.Babbit. Lions Gate Entertainment. 1999. DVD.
Calamity Jane. Directed by David Butler. 1953.
Cat on a Hot Tin Roof. 1958. Directed by Richard Brooks. Warner Home Video. 2000. DVD.
The Celluloid Closet. Directed by Rob Epstein and Jeffrey Friedman. Columbia Tristar. 1996.
Dangerous Living: Coming Out in the Developing World. Directed by John Scagliotti. First Run Features. 2005. DVD.
Daughter of the Sun. Directed by Maryam Shahriar. Farabi Cinema Foundation. 2000. DVD.
Dentelle. Directed by Inas Degheidi. 1993. DVD.
Diary of a Male Whore. Directed and screenplay by Twafiq Abu Wael. Trabelsi. 2001.
Firqat Banat Wa Bass. Dir. Sherif Shåban. c. 2003.
Genoun al-Shabab. Directed by Khalil Shawqi. 1980.
Ĥamam al Malatily. Directed by Salaĥ Abu Seif. 1973.
His Secret Life, dir Ferzan Ozpetek, Strand Releasing. 2002.
I Exist. Directed by Peter Barbosa. Arab Film Distributors. 2003.
The Last Supper Directed by Stacy Title. Screenplay by Dan Rosen. Sony Pictures. 1995.
Lil Rijal Faqat. Directed by Maĥmood Zulfikar. 1965.
Muthakarat Muraheeqa. Directed by Inas Degheidi. 2001.
al-Mutåt wal Åzab. Directed by Niasi Mustafa. c.1971.
Queen Christina. Directed by Rouben Mamoulian. 1933.
Quta Åla Nar/Cat on Fire. Directed by Samir Seif. 1977. Video cassette.
Shou Baĥibak/ Crazy of You. Directed and Screenplay by Akram Zåtari. Majnounak Distributors. 2001.
Some Like It Hot. Directed by Billy Wilder. MGM. 1959.
Steam: The Turkish Bath. Directed by Ferzan Ozpetek. Strand Releasing. 1998. DVD.
al-Suåood Ila al-Hawiya. Directed by Kamal Sheik. 1979.
Sukkar Hanim. Directed by al-Sayed Bedeir. 1960.
Tariq il-Ĥob/The Road to Love. Directed by Remi Lange. 2001. DVD.

Index